Breaking Away
Coleridge in Scotland

Portrait of Samuel Taylor Coleridge, by James Northcote, 1804.
Jesus College, Cambridge

BREAKING AWAY
COLERIDGE IN SCOTLAND

Carol Kyros Walker

2002
Yale University Press
New Haven & London

For my niece Pamela Bull and her son George

Set in Garamond by SNP Best-set Typesetter Ltd., Hong Kong
Printed and bound by C.S. Graphics, Singapore

Library of Congress Cataloging-in-Publication Data

Walker, Carol Kyros.
Breaking away: Coleridge in Scotland / Carol Kyros Walker.
p. cm.
Includes Coleridge's notes and letters from his tour of Scotland.
Includes bibliographical references and index.
ISBN 0-300-09641-0 (cloth : alk.paper)
1. Coleridge, Samuel Taylor, 1772-1834--Journeys--Scotland.
2. Travelers--Scotland--History--19th century.
3. Walking--Scotland--History--19th century. 4. Poets, English--19th
century--Biography. 5. Scotland--Description and travel.
I. Coleridge, Samuel Taylor, 1772-1834. II. Title.
PR4483.W24 2002
828'703--dc21
2002006607

CONTENTS

PREFACE

WHEN I COMPLETED work on Dorothy Wordsworth's *Recollections of a Tour Made in Scotland*, I realized I had left a tale untold. One of the original travellers on the six-week tour had parted company with the other two after the beginning of the third week. What happened to Coleridge after he left William and Dorothy Wordsworth at Arrochar, in sight of the Cobbler, near Loch Long? And what had been his experiences up to that point? The present book is meant to remedy this neglect, looking at Coleridge's journey with William and Dorothy from his point of view, and scouting out the Scottish tour he had on his own after leaving them.

Though I have intended *Breaking Away Coleridge in Scotland* to have an independent integrity, it is worth keeping in mind that much of Dorothy Wordsworth's *Recollections* includes accounts of days and episodes shared with Coleridge. There is an overlap between that book and this one; readers may find some exact repetition in parts of the Introduction and some of the notes. Ideally Dorothy's journal would be read as a companion to the present volume (and of course, the other way around). Though I have drawn from her memories to shed light on or to enlarge Coleridge's experiences, I have certainly not brought everything to bear that might be taken from her pages, leaving some research for the resourceful reader.

While Dorothy wrote her "journal" retrospectively, after she returned from the trip, Coleridge created his record spontaneously, as he travelled, keeping notes, making little drawings, and writing letters. There is a different feel to his travel literature, therefore, a higher energy in his writing. As a photographer I have sought here (as I did in my Keats book) to represent the imme-diacy and range of the traveller's experiences by using both color and black-and-white images, as distinguished from the consistent black-and-white I used to represent the quality of reflection for Dorothy's experiences.

Coleridge's travels reminded me as much of Keats's journey north as of Dorothy Wordsworth's—particularly the portion of Keats's route from Ballachulish to Inverness when Keats was fighting the onset of a severe (and ominous) sore throat as he perse-vered in his pedestrian tour with his friend Charles Brown, jotting letters and poems along the way. This was especially the case when I stopped to photograph Letterfinlay—the lonely building along General Wade's Great Glen road that had been an inn, providing shelter for Coleridge in 1803 after he explored Glen Nevis as well as Keats in 1818 after he had climbed Ben Nevis. The inn had deteriorated since I had photographed it for *Walking North with Keats*—there was no puff of smoke rising from its chimney now. But it still stands there, opposite Loch Lochy, storing its literary history behind a plain facade. The haunting simplicity of such places has left me with a sense of continuity in my work on three books about Romantic writers travelling to Scotland. And yet Coleridge has reminded me that the vision of a complex human being alters even the most common travel site. His notes and letters of the Scottish tour mix exquisite images of landscape, often made clearer with analogies to someplace at home, with startling revelations of his personal life—its upheavals, its accom-modation of strained loves and friendships, the yin and the yang of familial relationships. His physical being sometimes dominates the world through which he moves so dramatically that his ailments, his screaming nightmares attended by a sense of his own mortality, the gusto with which he consumes food, and his compulsion to walk speedily define the inns and measure the miles of Scotland as certainly as his meticulous descriptions of natural objects, especially trees, and man-made structures, notably bridges and forts, recreate the places he visited.

Acknowledgments

"Along the way" is an expression that has special meaning for a scholar-photographer like me, for it refers to how I do the kind of research that cannot be accomplished in libraries or on the internet. How do I find the little unpaved road that leads to . . . ? Have you ever heard of a place once called . . . ? More authoritative than any tourist information worker and indispensable to my geographical pursuits of Coleridge were many anonymous native English and Scots residents who sweetly paused from their own business to put me on my course, sometimes drawing maps on scraps of paper, always patient when I asked them to repeat some turn of phrase or pronunciation I didn't catch the first time. If they find their way to this book I hope they know how much I appreciated their help along the way.

Some inquiries lead to less fleeting encounters. I am enormously grateful to local historian Norman Douglas, F.S.A. Scot., of Arrochar, who invited me to tea with his wife Margaret so that I might regale him with questions about places in the area Coleridge mentions in his notes. Mr. Douglas's leads enabled me to locate and photograph virtually hidden places, like Pulpit Rock (Bull Stone), and the farm in Glen Falloch called Garbel. In subsequent correspondence he helped me sort out colloquial place names. Farther north in Scotland, Robert Steword, retired archivist at the Inverness Public Library, responded to my need to know the whereabouts and present nature of Moy House and found that we could talk best over lunch nearby. And an old friend I met trying to find the Cartland Crags for my last book thought it would be best if I stayed at her home while I tried again for Coleridge. Dorothy Leitch's hospitality at Carluke, near Lanark, gave support to my frustrating effort in the best Scots style.

Friends, scholars, and colleagues who were acknowledged in *Recollections* have my continued thanks here. Jack Stillinger has made special contributions to my Coleridge work. Carl Woodring's interest and support have sustained many a flagging stage of Coleridgean commitment. My husband and colleague Norman Walker dodged nary a request to proof read and critique, maintaining his curiosity down a long road. Jiro Nagasawa dispatched from Japan copies of maps he had used in his own work on Dorothy Wordsworth's later journey to the Arrochar area; his sharing made a difference. I have been fortunate receiving from Yale University Press the gifted and experienced attention of John Nicoll, designer of the book and my editor, and the thoughtful guidance of Mary Carruthers, graceful mender of my errant ways in writing and welcome beacon toward improvements.

Jenny Reynolds, practicing artist and graduate of the School of the Art Institute of Chicago, employed her command of computer skills in creating the maps of Coleridge's Scottish Tour, two of which she adapted from the Dorothy Wordsworth book. To John Nolan belongs the credit for translating some of the Latin in Coleridge's Scottish Notes.

The concept for *Breaking Away* enjoyed three permutations before it came to be a book. It was first presented as a paper at the Wordsworth Summer Conference in Grasmere in 1998. Considerably more focused, it was presented at a session of the MLA sponsored by the Wordsworth-Coleridge Association, in 1999 in Chicago. That paper was published in the *Wordsworth Circle* (Spring 2000). For these opportunities to explore my work with a select academic community I thank Jonathan Wordsworth and Marilyn Gaul.

I am grateful to Jonathan Miles of the Trumpington Gallery, Cambridge, for facilitating the reproduction of a print of the James Northcote portrait of Coleridge, and to the Master and Fellows of Jesus College, Cambridge, for permission to publish this portrait. The British Library made it possible for me to examine the manuscripts of Coleridge's Notebooks and granted permission to publish a detail of "A New and Correct Map of Scotland" (MAPS.C.40.F9). I appreciate the cooperation of Mrs. Joan Coleridge, of Chichester, in endorsing my application to Routledge for permission to publish material relevant to the Scottish tour from *The Notebooks of Samuel Taylor Coleridge*, edited by Kathleen Coburn, Vol. I (1957). The same material is published by permission of Princeton University Press and the Bollingen Foundation. Oxford University Press granted permission to publish Letters 1–7 from *Collected Letters of Samuel Taylor Coleridge, Volume II*: 1801–1806, edited by Earl Leslie Griggs (1956).

INTRODUCTION

A JOURNEY IS never bounded by its itinerary or duration when the traveller is a literary man of great talent. To open the account of only a day of his tour is to incise a complex personal history yoked to the moment. When thirty-year-old Samuel Taylor Coleridge set out on a tour of Scotland in the late summer of 1803 with his friends and fellow writers William and Dorothy Wordsworth, he had expectations of restoring his health and spirits while engaging in lively conversation and discovering the reputedly foreign culture and scenery of a part of his nation he occasionally referred to as N. Britain. In his three small notebooks he would capture impressions of what he saw, vent what he felt, and rough out, with itinerary and dates, a memoir of that brief period that would alter the direction of his life. For Coleridge was on a course of separating himself, from his present domestic life, from his deepest investment in poetry, and from the Wordsworths.

Home, Collaboration, and Health

The point of departure for Coleridge was his sizeable home called Greta Hall, once an observatory, atop a hill in Keswick, with a panoramic view of the Blencathra Mountain range and the River Greta flowing below. He had moved with his wife Sara and their first-born son Hartley, then four years old, from Nether Stowey, Somerset to Cumberland, in the Lake District, in July 1800, leaving behind loyal friends in order to be close to William and Dorothy Wordsworth and their home in Grasmere. He and William had already collaborated on

Lyrical Ballads, and their lives as poets and friends had been united in travel and talk. Indeed the early period of their relationship defined a magical coalescence of poetic minds and spirits, the figures themselves seeming the embodiment of Romanticism. Coleridge, still a bachelor, met Wordsworth for the first time in Bristol in 1795 at the town house of a mutual acquaintance, John Pinney. Not long afterwards Wordsworth, living rent-free then with his sister in a house owned by Pinney in Racedown, Dorset, sent a manuscript of his poem "Salisbury Plain" to Coleridge for comments before sending it to his publisher, and not long after that, Coleridge sent William his recently published *Poems on Various Subjects* (1796). A great deal of very fruitful poetic give and take was to follow. When Coleridge, now married to Sara, moved into a small thatched cottage on Lime Street in Nether Stowey, in December 1797 he found himself only forty miles from where William lived. On a fateful summer day, Coleridge set out to walk the distance to Racedown Lodge and the next afternoon leapt over a gate, gamboled down a path, and stepped into the lives of both William and Dorothy. During the two weeks he remained with his new friends, the poets read aloud to each other the plays they had been writing—*Osorio* for Coleridge, *The Borderers* for Wordsworth—exchanging critical comments, reacting, and generally offering whatever literary reinforcement was needed. Coleridge responded especially to William's need for critical direction, and William responded especially to Coleridge's need for encouragement. Dorothy was anything but a passive listener. The threesome took long walks, picnicked, laughed, considered nature and the sublime all about them, and discussed poetry.

By the time Coleridge left on 29 June, it was clear they all wanted more of each other's company, and Coleridge promoted a move to Somerset. William and Dorothy were in Nether Stowey by the beginning of July, and prepared to remain in the area. At first Coleridge squeezed them into his small house, finding great pleasure, whatever his wife may have felt, in having Dorothy under his roof: "Her information various—her eye watchful in minutest observation of nature—and her taste a perfect electrometer—it bends, protrudes, and draws in, at subtlest beauties & most recondite faults" (*Collected Letters*, I, pp. 330–31) But thanks to some help from Coleridge's good friend and neighbor Thomas Poole, William was soon signing a lease on a furnished mansion with nine bedrooms and three parlors that was available for one year at the extraordinarily low rent of £23 a year, including taxes. Only four miles west of Nether Stowey, Alfoxden (the name given to the house, the location, and the deer park in which it stood) made possible just the sort of regular interaction Coleridge and the Wordsworths desired; their friendship deepened and blossomed as they roamed the Quantock Hills and explored the Bristol coast on long walks, at all times of night and day, and in all weather. Their conversation turned on poetry, nature, art, the sublime, publication for their work, and schemes for collaboration. Stimulated by each other, by themselves, by the ever surprising landscape of the Quantock Hills, they wrote. Some of Coleridge's best known poems, "Kubla Khan," "This Lime-Tree Bower My Prison," "The Rime of the Ancient Mariner," flowed from their days of being neighbors. The ideas they shared would have reflected the values of the French Revolution, to which William and Coleridge had both subscribed, energetically in their university days and residually now. Liberty, equality, and respect for the common human being would extend from their talks to their poetry, for William and Coleridge, to her journal writing for Dorothy. Even

the way they were living now, heedless of social conventions, free to be themselves, suggested a taste for revolutionary modes. However, theirs tended to be an exclusive relationship, unfortunately for Mrs. Coleridge and even Tom Poole. When others were admitted into their world it was at dinner parties at Alfoxden, to which political radicals, literati, and local friends were invited and which Mrs. Coleridge could sometimes attend perhaps with little Hartley in hand.

It was during the Quantock Hills phase of their friendship, roughly the summer of 1797 through the summer of 1798, that the most important product of their collaboration was born. *Lyrical Ballads*, published anonymously in September 1798 in Bristol by Joseph Cottle, contained twenty-three poems, opening with Coleridge's "The Rime of the Ancient Mariner" and ending with Wordsworth's "Lines written a few miles above Tintern Abbey." A brief preface, called "Advertisement," put the reader on notice that something unusual was going to happen. "The majority of the following poems are to be considered as experiments. They were written chiefly with a view to ascertain how far the language of conversation in the middle and lower classes of society is adapted to the purposes of poetic pleasure" (Woodstock Facsimile edition). If the experiment with language was not a radical enough departure from poetic tradition, the focus on simple, uneducated country people as the subject of poetry confirmed an unprecedented literary concern for the common man and woman, and signaled a shift to modern literature with a democratic spirit. Beyond these movements away from the eighteenth century, Coleridge and Wordsworth determined a remarkable way to divide their work as collaborators. Years later, as he wrote his *Biographia*, Coleridge looked back on their conversations in 1797–98 and recalled the plan for *Lyrical Ballads*,

in which it was agreed, that my endeavours should be directed to persons and characters supernatural, or at least romantic; yet so as to transfer from our inward nature a human interest and a semblance of truth sufficient to procure for these shadows of imagination that willing suspension of disbelief for the moment, which constitutes poetic faith. Mr. Wordsworth, on the other hand, was to propose to himself as his object, to give the charm of novelty to things of every day, and to excite a feeling analogous to the supernatural, by awakening the mind's attention from the lethargy of custom, and directing it to the loveliness and the wonders of the world before us; an inexhaustible treasure, but for which in consequence of the film of familiarity and selfish solicitude we have eyes, yet see not, ears that hear not, and hearts that neither feel nor understand. (*Biographia Literaria*, II, pp. 6–7)

The immediate effect of *Lyrical Ballads* on critics and readers was modest, but it became, and remains, a landmark in the annals of English literature, regarded by literary historians as the single work that changed the course of British and American literature.

The collaborators moved on to another phase of their friendship at the end of the summer of 1798 when they all three picked up on plans Coleridge had worked out to go to Germany. Leaving the place where camaraderie and poetry had flourished so readily, the threesome sailed from Yarmouth to Germany in September, intending to immerse themselves in the culture and learn the language. Coleridge had the more specific aim to study German literature, science, and philosophy; and so he did, in the formal settings of first Ratzeburg and then Göttingen, where he enrolled at the university. William's aim to learn the language gave way to his urge to write more poetry. On an annuity of £150 Coleridge had recently received from Thomas and Josiah Wedgwood, sons of the famous pottery manufacturer, he could afford comfortable quarters and a sophisticated social life; William and Dorothy needed to stretch their relatively meager funds and settled in Goslar, a quiet town at the foot of the Hartz Mountains. They had all spent ten

days together in Hamburg before going in different directions. During the period of separation, Coleridge felt the absence of his friends deeply. A poem for them, written in English hexameters, communicated his sense of deprivation, ending with the lines: "William, my head and my heart! dear William and dear Dorothea! / You have all in each other; but I am lonely, and want you!" (*Collected Letters*, I, p. 452). Coleridge's elevation of William over himself in these lines had exhibited itself from the time their close friendship began. In June 1797 he wrote to his friend and publisher Cottle: "I speak with heart-felt sincerity & (I think) unblinded judgement, when I tell you, that I feel myself a *little man by his* side; & yet do not think myself the less man, than I formerly thought myself" (I, p. 325). The next month he told Robert Southey, "Wordsworth is a very great man—the only man, to whom *at all times* & in *all modes of excellence* I feel myself inferior . . ." (p. 334). The ring of idolatry in proclamations like these worried Coleridge's closest friends (the Wedgwood brothers, Tom Poole, Charles Lamb), who were concerned that William's influence was too strong; they rejoiced in the news that the friends had gone their separate ways in Germany.

William and Dorothy returned to England in early May; faced with the question of where to live, they stayed for seven months on the farm of the family of Dorothy's friend Mary Hutchinson at Sockburn, a village in the northeast of England below Darlington. Coleridge, accompanied by his friend and publisher Cottle, visited Sockburn while the Wordsworths were there and embarked on a walking tour guided by William, of the places of William's boyhood in the north, during which journey Coleridge had his first dazzling glimpses of high fells, lakes, waterfalls, rivers, and valleys of the Lake District. One mountain struck him as "a most sublime Crag, of a violet colour, patched here & there with islands of Heath plant & wrinkled & guttered picturesquely" (*Notebooks*, I, 537, f41). This was Helm Crag the peak that overlooks the village of Grasmere where William and Dorothy were soon to take up residence in a place they could at last call their own, Dove Cottage. Later he discovered the peaks near Keswick, where—though he did not know it yet—his home would be. "[T]he Mountains stand one behind the other, in orderly array as if evoked by & attentive to the assembly of white-vested Wizards—N.B. The Keswickians have been playing Tricks with the stones" (I, 543, f29).

Coleridge did not return from Germany until late July. He faced grief and recriminations from his wife, their second child, Berkeley, having been born and died while he was away. After a spell of alternately welcoming and rejecting each other's company, the Coleridges moved to London where Coleridge could earn a living writing for the *Morning Post*. As for ties with the Wordsworths, William, apparently having settled on his own plans before leaving Germany, broached the subject of a move north for Coleridge. Coleridge wrote to the friend he called his "anchor," Tom Poole, "It is painful to me too to think of not living near him; for he is a *good* man and a *kind* man, & the only one whom in *all* things I feel my Superior . . ." (*Collected Letters*, I, p. 491). If his words betrayed a continued tendency toward idolatry, they more importantly predicted a departure from Somerset for the Lake District.

Before actually relocating with his wife and child, however, Coleridge made two significant trips to Grasmere to see William and Dorothy, in April 1800 and again in June, both times to work with William on his plan to reissue the 1798 *Lyrical Ballads* and to get out a second volume with new poems, to be published under William's name. The Preface to that second volume would be written in September and October, after Coleridge moved there. In the meantime, Coleridge invested time and energy in negotiating the publication of the volumes with Longman. Assisting him in this now, and for a time to come, was his friend Humphry Davy, the Bristol scientist and poet.

"I would that I could wrap up the view from my House in a pill of opium, & send it to you!" he wrote to Davy about his new "permanent" home in Keswick (I, p. 605). Of all the things that lured him to this part of England, the affinity he felt with William and Dorothy and their continued work on *Lyrical Ballads*, with the promise of more poetry to come out of the collaboration, was the most compelling. He must have regarded the change of scene as an opportunity to put his marriage on track, supposing that a house that was even larger than Alfoxden would please Sara, enrich their child's life, and provide comfortable space for visiting friends, of which there were to be many. But this was a secondary motive, as was the appeal of the gorgeous scenery of the Lakes, with which he was to engage day-to-day and which were so profoundly satisfying to him as a writer, a thinker, and a trekker. His great pleasure in walking thirteen miles (as he measured it) to see Wordsworth in Grasmere came from taking command of mountains and Romantic paths (as well as imbibing now and then at the Swan along the way).

His work with William on the new volumes of *Lyrical Ballads* and the Preface occupied him through October 1800, and probably seemed to him to be setting the pace for how their lives as poets would proceed for the duration of their being neighbors again. But the months that lay ahead proved complicated for Coleridge. He hit a slump as a poet, noticeable in his correspondence starting December, when, on the 17th, he wrote to a friend: "As to Poetry, I have altogether abandoned it, being convinced that I never had the essentials of poetic Genius, & that I mistook a strong desire for original power" (I, p. 656). Two days later he told another friend, "As to our literary occupations they are still more distant than our residences—He is a great, a true Poet—I am only a kind of Metaphysician" (I, p. 658). The saddest was the ironically poetic confession to William Godwin the following March: "The Poet is dead in me—my imagination (or rather the Somewhat that had been imaginative) lies, like a Cold Snuff on the circular Rim of a Brass Candle-stick, without ever a stink of Tallow to remind you that it was once cloathed & mitred with Flame" (II, p. 714). Literary critics today identify this as a loss of confidence brought on by Coleridge's having forfeited recognition for his work and space in the new volume for his own poetry as he yielded to Wordsworth's controlling influence in their recent collaboration on *Lyrical Ballads*. Coleridge himself seems not to have made a connection yet between turning over power to Wordsworth and feeling inadequate as a poet.

Aside from *Lyrical Ballads* Coleridge had some projects of his own he should have attended to—a Life of Lessing he had promised the Wedgwoods he would write; a piece of travel writing about his German trip for the publisher Longman for which he had received an advance; a piece to be called Essay on the Elements of Poetry, "in reality . . . a *disguised* System of Morals & Politics," he indicated to Humphry Davy (I, p. 632). He told Tom Poole, to whom he most often opened his heart, about a plan to publish his long poem "Christabel" (omitted from the new *Lyrical Ballads* on a decision by William) under a separate cover with two essays, one on the "Praeternatural" and the other on "Metre." Moreover, he wanted to produce a work in which he would discredit the systems of Locke, Hobbes, and Hume and then ask Longman to accept it in substitution for the German travel work, which embarrassed him, "because it brings me forward in a *personal* way, as a man who relates little adventures of himself to *amuse* people—& thereby exposes me to sarcasm & the malignity of anonymous Critics, & besides is *beneath* me" (II, p. 707). In this same letter of 16 March 1801 he revealed to Poole that he had been studying intensely notions of time and space and David Hartley's doctrine of association, and that he was striving to deduce from the five senses one sense and thereby "solve the process of Life & Consciousness," endeavors which Wordsworth urged him to give up because they were making Coleridge "nervous & feverish."

From this spring until the spring and summer of 1803 and the Scottish tour Coleridge's intellectual and literary life followed a pattern, suggested in this letter, of plans for writing that did not get off the ground, explorations of major philosophical concepts, adventures into scientific principles, intentions to accomplish some work that would please his benefactors, thoughts about poetic theory. His flashes of brilliance seemed not to have found a controlling force to guide them to full articulation. What might be put down to grandiosity in one for whom they had less affection, must have been perceived by the good friends with whom Coleridge corresponded as a teeming brain temporarily inhibited in the north. That Coleridge was in search of a medium other than poetry in which to express the ideas of German philosophy, especially the metaphysical Kant, was something only later friends and critics could recognize.

Through all, Coleridge maintained a warm friendship with William and Dorothy, with joyful romps in the fells and lakes between their homes, often reminiscent of their time in the Quantocks. Dorothy chronicled such an experience of their being together in the old way on a warm day in May 1802 when she and Wordsworth were joined by Coleridge in the hills near Wythburn:

We came down & rested upon a moss covered Rock, rising out of the bed of the River. There we lay ate our dinner & stayed there till about 4 o clock or later— Wm & C repeated & read verses [of William's "Leech Gatherer"]. I drank a little Brandy & water & and was in Heaven. The Stags horn is very beautiful & fresh springing upon the fells. Mountain ashes, green. We drank tea at a farm house. . . . We parted from Coleridge at Sara's Crag after having looked at the Letters which C carved in the morning. I kissed them all. Wm deepened the T with C's penknife. We sate afterwards on the wall, seeing the sun go down & the reflections in the still water. C looked well & parted from us chearfully, hopping up upon the Side stones. (*Grasmere Journals*, p. 95)

Life altering events occurred during this time too.

Coleridge's wife gave birth to a girl, named Sara, on 23 December 1802, increasing his family to three surviving children (the second, Derwent, having been born 14 September 1800, relatively soon after their arrival at Keswick). Correspondingly, but not as a consequence, Coleridge's relationship with his wife spiraled downward into dire incompatibility, his health had steadily deteriorated, and he needed to worry about money. By the end of January 1802 he admitted to William Godwin that he was "struggling with sore calamities, with bodily pain, & languor,—with pecuniary Difficulties—& worse than all, with domestic Discord, & the heart-withering Conviction—that I could not be happy without my children, & could not but be miserable with the mother of them" (*Collected Letters*, II, pp. 783–84). Since his arrival at the Lakes, Coleridge had fallen in love with yet another Sara, the sister of Mary Hutchinson, who was to become William's wife. On William and Mary's wedding day, 4 October 1802, Coleridge had a poem published in the *Morning Post* as a wedding gift. "Dejection: An Ode" was weighted with significance. In an unusual mode of collaboration, it was written in response to William's recently composed "Ode: Intimations of Immortality." Beyond that, it was an edited-down (and improved) version of a poem Coleridge wrote 4 April addressed to and concerning Sara Hutchinson, though her name did not appear in the latest version. And finally, the date of publication marked not only William's marriage day but also the seventh anniversary of Coleridge's marriage to his wife Sara.

By the time of the Scottish expedition, then, the rewards of the move to Keswick were not entirely clear. William's life had gelled in most desirable ways. His marriage to Mary Hutchinson had proved happy, and their first child, John, had been born only a few months previously. Dorothy, who had lived with William at Dove Cottage before his marriage, was now an integral part of his harmonious household. Best of all, William was entirely clear about committing himself to a career as a poet. He had returned from Germany with the Lucy poems and the first two books of the *Prelude* already written and he rode on the wave of these accomplishments, as well as the work on the new *Lyrical Ballads*, always confident that more would follow. Now he was enjoying a period of high creativity.

Coleridge's life, on the other hand, had not taken such positive turns. The youngest of the three at thirty (Dorothy was thirty-one and William thirty-three) he was dealing with both gout and an opium addiction. Though he loved his three children, his marriage became more and more unbearable, and he and his *wife* Sara had discussed separation. To further complicate matters the love he felt for the other adult Sara in his life, Sara Hutchinson, whose name he spelled Asra in his poems and private notes, by scrambling the letters, became obsessive. And having slipped off the crest of inspiration that came in the Quantocks once he arrived in the Lakes, he seemed to be floundering in his creative life. Coleridge had taken a number of journeys since making his home at Greta Hall, ostensibly for health or for professional work, but actually for putting some distance between himself and his wife. (One journey that prefigured in some ways the ending of the one he was about to take was a solitary excursion, 1–9 August 1802, of the major fells of Cumberland, scrupulously recording his observations in a notebook as he climbed and trekked, and reporting them in letters to Sara Hutchinson.) A trip to Scotland should accomplish desired relief from domestic stress and restore him to health. But more importantly, travelling with Dorothy and William might revive the generative relationship and creative spirit that prevailed when the three had walked in the Quantocks talking about what was to become the brilliant and daring *Lyrical Ballads*.

"I never yet commenced a Journey with such inauspicious Heaviness of Heart before," Coleridge admitted, however (II, p. 975). His worry was about his health, which having taken a turn for the worse just before leaving, seemed likely to stand in the way of pleasure and rapport. From the time he arrived in Keswick he had suffered from a panoply of serious ailments and peculiar symptoms. By the end of January 1801 he reported he had been confined to bed for five weeks with rheumatic fever, accompanied by a pain in his hip, swollen eyelids, boils behind his ears, and a swollen left testicle whose problem he identified as a "hydrocole." By May he concluded his illness was "irregular Gout," which was accompanied by "frequent nephritic attacks" affecting his fingers, his toes, his right knee and ankle, but mostly his left knee and ankle. He had shivering fits and feverishness. He was convinced that the damp weather and the cold exacerbated his gout and contrived to travel to a warm climate for the winter months (leaving Mrs. Coleridge and the children in Keswick). When Dr. Beddoes, the Bristol physician for whom Coleridge had such high regard, disabused him of the notion that gout was affected by cold and dampness, he gave up dreams of going to the Azores, or even just Cornwall for relief, but now that he was off to Scotland he returned to his original theory that exposure to cold rainy weather could be dangerous for him. Moreover, he had zeroed in on his medical problem anew through research in the *Encyclopedia Britannica*, announcing to his brother-in-law, Robert Southey, that he had "Atonic Gout," and elaborating, "I have been very ill, & in serious dread of a paralytic Stroke in my whole left Side. Of my disease there now remains no Shade of Doubt: it is a compleat & almost heartless Case of Atonic Gout" (p. 974). His local doctor, the Keswick surgeon-apothecary John Edmondson, advised Coleridge in favor of travelling to Scotland, urging that "Exercise & the Excitement" would offset the dangers of wet and cold. Edmondson prescribed "Carminative Bitters" to relieve what Coleridge describes as "this truly poisonous, & body-&-soul-benumming Flatulence and Inflation" (p. 974), symptoms that did not bode well for the desired intimacy with friends in travel.

His present addiction to opium was bound to complicate his physical condition even more. In his letter to Southey he enumerated symptoms of addiction and withdrawal that would be repeated in more horrific terms in later letters from Scotland—"frightful Dreams with screaming—*breezes* of Terror blowing from the Stomach up thro' the Brain . . . frequent paralytic Feelings—sometimes approaches to Convulsion fit—three times I have awakened out of these frightful Dreams, & found my legs so *locked* into each other as to have *left* a bruise" (II, p. 976). Coleridge had been medicating himself, applying laudanum to the joints directly and taking it internally to relieve what he thought were his symptoms of gout. He told Poole in May 1801 that he had had to use brandy and laudanum (presumably the one in the other) to relieve stomach fits and nephritic pains in his back, and described the "Disgust, the Loathing" that he felt as a consequence (p. 731). But his drug use predated this instance of consumption. He had been using addictive drugs, under the labels of laudanum, morphine, or simply opium, prescribed to him for health problems or purchased to treat an underlying psychological need for sedation well before his life in the Lake District. Drugs were easily accessible in Bristol; now he had the option of a locally produced product—the Kendal Black Drop, an extra-strength laudanum solution advertised as a remedy for any number of common health problems. Having availed himself of addictive medication, probably to a far greater extent than those closest to him realized, he now exhibited classic signs of drug dependency. On the Scottish tour he appears to have taken a smaller amount of morphine with him, possibly to use the journey as an opportunity to wean himself from this drug. Writing from Perth, near the end of his journey, he aimed to give Southey the impression he had succeeded in this effort: "I have abandoned all opiates except Ether be one; & that only in *fits*" (p. 982).

Issues of his health had constituted a running story-line in his letters, and Southey had been a regular recipient of the details. His presence in Coleridge's life in 1803 proved to be critical; his ties to Coleridge were both familial and literary, and at the beginning of their friendship, collaborative. The two met in 1794, while Southey (twenty at the time) was a student at Oxford, and Coleridge (twenty-one) was passing by from Cambridge on his way to Wales. In a rush of idealism nourished by the spirit and values of the French Revolution, and mutually sympathetic with Jacobinism, the two young men worked on a plan for a kind of utopian community bound by a belief in Pantisocracy. No small vision, it was to be a settlement in America, in the Susquehanna Valley. Twelve men were to make up the basic emigrant party. One of them, Robert Lovell, had married one of three sisters, Mary, in a family called Fricker. Southey, conveniently enough, fell in love with and married another sister, Edith. When Coleridge became a part of the Pantisocracy fellowship, he was introduced to the third and remaining sister, Sara, and he soon felt pressure from Southey to marry her, for the good of the cause, though he was in love with another woman, Mary Evans. Coleridge acquiesced, but the scheme for the Pantisocratic community disintegrated, and the residue of its failure, which resulted from insufficient funds to carry out the group emigration, was a severely fractured relationship between the two poets. When Southey accepted an offer from his uncle to go to Portugal in 1795, Coleridge grew angry with Southey for entirely abandoning his utopian ideals. Before breaking off relations, the two had collaborated on a political play, *The Fall of Robespierre*, and given a series of lectures together in Bristol to raise money for their movement. But the rift that occurred was for Coleridge irremediable. In future years there were reconciliations and further fallings out; they read and criticized each other's work. Coleridge regarded himself as the superior poet, but Southey distinguished himself with self-discipline and responsible conduct.

In June of 1797 Coleridge moved on to a spiritual and literary partnership that profoundly eclipsed his friendship with Southey as he discovered a collaborative and personal bond with William Wordsworth. Yet Southey was often still to prove an invaluable friend and relative,

never more so than in 1799 when Coleridge's son Berkeley died while he was miles away in Germany. Southey came to the aide of the distraught Sara Coleridge, taking her into his home to be comforted by his wife, Sara's sister Edith, and himself, and looking after the burial of the child. The opportunity to reciprocate this kindness at the time of tragedy was afforded to Coleridge at the end of his Scottish tour. In a reversal of misfortune, Southey suffered the loss of his only child and Coleridge fervently welcomed Southey, his wife, and the third Fricker sister, now a widow and living with the Southeys, to Greta Hall, which would remain their home for a very long time—beyond Southey's becoming Poet Laureate in 1817 and beyond Coleridge's defection to London.

The Irish Jaunting Car

In the planning stages of the Scottish tour Coleridge and Wordsworth communicated about how they would travel, and the idea of an economical vehicle to transport the travelling party and their belongings was proposed. Coleridge would have preferred to make this a walking tour, but Wordsworth favored wheels. The business of finding an affordable horse and cart fell to Coleridge, who despite the marvelous skill he exhibited for arriving at contracts with publishers, was stymied by the prospect of buying a horse and cart. Finding no car locally, he corresponded with an acquaintance in Devonshire, Col. Nathaniel Moore, who had an Irish Jaunting Car to sell. His asking price was firm, but in the letter he wrote Coleridge on 17 July he left a margin for a discount: "It is worth £15—that I often refuse—deduct from it what you please" (*Collected Letters*, II, p.957,n.). The problem of the cart solved, there was still the matter of the creature to pull it. "What the devil to do about a Horse!" he wailed to Wordsworth on 23 July (p. 957). There seemed to be none for sale in Keswick. Frustrated, he complained, "I begin to find that a Horse & Jaunting

Car is an anxiety—& almost to wish that we had adopted our first thought, & *walked*: with one pony & side saddle for our Sister Gift-of-God [Dorothy]" (pp. 957–58). Which of the two poets finally succeeded in finding a horse is not clear, but Coleridge was ebullient when he could announce to Southey just before the journey began:

We have bought a stout Horse—aged but stout & spirited—& an open vehicle, called a Jaunting Car—there is room in it for 3 on each side, on hanging seats—a Dickey Box for the Driver / & a space or hollow in the middle, for luggage—or two or three Bairns.—It is like a half a long Coach, only those in the one seat sit with their *back* to those in the other / instead of face to face.—Your feet are not above a foot—scarcely so much—from the ground / so that you may get off & on while the Horse is moving without the least Danger / there are all sorts of Conveniences in it. (p. 975)

This half-a-coach was cleverly enough outfitted to intrigue Coleridge and sufficiently rudimentary to contradict any appearance of fashionable travel. The eccentric little vehicle was appropriate for three English Romantics heading into Scotland, and for Coleridge the possibility of being able to leap off of it on impulse must have held special appeal.

Horse, cart, and passengers got off to a perilous start. They had just turned off what is now the A66 at the White Horse and taken a little winding road toward Mungrisdale. Then, Dorothy recalls, "our horse backed upon a steep bank where the road was not fenced, just above a pretty mill at the foot of the valley; and we had a second threatening of disaster in crossing a narrow bridge between the two dales," though she was quick to add, "but this was not the fault of either man or horse" (*Recollections*, p. 39).

Horse and man adjusted to each other predicament by predicament. Inept and inexperienced, William proved a slow learner in the management of creature and cart. A local Scot talked him through the mending of a wheel as the party approached Crawfordjohn. When they pulled into the stables of the pleasure grounds of Bothwell Castle, "there was no one to unyoke the horse, so William was obliged to do it himself, a task which he performed very awkwardly, being new to it" (*Recollections*, p. 71). As for the aged, stout horse, he was to encounter problems that went beyond William's capacity to deal with him. The worst came after Coleridge had left the Wordsworths, but there is little doubt the drama would have commanded a vivid report in his notebook if he had been a witness.

The incident occurred at the ferry crossing at Connel; it involved wicked ferrymen, an outraged Dorothy, and a terrified horse. Dorothy's account indicts the abusers of her animal, who was "harshly driven over rough stones" to reach the boat, then beaten and pushed onto a ferry boat. "A blackguard-looking fellow, blind of one eye, which I could not but think had been put out in some strife or other, held him by force like a horse-breaker, while the poor creature fretted, and stamped his feet against the bare boards, frightening himself more and more with every stroke" (p. 140). Nor did the unfortunate horse make it to shore without further assaults. "All the while the men were swearing terrible oaths, and cursing the poor beast, redoubling their curses when we reached the landing-place, and whipping him ashore in brutal triumph" (p. 154). The horse was never the same after this treatment. He had developed such a serious fear of water that the Wordsworths would have to remain on guard for the duration of the journey. Later the same day with another ferry crossing ahead, they decided to have the horse swim across the water rather than subject him to another boat ride. Once out of the water on the other side, the horse experienced more stress. "Poor creature! he stretched out his nostrils and stared wildly while the man was trotting him about to warm him, and when he put him into the car he was afraid of the sound of the wheels" (p. 142). An accident only a day after his traumatic ferry ride and subsequent swim confirmed his vulnerability:

> We travelled close to the water's edge, and were rolling along a smooth road, when the horse suddenly backed, frightened by the upright shafts of a roller rising from behind the wall of a field adjoining the road. William pulled, whipped, and struggled in vain; we both lept upon the ground, and the horse dragged the car after him, he going backwards down the bank of the loch, and it was turned over, half in the water, the horse lying on his back, struggling in the harness, a frightful sight! I gave up everything; thought that the horse would be lamed, and the car broken to pieces. (p. 147)

Again the car and its distressed horse taxed the skills of the amateurish travellers. William needed and got some help. "Luckily a man came up in the same moment, and assisted William in extricating the horse, and, after an hour's delay, with the help of strings and pocket-handkerchiefs, we mended the harness and set forward again" (p. 147).

From the start the Irish Jaunting Car had demanded more maintenance than Coleridge and the Wordsworths had counted on. Had they been travelling in a chaise with a servant or groom, as most English tourists did when they ventured into Scotland, their tale would have been much different. But their "one single horse and outlandish Hibernian vehicle" (p. 89), as Dorothy characterized it, charming and Romantic though it may have been, always meant more work. Coleridge and Wordsworth were sometimes too self-absorbed to even consider behaving chivalrously, so the work often fell to Dorothy, indeed their "Sister Gift-of-God." Samuel Rogers encountered the Coleridge-Wordsworth party in Dumfries, while on a Scottish tour with his own sister, and noted the peculiar cart and even more peculiar distribution of labor with obvious amusement:

> During our excursion we fell in with Wordsworth, Miss Wordsworth, and Coleridge, who were, at the same time, making a tour in a vehicle that looked like a cart. Wordsworth and Coleridge were entirely occupied in Talking about poetry; and the whole care of looking out for cottages where they might get refreshment and pass the night, as well as of seeing their poor horse fed and littered, devolved upon Miss Wordsworth. She was a most delightful person,—so full of talent, so simple-minded, and so modest! (*Table Talk*, pp. 208–209)

Observers with no literary claim to importance also found the Irish Car and its passengers curious. In Glasgow, a city of international commerce where alien images should not have turned heads, the Irish Jaunting Car and its English passengers drew bemused expressions. Dorothy recalled the entertainment they provided as they departed: "We were obliged to ride through the streets to keep our feet dry, and, in spite of the rain, every person as we went along stayed his steps to look at us; indeed, we had the pleasure of spreading smiles from one end of Glasgow to the other—for we travelled the whole length of the town" (*Recollections*, p. 75). Excited schoolboys followed the cart, trying to jump aboard, and finally succeeding, much to the passengers' pleasure.

The cart may have served the Wordsworths well on the journey, but it was not entirely satisfactory for Coleridge, who soon enough found the grating of the wheels annoying. Further, he either did not want to, or could not take command of the vehicle. Mrs. Coleridge, writing to Southey about the plan for the trip, claimed, "W. is to drive all the way, for poor Samuel is too weak to undertake the fatigue of driving" (*Collected Letters*, II, p. 975n). Never to take the reins would have signified an absence of power for Coleridge, a condition that was antithetical to his independent spirit. He began to find excuses not to ride in the cart. When Coleridge and the Wordsworths separated midway through the journey, the cart went off with William and Dorothy in the direction of Inverary. Coleridge did not miss it or see it again until the three met once again in the Lake District. It remained in the Wordsworth household for many years after the journey was over, and William drafted it into service for another Scottish tour in 1814 with his wife Mary and her sister Sara (Asra), with his eleven-year-old son John riding along separately on his own pony.

Breaking Away

An entourage of family members—Wordsworth, his wife Mary, his sister Dorothy, his baby boy John, Coleridge, his sons Hartley and Derwent—, and the Coleridges' servant Mary Stamper, with William in the Dickey Box driving, had brought the cart up to Keswick from Grasmere earlier in the week, on Thursday 11 August, and on Sunday Mrs. Coleridge and little Sara replaced Coleridge as the party drove Mrs. Wordsworth and Johnny half way back to Grasmere. It was a cheerfully supported beginning. William, Dorothy, and Coleridge were on their way the next day: "Monday, Morning 20 minutes after 11, August 15, 1803," Coleridge recorded precisely (*Scottish Notes*, below, p. 1). Dorothy remembered, "The day was very hot . . ." (*Recollections*, p. 39).

There was much to enjoy before ever crossing into Scotland—Mr Younghusband's good public house in Hesket Newmarket, the Howk, or "fairy Breaks," in Caldbeck, Rose Castle, rosy in the color of its stone and warm in its pastoral setting. Carlisle had been a-buzz with the trial of a colorful criminal. Coleridge put on a madcap performance in the courthouse where John Hatfield, whose case he had covered in a series of sensational articles for the *Morning Post*, was being sentenced for forgery—though his greater crimes were bigamy and the exploitation of the "beautiful maid of Buttermere." "I alarmed the whole Court, Judges, Counsellors, Tipstaves, Jurymen, Witnesses, & Spectators by hollooing to Wordsworth who was in a window on the other side of the Hall—Dinner!" (*Scottish Notes*, p. 133). Coleridge, Dorothy and William, at Dorothy's instigation, paid a visit to Hatfield at the jail. Spirits were high; the *Lyrical Ballads* partners recovered their old camaraderie.

"Enter Scotland, on foot—over a Bridge of the scanty River Sark, that winds like the convex edge of a crescent of sand/ then rolls dark over its red brown Stones . . ." (*Scottish Notes*, p. 134), Coleridge wrote in his notebook, as if marking a ceremonial passage to a new place. With Springfield and Gretna came the satisfying sense of being in the Scottish Lowlands. To this point, a few days into the trip, Coleridge's health had stood up well to the rigors of travel and sight seeing. The accord and simpatico he felt with his fellow literary travellers was releasing his better spirits. It would seem the journey was answering just the needs he had hoped it would.

Their route took them next through Dumfriesshire and Burns country and on to Lanarkshire. Coleridge the political essayist, whose anti-slavery tracts filled pages of *The Watchman*, the inflammatory periodical he launched in his radical Bristol days, published by subscription from March 1795 to May 1796, made a comeback when they stopped at a turnpike house managed by a well-travelled bachelor. "Coleridge gave our host a pamphlet, 'The Crisis of the Sugar Colonies,'" Dorothy noted (*Recollections*, p. 46)—though why Coleridge was carrying this pamphlet with him into Scotland and how he decided this man needed to read it remains as mysterious as why and how the Ancient Mariner knew when and to whom to tell his tale.

When little boys from the mountain mining village of Wanlochhead told the English visitors that they went to school and learned Latin and Greek, Coleridge, instead of being generous enough to appear impressed, asked questions about their education, and fearing that this English stranger "would examine them" (p. 48), as Dorothy put it, they scampered off. This perverse way of amusing himself was part of a pattern of not being able to shed the persona of the learned, analytical man long enough to simply enjoy chance encounters. He pronounced the Latin of the inscription on a proud monument to Smollett "miserably bad" (p. 81). At the Falls of the Clyde he fell into a conversation with a man who commented that it was "a majestic waterfall."

> Coleridge was delighted with the accuracy of the epithet, particularly as he had been settling in his own mind the precise meaning of the words grand, majestic, sublime, etc. And had discussed the subject with William the day before. "Yes, sir," says Coleridge, "it is a majestic waterfall." "Sublime and beautiful," replied his friend. Poor Coleridge could make no answer, and not very desirous to continue the conversation, came to us and related the story, laughing heartily. (p. 64)

Dorothy was charmed by the little girl who guided them at the Falls of the Clyde, but Coleridge had this snide observation for his notebook: "The little Girl sent to *dog* & guide us, yawning with stretching Limbs a droll dissonance with Dorothy's Raptures" (*Scottish Notes*, p. 141). Perhaps the meal he and Dorothy ate at their inn in Lanark had given a dispeptic turn to his thoughts. "[The] . . . dish was true Scottish—a boiled sheep's head, with the hair singed off; Coleridge and I ate heartily of it; we had barley broth, in which the sheep's head had been boiled" (*Recollections*, p. 65).

At the Cartland Crags Coleridge thought longingly of Asra: " Wherever I am, & am impressed, my heart akes for you, & I know a deal of the heart of man, that I otherwise should not know" (*Scottish Notes*, p. 142). In Glasgow he relished the grotesque: "Here I stood beside an asthmatic Town-Cryer, a ludicrous Combination // a woman—Shaver, & a man with his lathered Chin most amorously Ogling her as she had him by the Nose" (p. 144). Yet Asra still haunted him: "The still rising Desire still baffling the bitter Experience, the bitter Experience still following the gratified Desire" (p. 144).

However, early on there were symptoms of a problem in the party of three. Coleridge sniped at William in his notebook, accusing him of being "*Feckless in an Inn*" adding that he "wants Dignity & courage" (p. 136)—this because it was Coleridge who had to offer to sleep on chairs in the parlour when they encountered difficulty in obtaining three beds together where they had stopped for the night. And Dorothy chronicled what might be called the "Poor Coleridge" syndrome. On 18 August at the lonely inn at Brownhill, "Coleridge was not well, and slept upon the carriage cushions" (*Recollections*, p. 44) while William and Dorothy went for a walk after dinner. Earlier that day he had not gone with them to visit Burns's house and grave in Dumfries. At the inn in Leadhills on the 19th, "Coleridge was weary; but William and I walked out after tea" (p. 51). On the 20th, they arrived at Lanark in the evening and Dorothy wanted to see the celebrated waterfall. "Poor Coleridge was unwell, and could not go" (p. 59). By the 23rd, in Dumbarton, "We went early to bed; but poor Coleridge could not sleep for the noise at the street door; he lay in the parlour below stairs" (p. 77). The next day, when they arrived at Luss, the gateway to the Highlands on Loch Lomond, and the point where the language they heard was now Gaelic, or Erse, "Coleridge was not well, so he did not stir out, but William and I walked through the village shore of the lake" (p. 84). He rallied for the journey to Loch Katrine and the Trossachs, but when a ferryman was found to row them down the lake, "Coleridge was afraid of the cold in the boat, so he determined to walk down the lake, pursuing the same road we had come along" (p. 101) .

As much can be gleaned from what Coleridge did not say or do as from what he did. Burns was *the* celebrated Scottish poet, yet Coleridge could not overcome his physical condition to visit his grave or his home, missing, as we travellers would say today, the opportunity of a lifetime. Tobias Smollet was a man of great learning, but Coleridge could only carp at the Latin inscription on his monument. Robert Owen's socialistic working settlement at New Lanark should have struck a chord in the heart of one who in his younger days considered living in a Pantisocratic commune in America, but Coleridge notices only the "Huge Cotton Mills." The same social conscience that had led him to bring an anti-slavery pamphlet into Scotland should have inspired Coleridge to admire the provision of schooling and libraries for miners in Wanlockhead and Leadhills, where another experiment in communal living for workers was going on, but had it not been for Dorothy's account of his teasing the boys, we would never know Coleridge had been there. This is true also of his meeting with Samuel Rogers and his sister in Dumfries. Although he did not like Rogers—having tea and spending the evening with him in Grasmere, for example, "had produced a very unpleasant effect on my Spirits" (*Collected Letters*, II, p. 964)—it would have been more natural for Coleridge to take a jab at him in his notes than to ignore him altogether. Both Rogers and Dorothy record the meeting; for Coleridge, it did not happen. Clearly the vastly associative mind of the poet of "Kubla Kahn" and "The Rime of the Ancient Mariner" had been short circuited by some negative influence.

Coleridge had once said of his closeness with William and Dorothy that "tho' we were three persons, it was but one God" (*Collected Letters*, II, p. 775). This was not something he could say now. The unity in that friendship he had trusted as he agreed to a journey to Scotland, hoping that their extraordinary companionship and the act of travel would restore his health and ignite a creative effusion, had miscarried. This was not the togetherness they had known in the Quantock hills, or in the best of times in the Lake District. Coleridge was not going to complete the journey, partly because he was still very ill and partly because the dynamics among the travellers had disappointed him. From the point of view of the Wordsworths, this might have been a relief, for Coleridge, despite the wit and brilliance of his conversation (which must have been especially welcome by Dorothy when her brother hit one of his introverted

spells), could be a difficult companion. If he had articulated his physical complaints to them in even half the detail he had given Southey before leaving Keswick, they would have known more than they wanted to know. If he had not been able to stave off the symptoms that plagued his sleep, his stomach, and his bowels (if the Carminative Bitters had not worked), they had witnessed more than friends should be expected to. For his part, Coleridge must at times have wished for privacy to avoid embarrassment and to manage his opium addiction and its effects in his own way, alone. This and the realization that his genius had not received nourishment from his companions, and that brother and sister seemed to be content in each other's company, made it easy for Coleridge to reach a decision to reduce a trinity by one.

On the rainy day of 29 August, following their excursion to Loch Katrine and the Trossachs, the three landed at Tarbet, on Loch Lomond, and proceeded two miles along the road to Arrochar, where they dined at an inn and absorbed the view of the mountain called the Cobbler across Loch Long. At 4:00, when the rain had stopped, they set out upon independent routes—the Wordsworths to Cairndow and Coleridge, allegedly to Edinburgh and then home to Keswick. "We portioned out the contents of our purse before parting; and, after we had lost sight of him, drove heavily along" Dorothy wrote (*Recollections*, p. 117).

What Coleridge subsequently gave as his reason for returning depended on his audience. To his wife (2 September 1803) he wrote: "We returned to E. Tarbet, I with the rheumatism in my head / and now William proposed to me to leave them, & make my way on foot, to Loch Ketterine, the Trossachs, whence it is only 20 miles to Stirling, where the coach runs thro' for Edinburgh . . ." (Letter 1, below).

Falling back on his stubborn belief that exposure to dampness was a threat to his health and at the same time betraying his sense of not being at ease with the Wordsworths, he added defensively: "I eagerly caught the Proposal: for the *sitting* in an open Carriage in the

Rain is Death to me, and somehow or other I had not been quite comfortable" (Letter 1). A note of acrimony could be detected in his resentment over the way the funds had been divided: "The worst thing was the money—they took 29 Guineas, and I six—all our remaining Cash!" (Letter 1).

Sir George and Lady Beaumont, friends to all three travellers, needed to have another kind of explanation. Coleridge gallantly took the blame entirely on himself: "I left Wordsworth & his Sister at Loch Lomond / I was so ill that I felt myself a Burthen on them / & the Exercise was too much for me, & yet not enough" (22 September, *Collected Letters*, II, p. 994). But for Thomas Poole, ever on Coleridge's side, it was right to shift some blame to Wordsworth: "I soon found that I was a burthen on them / & Wordsworth, himself a brooder over his painful hypochondriacal Sensations, was not my fittest companion . . ." (3 October, p. 1010).

The parting of the ways encouraged by Wordsworth, whatever spin Coleridge put on it in letters to others, followed the happiest night he had experienced since leaving home, an evening of laughter and mellow conversation with Dorothy and William and an artist who had temporarily joined their party, before a fire in the ferryman's hut on Loch Katrine. "This was the pleasantest Evening, I had spent, since my Tour: for [Wordsworth's] Hypochondriacal Feelings kept him silent, & [self]-centered—," he told his wife (Letter 1). He should have had every expectation that he would continue on his journey after such an evening. Wordsworth's proposal that he go home at just that point must have taken him aback. The event would not be forgotten, as a glimpse into the future reveals.

A severe breach of trust between Wordsworth and Coleridge that occurred many years later, in 1810–12, highlighted the significance of that separation at Arrochar for Coleridge and sent him back to his Scottish tour notebooks to write an emendation of the term "friend." On 5 June 1812, returning to the entry for 27 August 1803 about the ferryman's hut on Loch Katrine and his note that "we slept in the Barn upon the Hay/ My Friend . . . & the Artist," Coleridge inserted, after the word "Friend," the remark: "O me! What a word to give permanence to the mistake of a Life!" (*Scottish Notes*, p. 151). And to the entry of a few days later, 30 August, concerning the point at which he realized he would have to "make my way alone to Edinburgh," he superimposed another 1812 revisionary remark: "O Esteesee! That thou hadst from thy 22nd year indeed made *thy own* way & *alone*!" (p. 152).

The full blown crisis of relationship for Coleridge began in August 1808, when after completing a successful lecture series, for which he received considerable recognition, he left London, where he had been living in the Strand, and headed to the Lake District for an open-ended visit. He had just started work on a new literary enterprise, a weekly newspaper filled with original writing, called *The Friend*. He was also attempting an opium cure. Much of the time he stayed with the Wordsworths in their new, spacious home in Grasmere called Allen Bank. The household now included Mrs. Wordsworth's sister, Sara Hutchinson, Coleridge's Asra, who assumed the sensitive, invaluable role of amanuensis to him, sitting by his side as he prepared manuscript for his newspaper. Other times he resumed residence at Greta Hall, where he could enjoy and influence his children. His wife Sara, from whom he had been agreeably separated for some time, and with no thought of reconciliation, greeted him cordially. Southey had by this time effectively assumed the role of man of the household. Weeks stretched into months, and by the autumn of 1810 Coleridge, living at Greta Hall, grew restless, so that when an opportunity offered itself to return to London, he seized it.

That opportunity came from an old friend of Wordsworth's, Basil Montague, who came to visit the Lake District while touring with his new wife. The prosperous Montague, sensing Coleridge's need for change, invited him to return to London and stay with him and his wife in their fashionable home in Holburn for the winter. Coleridge's acceptance of this welcome invitation precipitated the final curtain of the Wordsworth-Coleridge drama. William had a conversation with Montague in which he warned him that Coleridge would be a difficult house guest, apparently offering documentation from his own experiences. As Dorothy put it in writing to her friend Catherine Clarkson, "William spoke out and told M. The nature of C's habits . . ." (*Letters of William and Dorothy Wordsworth, II, The Middle Years*, pp. 488–89, 12 May 1811). As a result, when the Montague coach arrived in London, Coleridge was deposited not at the fashionable town house to which he had been invited but at a residence in Soho that had belonged to Mrs. Montague's family. Here the ambience was not what Coleridge had had in mind. At some point he complained to Montague that not enough wine was served him at dinner, when he had a guest. Whereupon Montague revealed to Coleridge all that Wordsworth had said about him, adding insult to injury by indicating that Wordsworth wanted him to do so. Coleridge was deeply hurt by this revelation. Realizing he had been betrayed, he moved out to a hotel.

The wound to Coleridge cut so deep and the news of the rift spread so widely among friends, that something resembling the feuding of political parties began. Coleridge's bitterness festered; friends of the two literary giants took sides. Asra was in the Wordsworth camp. Coleridge looked for an apology from Wordsworth, but it never came. A long silence continued until April 1812 when William arrived in London to resolve the quarrel. A veritable negotiating team was needed to provide communication between the two men. Wordsworth wanted to clarify what he had actually said to Montague and whether or not he had intended Montague to communicate this to Coleridge. The two men never did meet alone to speak face to face. Wordsworth enlisted Henry Crabb Robinson, journalist, diarist, and most importantly, friend to all in the Coleridge-Wordsworth circle, to act as intermediary, a job Robinson, who was soon to be practicing at the bar, executed with legalistic

diplomacy. Coleridge was at last given to understand that William had admitted to telling Montague that he "had no hopes of Coleridge," and that he cautioned Montague against Coleridge's drunkenness, his opium habit, and his outbursts. However, Wordsworth denied having urged Montague to communicate the substance of his conversation to Coleridge.

Thus, by 5 June 1812, when Coleridge went back to his Scottish tour notes, he was still smarting from the wounds of the Wordsworth-Montague incident. Reviewing the 1803 tour, he relived the separation from the Wordsworths at Arrochar, focused sharply on Wordsworth's proposal that Coleridge should return home alone, and understood it in a new light, as prophetic of the recent breaking away and wished bitterly that he had broken free earlier.

To return to the central thread of the 1803 tour, almost the first remark Coleridge jotted in a notebook after bidding farewell to the Wordsworths was a cutting: "*utinam nonq. Vidissem!*" ("Would that I had never seen them!") (*Scottish Notes*, p. 152). This loaded declaration stood without amplification, the tiny pages allowing little space for more and his mood inclined to action rather than composition. Had he been in a more contemplative frame of mind he could easily have cited some serious personal and professional injuries endured from the time he had responded to Wordsworth's appeal to come north to the Lakes and collaborate on a new edition of *Lyrical Ballads*. He had given up proximity to his constant and admiring friend Thomas Poole; his already problematical marriage was now in a shambles; he was losing opportunities to make money. Worse, his confidence in himself as a poet had been broken. Wordsworth had rejected "Christabel" for *Lyrical Ballads*. He had even planned to omit the "Ancient Mariner," which occupied the opening pages of the 1798 *Lyrical Ballads*, and though he ultimately retained it, he shifted this major work to the end of volume I, and added a note to the reader about its "defects." Coleridge found himself agreeing to allow the new edition to be published under Wordsworth's name only. His role at one point was reduced to copying William's poems for the publisher. As for the new and now famous Preface, Wordsworth never adequately acknowledged the contribution of his brilliant collaborator whom he had summoned from the south. (Coleridge told Southey in 1802: "Wordsworth's Preface is half a child of my own Brain / & so arose out of Conversations, so frequent, that with few exceptions we could scarcely either of us perhaps positively say, which first started any particular Thought" [*Collected Letters*, II, p. 830]) And Dorothy had complicity in all of her brother's efforts to relegate Coleridge to a secondary status. "*Utinam nonq vidissem!*" came from a deeper source than simply the Scottish tour.

It was clearly in the spirit of good riddance that he proceeded after the separation at Arrochar. His first moments, indeed his first days away from his professed friends reveal a man celebrating independence and solitude. Dorothy and William had arrived at the Romantically gloomy Glen Croe probably about the time Coleridge returned to Tarbet. In Dorothy's melancholy record: "Our thoughts were full of Coleridge . . . I shivered at the thought of his being sickly and alone, travelling from place to place" (*Recollections*, p. 118). Coleridge hardly required such sympathy. His note for the following day contained joyful imagery: "The Rain drops on the Lake to an army of Spirits, or Faeries, on a wilderness of white Sand . . ." (*Scottish Notes*, p. 152). As well, there was a bright account of his negotiations as he commenced his return trip—waving and shouting and making hand signals to a ferry. He was excited over wild flowers the next day: "Among the Beauties of the Highlands in Aug. & Sept. let me not forget the Fumitory with its white flower on the Hovels & Barns/ & the Potatoe fields with white Blossoms—appearing to my eye the loveliest & richest flower of Gardens—" (p. 155). For a man considered too unwell to go any further, Coleridge was carrying on happily and with perfect competence and consummate self-sufficiency.

Coleridge experienced a great surge of energy when he was relieved of dealing with two other people, the creaking cart, and the stout horse, and responded to his independence like a coiled spring suddenly released. After four days of "freedom" he wrote to his wife: "I am enjoying myself, having Nature with solitude & liberty; the liberty natural & solitary, the solitude natural & free!" (Letter 1).

This pleasure in liberty, in being totally in charge of his own life must account in part for his decision not to return to Keswick immediately. If Coleridge had had serious intentions of heading home, as the Wordsworths assumed he would after the farewells, he quickly gave them up and set upon a Highland journey of his own that would defer his homecoming for seventeen days. The Wordsworths were left to wonder why as they continued their journey they would learn at the inns they checked into that Coleridge had already been there—perhaps just a few days before. He made a number of decisions impulsively and often travelled at breakneck speed.

Wordsworth's recommendation had been for Coleridge to make his way on foot to the Trossachs, which would have meant walking to the head of Loch Lomond and beyond to Glen Falloch and then climbing over a mountain following a crude path that would bring the traveller down at Glengyle, at the Head of Loch Katrine. From there he could walk to the Trossachs, "whence," Wordsworth had said, "it is only 20 miles to Stirling, where the Coach runs thro' for Edinburgh" (Letter 1). It was a plan the Wordsworths themselves would follow on their return to the Trossachs as part of their tour, and one the three of them had probably discussed. But Coleridge ignored this advice and first attempted to catch a ferry to Inversnaid, which would have cost a little more but have been more direct and less strenuous. He could then have simply retraced the route he had already so recently followed—taking the road that went past the Garrison to Loch Katrine, proceeding up to the head of Loch Katrine, coming down the other side of the loch, past the treasured ferryman's hut, to the Trossachs, then east to Callander and down to Stirling. But his adventure in hiring a boatman resulted in an interesting digression and delay.

Frustrated after an hour of trying to hail a ferry to take him across Loch Lomond, he detoured to a cottage on the shore in front of which there was a little boat. With the idea of engaging the owner to take him over, he entered what turned out to be a "small Slaughter House." There a man to whom he gave two shillings for a boat ride insisted that he have a glass of whisky with him. That led to another detour in the opposite direction of where he was trying to go—up the River Douglas, or Inveruglas ("Inveydougle" to Coleridge) to a remote spot inland, where there was a distillery on a farm in the mountain hidden among the foliage and the hogs. Returning to Loch Lomond after his whisky, he headed up a road that followed the loch to its head and on to Glen Falloch, stopping to look at Pulpit Rock (the "Bull Stone"). He continued until he reached a dram house called Garbel ("a Cottage Inn," as he described it to his wife), where he spent the night.

At this point he had another opportunity to take the route Wordsworth had advocated but again he did not. The "gude man of the House" at the inn told him it was only forty miles to Glen Coe (north, and entirely the opposite direction of home), and he seized on the idea of going there as if the plan had issued from the mouth of an oracle. He now began a solo journey that took him on a major circuit of the northern Highlands—a journey that would be a good deal more adventurous than the Wordsworths'. His first taste of freedom after two weeks of intimacy with William and Dorothy brought an unexpected charge of ambition.

A Journey Alone

His solo journey was to take him to some of the most celebrated points in Scotland—the embracing mountains and historic site of clan conflict in Glen Coe, the meandering road through Glen Nevis in the shadow the highest mountain in Great Britain, Ben Nevis, the Falls of Foyers; as well there would be artful bridges, moors, distant castles, and an insider's view of the prison at Fort Augustus.

Easily enough, he made his way to Glen Coe by way of Tyndrum, and then on to Ballachulish, and up to Fort William, the beginning of the "line of the forts," taking the time to explore Glen Nevis but not climbing Ben Nevis. He continued on to Letterfinlay, beyond to Fort Augustus, up the east side of Loch Ness, stopping to visit the famed Falls of Foyers, and proceeded as far north as Inverness, nodding to or visiting Fort George. By then eleven days had passed since he had left his friends. Coleridge did not have a map (William and Dorothy had apparently kept it, assuming, fairly enough, that Coleridge no longer needed it), but he managed well without it. As Keats would in 1818, he followed his nose to the north. His route to the distant Highlands was the classic one that took him across the Great Glen of Scotland, sometimes on General Wade's road, sometimes where he could see the work beginning on the Caledonian Canal. He could easily find his way by asking directions locally. Besides, Coleridge would have remembered what he had read in the new travel work of his acquaintance John Stoddart, popularly known as "Stoddart's Tour" (*Remarks on Local Scenery and Manners in Scotland during the years 1799 and 1800. 2 vols, 1801*).

The next seven days constituted a southward journey; Coleridge seemed at last to be homeward bound. From Inverness he dropped in a generally southeasterly direction, to Aviemore, Kingussie, Pitmaine, Dalwhinnie, Kenmore, Methven, and at last to Perth, where he found two disturbing letters from his brother-in-law Southey: "—his little Girl, an unexpected Gift after 7 years' marriage, died of water on the Brain from teething—and Southey & and his Wife, almost heart-broken, immediately left Bristol, & came to Keswick, Southey for the comforts, he expected from my society, & Mrs Southey to be with her Sister" (to George Coleridge, *Collected Letters*, II, p. 1006). The news snapped Coleridge out of his self-absorption; he leapt into action to arrange a hasty return to Keswick. He had arrived at Perth at 8:30 in the evening. By 9:00 he had read and responded to Southey's letters. By 4:00 the next morning he was on a mail coach to Edinburgh. Rushed though he was, he could not ignore the appeal of this cultivated metropolis: "What a wonderful City Edinburgh is!" (Letter 6). He remained there only two nights, at the Black Bull, in Grassmarket, down the road from the White Hart, where the Wordsworths were to stay a few days later, but he took the time to see some of the major sights—Arthur's Seat, Holyrood House and its adjacent abbey, the Calton Hill observatory, the ships in the Firth of Forth. Interestingly, considering he had not been able to drag himself to visit Burns's home in Dumfries, he took time to seek out Scott's residence on Castle Street—"his House in Edinburgh is divinely situated—it looks up a street, full upon the Rock & the Castle, with its zig-zag Walls like Painters' Lightning—" (Letter 6). The motive for finding Scott's home and noting that he was not there but at Lasswade sprang from discussions Coleridge and Southey had had about producing an encyclopedia of British literature, *Biblioteca Britannica*, and inviting Scott to contribute an article on Scottish poets. Edinburgh was alluring enough to make him wish he could stay longer, but having retrieved the clothes and other belongings he had forwarded from Tarbet, he hurried away on a coach the second morning after he had arrived, and was home at Greta Hall, Keswick by noon on Thursday, 15 September, ten days before the Wordsworths returned to Grasmere, on 25 September.

Coleridge's letters and notes reveal several sides of a complex man. The text ranges from Gothic to pastoral, with a philosopher and a poet breaking through along the way. By far the most entertaining letters and notes are those written in the first eleven days after leaving the Wordsworths. The notebooks contain treasures of poetic images buried among the details of geological shapes and analyses of natural settings. As well there are glimpses of unexpected curiosities—a thigh bone and shin on a bank of earth next to a dug grave with two spades in it at the Burial Ground of Stratherrich "40 strides long, 35 broad" (*Scottish Notes*, p. 170) or "a cornfield [and] two burnt down Huts bearing every mark as if the owners had burnt them in heart's-spite-Joy before their Emigration—" (p. 170). In his letters he reported wonderful tales to be circulated. There was the problem of the shoes that he had burnt while trying to dry them at the "Boatman's Hovel" on Loch Katrine. "The shoes were all to pieces / and three of my Toes were skinless, & and I had a very promising Hole in my Heel" (Letter 4). Short of money because of the way it had been divided up with the Wordsworths, who must have assumed Coleridge would need less since he was going home, he told Sara "I expect to enter Perth Barefooted" (Letter 2) and impressed on her the urgency of borrowing £10 and directing it to him at Perth. Resourceful as usual, however, he somehow managed to buy new ones at Fort Augustus, not long after he posted the letter at Ballachulish.

One of the best tales was of being taken for a spy, seized, along with part of a letter he was writing to Sara, and "clapped into Fort Augustus" (Letter 3). It was "the Governor & his wise Police Constable" (Letter 4) who nabbed him, and in his notebook he wrote of "having breakfasted with the Governor" (*Scottish Notes*, p. 167). It was a brush with the law best not spoken of in detail considering the climate of suspicion in Great Britain at that time, for the Peace of Amiens had been broken in May and the nation seemed poised for a French invasion. Danger put a nice edge on Coleridge's spy story.

A good traveller reports on food and lodging, and Coleridge conforms here. Arriving at the inn at Letterfinlay at 9:00 p.m. He found "all in *bed*—they got up—scarce any fire in; however made me a dish of Tea & I went to bed—Two blankets & a little fern & yet many Fleas!—Slept however till 10 the next morning/ no more

Tea in the House—3 Eggs beat up, two glasses of Whisky, sugar, & $\frac{2}{3}$rds of a Pint of boiling water I found an excellent Substitute" (p. 166). Farther north, at the General's Hut in Foyers, he "Dined on lean mutton, & good Tea, & supt on Sewens & roasted Potatoes" (p. 169). And yet he told Sara that for three days "I have lived wholly on Oat cake, Barley Bannock, Butter, & the poorest of all poor Skim-milk Cheeses . . ." (Letter 4).

As if anticipating a wide reading audience at home, he filled his notes and letters with analogies to the Lake District. There were only four, perhaps five things worth going to see in Scotland for anyone who had been in the Lake Country, he told Southey at the end of his journey: the view of the islands at the foot of Loch Lomond as seen from the top of the highest island, Inchtavannach, the Trossachs, the Falls of Foyers, and the city of Edinburgh, with Glen Coe contending as a possible fifth. These were all touted tourist sites and revealed little original thinking for a man of his sophistication, though what appears to be a flip dismissal of the landscape with which he had been in such intimate contact as he walked alone could just as well be construed as an expression of renewed appreciation for home. Coleridge had not engaged with the Scots themselves sufficiently to know them or speak of their culture. No Highland lass had entered his consciousness deeply enough to produce a poem; he had not been touched by a question like "What? You are stepping westward?"

Yet his solitary if athletic excursion had been haunted by opium related nightmares. He defined his pain to Southey: "My spirits are dreadful, owing entirely to the Horrors of every night—I truly dread to sleep / it is no shadow with me, but substantial Misery foot-thick, that makes me sit by my bedside of a morning, & *cry*—" (Letter 3). Having professed abstinence from opium and an end to hard liquor ("when you see me drink a glass of Spirit & Water, except by prescription of a physician, you shall despise me"), he offers "a true portrait of my nights" in the form of a poem later to be called "The Pains of Sleep." The work is a veritable exposition of his anguish and agony, weaving fear, guilt, shame, terror, screaming, crying, self-loathing, and powerlessness in verse that signals alarm to a stable reader. A second less famous poem from his northern exposure inspires equal concern in only a few lines. It is his own epitaph, composed in his sleep Tuesday 13 September at the Black Bull in Edinburgh while dreaming that he was dying:

Here sleeps at length poor Col, & without Screaming,
Who died, as he had always liv'd, a dreaming:
Shot dead, while sleeping, by the Gout within,
Alone, and all unknown, at E'nbro' in an Inn.

(Letter 7)

Coleridge's health, both physical and psychological, jinxed his Scottish tour. It drove his decisions, generated his worries, and consumed much of his creative energy. His descriptions of what ailed him often rose to such heights of documented drama that they eclipsed the travel writing. When Southey, whose child had died, should have been reading some uplifting thoughts and eloquently turned phrases of consolation, Coleridge offered him this report on his own condition:

I am tolerably well, meaning, the Day Time, for my last night was just such a noisy night of horrors, as 3 nights out of 4 are, with me. O God! When a man blesses the loud Scream of Agony that awakes him, night after night; night after night!—& when a man's repeated Night-screams have made him a nuisance in his own House, it is better to die than to live. I have a Joy in Life, that passeth all Understanding; but it is not in it's present Epiphany & Incarnation. Bodily Torture! all who have been with me can bear witness that I bear it, like an Indian / it is constitutional with me to sit still & look earnestly upon it, & ask it, what it is?   (Letter 6)

If one of the benefits of his Scottish tour was to learn that he functioned better without the Wordsworths, another was to realize that he had tested his physical state and found himself more than equal to arduous travel on a low budget in a country that was not geared to comforts and hospitality. As we saw earlier, Mr. Edmundson, his doctor, thought that the exercise and excitement would be good for his gout if he travelled; Coleridge converted that advice into a maxim. It served as a fine explanation to others of his superhuman exertions. He told one man that he had gout in his stomach and "that this Tour was an experiment for Exercise" (Letter 2). To Welles, an acquaintance claiming expertise in medicine and drugs, he wrote that he walked 263 miles in eight days "in the hope of forcing the Disease into the extremities" (Letter 5). Thomas Wedgwood and Sir George and Lady Beaumont heard the same odd theory, and further that "so strong am I that I would undertake at this present time to walk 50 miles a day for a week together" (*Collected Letters*, II, p. 993). He was keen to present a portrait of competence to his friends.

Bless Wade!

A rhythmic lapping of miles covered pages of one of his small notebooks with an almost musical log of his march toward Perth from Inverness. The report flows milestone by milestone, in a detached voice. "The 9th mile-Stone locks me in completely with Heath-hills" he writes; "beyond the 12th mile stone a Square Furlong of perfect level"; "39th mile, a hugh house to my Right, Mr Macpherson's—40th a new or new-making Village, Kingussie"; "Dalna Cardach/ . . . turned off over the Bridge—/ Between the 73 & 74th Stones a Bottom, with a stream, pleasant Fields—& human white Houses" (*Scottish Notes*, pp. 172-74)—and so on, without Coleridge's tiny line drawings of shapes and designs that illustrate his other descriptive pages.

Coleridge may not have known the lines, but he certainly had cause to appreciate the sentiment of a popular couplet,

Had you seen these roads before they were made,
You would lift up your hands and bless General Wade

Two eighteenth-century military figures, General George Wade, and his successor William Caulfield, had paved the way—literally—for Coleridge's travel from the time he separated from the Wordsworths. Under George I, Wade had been assigned the enormous task of establishing a network of roads, with bridges and forts, in the Highlands of Scotland in response to alarm on the part of the Hanoverian government that there might be further rebellion from Jacobites. The uprisings of 1715 and 1719 were over, but, in 1724 the king had received warnings of substantial Jacobean support. This meant government troops needed roads in order to move rapidly through the Highlands to quell trouble. Barracks and forts would be needed to house the soldiers and make their presence known.

Wade's major initial effort was what today is known as the Great Glen Road, running from Fort William to Inverness. He was responsible for the fortification at Fort Augustus, and his bridges were remarkable—the one over the River Spean, called Highbridge, warranting a lyrical description in Coleridge's notebook:

Highbridge . . . The desolation dreamlike of the fine Road, of the ghost-like "High Bridge" & its 2 arches, & $\frac{1}{2}$ —the Mountain ridges so backlike, odd & void of connection or harmonizing Principle . . . O it is indeed a High Bridge. What can Sappho's Leap have been beyond this?—The building of the Bridge mixes so indistinguishably with the schistous slanting Strata, that form the Banks of the River. (*Scottish Notes*, p. 165)

The spectacular 1736 Highbridge joined the Inverness to Fort Augustus road, completed in 1726, to the more recently completed Fort William to Fort Augustus road, inspiring admiration in early travellers.

Virtually all the roads Coleridge trod were military

roads, though not all built by Wade, whose active period of road making ended in 1740, when he left Scotland. He handed over his work to William Caulfield, whom he had appointed Inspector of Roads. Major Caulfield carried on the project until 1767, creating a latticework of roads and bridges in the Highlands, many of which were later erroneously attributed to Wade. During his watch the final devastating Jacobite uprising, fought and nearly won at Culloden in 1745–46, gave reason for further government investment in military roads. By the time Coleridge routed himself through the Highlands in 1803, there were military roads from Inverness to Dunkeld, from Inverness to Aviemore, down to Ruthven Barracks, Dalnacardoch, and well on to Amulree. A good road lay all the way from Dumbarton to Tyndrum, to Kingshouse, to Fort William. Needless to say, the Fort George-Culloden-Inverness hub fell under close surveillance.

Military roads, marked with milestones and measured in English miles, as opposed to Scottish miles (three Scottish equalling two English), made it possible for Coleridge to track his route without a map and to calculate his staggering records of per diem miles and speed. Far and away his flashiest claim, and the one that made all the letters home, was of his speed and endurance in walking: "I can walk 24 miles a day" (Letter 1); "and now I have walked 28 miles in the course of the Day" (Letter 2); I have walked 263 miles in eight Days" (Letter 3). This last most spectacular announcement went out similarly phrased with qualifications—he walked "briskly," he had no unpleasant fatigue, he averaged thirty-four miles a day—to all his readers: Southey, Welles, Wedgwood, his wife Sara, and his brother George. The claim of walking 263 miles in eight days may still raise the eyebrows of skeptical readers, but it need not. It was made in a letter to Southey written 11 September (though erroneously dated "10 Sept."). Counting back eight days we can place Coleridge in Glen Coe at Kingshouse. By adding miles from point to point using the figures given on modern maps, the

distance from Kinsghouse to the Inverness area with a return south as far as Perth can be calculated. Where figures are lacking but a scale given, one whips out a ruler and measures (five miles to the inch, for example). Disregarding his foray into Glen Nevis, but figuring in a walk, or coach ride, as far northeast as Fort George, such amateur computing yields a total of 266.5 miles, perhaps not precisely accurate but very close to Coleridge's figure of 263 miles. It also authenticates Coleridge's claim that he walked 30 to 35 miles per day for eight days, as the estimate squares nicely with his total of 263 miles in eight days. The extraordinary achievements of a supposedly sick man owe much to the military road making.

Despite the reliability of these roads, there are stretches of Coleridge's route that cannot be accounted for unequivocally. His notes do not leave a record of how he approaches his return southward through the Grampian Highlands after reaching the northern end of the Great Glen Road. An entry in his notebook reports: "Left Inverness in a return post Chaise Thursd. Sept. 8. with a mad drunk Post Boy whom I was soon obliged to quit" (*Scottish Notes*, p. 172). He then describes the countryside through which he passes, after leaving the post boy, up to the ninth milestone, and onward to Moy Hall. This would have been the reasonable route to take on foot, following General Wade's military road, with its dependable milestones to mark the distances. What puts this route into question is the letter he wrote to Sir George and Lady Beaumont two weeks later, after he had returned to Keswick, in which he gives a condensed version of his journey that includes this puzzling claim: "I sent my cloathes forward to Edinburgh / & walked myself to Glen Coe, & so on as far as Cullen, then back again to Inverness, & thence over that most desolate & houseless Country by Aviemore, Dalnacardoch, Dalwhinny, Tummel Bridge, Kenmore, to Perth, with various Digressions & mountain climbings" (*Collected Letters*, II, p. 994). Cullen is the sticking point here. There would have been no sense to his walking to Cullen, a coastal town roughly fifty miles northeast of Inverness. Coleridge surely meant "Culloden" when he wrote "Cullen." In the manuscript of the letter to the Beaumonts, now in the Pierpont Morgan Library in New York, the word "Cullen" is entirely legible, unmistakably what it is. But neither "Cullen" nor "Culloden" appears in his notes or letters, which gives the impression that after returning he tried to reconstruct his travels in the Inverness area and chose a place name that was close to what he vaguely recalled. I maintain he intended to write Culloden because Culloden is only five miles from Inverness, on a coaching route, and on Wade's route as well. Also, in his notebook entry for 2 September Coleridge had written that it was eighty-four miles from Glen Coe to Inverness. There is absolutely no evidence in his notebooks that he went as far northeast as Cullen; there is substantial evidence that he was not only in but around Inverness.

A related Inverness question is this: did Coleridge see Fort George? In his notes, he suggests he did, or meant to, see the fort. "When I come within view of Inverness, stop—take the view of the river—the Town of Inverness & Fort St George—From Inverness to Fort George" (p. 156). Eleven miles northeast of Inverness, Fort George had been built after the Battle of Culloden (1746) and was occupied by the Hanoverian army of King George II. It had inspired a visit by Boswell and Johnson in their 1773 tour of Scotland. Whether it attracted Coleridge to the point of an actual visit or whether he simply acknowledged its proximity on the way to or from Culloden, or when riding with the drunk post boy is not clear. Everything else in the passage is consistent with the directions and sightseeing advised by Hay Drummond, whom Coleridge met in Glen Coe at Kingshouse, 1–2 September.

By what means Coleridge travelled on the final leg of his journey, from Carlisle to Keswick, is the remaining loose end. When he wrote to Southey from Edinburgh on Tuesday 13 September he was not sure whether he would walk from Carlisle all the way to Keswick or take the coach to Penrith.

If the Coachman do not turn Panaceist, and cure all my Ills by breaking my neck, I shall be at Carlisle on Wednesday Midnight—& whether I shall go on in the Coach to Penrith, & walk from thence, or walk off from Carlisle at once, depends on 2 circumstances— whether the Coach goes on with no other than a common Bait to Penrith & whether—if it should not do so—I can trust my cloathes &c to the Coachman safely, to be left at Penrith—There is but 8 miles difference in the walk—& eight or nine Shillings difference in the expense.   (Letter 6)

He promised Southey that in either case he would be home on Thursday in time to dine with him "if you dine at $\frac{1}{2}$ past 2 or 3 o clock." And he was. In fact, he was there by noon, according to his letter to Wedgwood written on Friday. In the light of this marvelous punctuality, it hardly seems important whether he arrived by coach or his inimitable speed walking.

EPILOGUE

His GOUT HAD not been driven out through his extremities by the time he returned home on 15 September, however. He continued to write to friends about the night screams. His relationship with his wife did not improve, and his relationship with William and Dorothy required a cooling off period. Visits between the poet in Grasmere and the poet in Keswick were rare, and Coleridge took umbrage at William's failure to be attentive. In October he reflected to Poole, "I was at one time confined for two months, & he never came to see me / me, who had ever payed such unremitting attention to him" (*Collected Letters*, II, p. 1013). Casting a more cynical eye on his erstwhile collaborator he continued, "I saw him more and more benetted in hypochondriacal Fancies, living wholly among *Devotees*—having every the minutest Thing, almost his very Eating & Drinking, done for him by his Sister, or Wife—& I trembled, lest a Film should rise, and thicken on his mortal eye" (p. 1013). By November Coleridge was requesting of John Thelwell that he purchase drugs for him in Kendal—"an Ounce of crude opium, & 9 ounces of laudanum" (p. 1019).

Before leaving for Scotland he had considered as an alternative going to a warm climate; Madeira or Malta were the choices, and they now seemed desirable possibilities again. In December Coleridge went to Grasmere with his son Derwent to pay a farewell visit to the Wordsworths, intending to leave Derwent there and proceed to one of the foreign countries. His illness flared up, and his visit to Dove Cottage stretched out to a month. Dorothy and Mary, William's wife, nursed him "with more than Mother's Love," as he put it. His relationship to William continued to be idolatrous at

Coleridge's expense: "Wordsworth is a Poet, and I feel myself a better Poet, in knowing how to honour *him*, than in all my own poetic Compositions, all I have done or hope to do—" he told Poole after he left Grasmere (p. 1034). Nor had his envy subsided, as he observed Wordsworth's women catering to his every personal and professional need. When Coleridge left Dove Cottage in January, Dorothy, no doubt having tapped his memory of their journey, resumed the project Coleridge's visit had interrupted—the composition of her *Recollections of a Tour Made in Scotland, 1803*. And on 9 April, Coleridge, responding at last to an invitation John Stoddart had extended before the Scottish tour, sailed for Malta from Portsmouth, for a warmer climate, putting a great distance between himself and all that was the Lake Country.

Coleridge landed in Malta on 18 May and soon enough was earning a salary as Private Secretary to Sir Alexander Ball, the Governor of Malta, carrying out his responsibilities, whatever personal and health problems impinged, with perfect equanimity. The following January he was promoted to Public Secretary. After his return to English soil two years later, on 17 August 1806, his visits to Keswick were temporary and short. The larger picture of Coleridge's life from that point on finds him calling London and environs home, until his death, in 1834, at sixty-one.

During those years he gained celebrity in ways that would not have been possible in his Lake District days. Aesthetic concepts that lay in the back of his mind now found sophisticated audiences. In his lecture series for the Royal Institution in 1808 he articulated the signature principles and psychology of Romantic imagination. His brilliant 1810–11 lectures on Shakespeare, for the Philosophical Institute at Corporation Hall in Fleet Street, turned literary London on its ears, offering readings of the major plays that altered the way we see and read Shakespeare to this day. In 1816 he moved into the home of a generous friend, James Gillman, in the north London suburb of Highgate. Gillman offered not only hospitality but also medical expertise, for he was a physician and in that capacity undertook to monitor Coleridge's intake of opium. As a Highgate resident Coleridge illuminated the worlds of all who came into his midst—as well as those who chanced upon him in the streets, as did a twenty-three-year-old John Keats, who wasted no time writing to his brother George in America, with some amusement, about the meandering one-sided conversation (that "broached on a thousand things") with the celebrated senior poet. When in 1823 Gillman purchased a larger home in Highgate, the best bedroom, a large, airy attic space with an attractive view, went to Coleridge, who by then had come to be known as "the sage of Highgate." He drew to him some of the best minds of his time, including the young Thomas Carlyle, John Stuart Mill, Gabriel Rossetti, and from America, Ralph Waldo Emerson. Still more gathered around for conversation when Coleridge began his "Thursday evenings at home." The London-Highgate years saw Coleridge's poetry gathered into a volume called *Sibylline Leaves*, published in 1817. But the product of his mid-life for which posterity honors him the most, published in the same year, was an epoch making work that has defined literary theory for generations, his *Biographia Literaria*.

SCHEDULE AND ITINERARY

FIRST WEEK

15 August, Monday
Leave Keswick with the Wordsworths 11:20 a.m. On to Threlkeld—turn off at the White Horse—Grisdale—Carrock—Hesket Newmarket (staying at the Queen's Head), visits Caldbeck after dinner.

16 August, Tuesday
Leave Hesket Newmarket 9:00 a.m.—Rose Castle—Hawksdale Bridge—Carlisle—(visit court, see Hatfield in jail, dine)—Longtown. Arrive 8:30 p.m. (staying at the Graham Arms).

17 August, Wednesday
Leave Longtown 9:00 a.m. Enter Scotland over River Sark—Springfield—Gretna Green. Arrive at Dumfries in the evening.

18 August, Thursday
Leave Dumfries 11:30 a.m.—up valley of the Nith, passing Ellisland Farm—Brownhill (staying at Brownhill Inn)—problem with beds, Wordsworth "Feckless."

19 August, Friday
Leave Brownhill—Thornhill—Drumlanrig Castle—Mennok, turnpike house—"up the Coomb in 9 long reaches" to Wanlockhead and Leadhills (staying at Mrs. Otto's in Leadhills)—the Library.

20 August, Saturday
Leave Leadhills—Crawford John—Douglas Mill (dine)—Lanark (staying at the New Inn).

21 August, Sunday
See Falls of the Clyde and go on—Cartland Crags—follow the River Clyde—arrive at Hamilton 9:00 p.m. (staying at an inn).

SECOND WEEK

22 August, Monday
In Hamilton attempt to see Duke of Hamilton's House and picture gallery—Bothwell Castle—Abbey of Blantyre—proceed to Glasgow—arrive Glasgow 4:00 p.m. (staying at Saracen's Head).

23 August, Tuesday
Visit Glasgow Green, the Drying Ground—dine—leave Glasgow in the afternoon in heavy rain—Bowling—Dumbarton (staying in an inn)—cannot sleep because of noise at the street door.

24 August, Wednesday
Visit Dumbarton Rock, note the Governor's House—leave Dumbarton about 11:00 a.m.—Renton, Smollett's monument, Leven Water—Loch Lomond—Luss, enter the Highlands here (staying at an inn by the roadside), does not stir out of the inn.

25 August, Thursday
Morning, note the cottages, fern roofs, chimneys of Luss—Ben Lomond—drop back to visit island of Inchtavannach, climbing to the peak for fine views—proceed up Loch Lomond, catching sight of the Cobbler, to "E. Tarbet" (staying at an "hospitable Inn" where Gaelic was spoken).

26 August, Friday
Go across Loch Lomond with a "Jacobin Traitor of a Boatman" to Rob Roy's Caves then Inversnaid ferry landing—walk to the Garrison, on to Loch Katrine, see gentlemen's houses (staying in one, Mr. Mcfarlane's in Glengyle). Wishing to visit the Trossachs.

27 August, Saturday
Morning, go $3\frac{1}{2}$ miles down the opposite side of Loch Katrine to Ferryman's House (of Gregor MacGregor). The Wordsworths ride in ferryman's boat, but Coleridge walks—down to the foot of the loch, in the heart of the Trossachs. All return to the Ferryman's Hut, Coleridge again by foot. An artist from Edinburgh, whom they met in the Trossachs has joined the party. They have a "merry meal" at the Ferryman's House. The men sleep in the barn, Dorothy in the house. The "pleasantest Evening" of the tour.

28 August, Sunday
Morning. Take boat across Loch Katrine, retrace route to the Garrison and Inversnaid. Stay all day at the ferry house. Highland lasses tend to them, serve meal. Observe waterfall—wait for ferry boat to return from a preaching—cross Loch Lomond to Tarbet—artist still with them (staying in the same inn they had come to on Thursday).

29 August, Monday
Accompanies the Wordsworths to Arrochar—dine at the New Inn on Loch Long, formerly a gentleman's house, look at the Cobbler. Heavy rain. Accommodations for William and Dorothy not available at the inn. Rain stops. About 4:00 p.m. the separation begins with the Wordsworths going on to Inverary and Coleridge returning alone to Tarbet (staying at the inn).

30 August, Tuesday
Is to make his own way alone to Edinburgh but goes in another direction. Walks up the shore of Loch Lomond to a place that turns out to be a slaughter house, hires a man to take him by boat to Inversnaid but instead goes with the man inland, up the River Douglas to a small distillery for whisky. Returns to Loch Lomond, walks up, stopping to visit Pulpit Rock ("Bull Stone"), proceeding up to Glen Falloch (staying in a dram house or "Cottage Inn" at Garbel).

31 August, Wednesday
Host tells him it is only 40 miles to Glen Coe, and he decides to go there—Tyndrum, dines well there—on to Inveroran—(presumably spending the night in Inveroran, at Inveroran Inn).

1 September, Thursday
"I have walked from Inveroran to Kingshouse." Meets Dr. Hay Drummond this day or next morning—(staying at the Kingshouse)—the drovers at Kingshouse rowdy.

2 September, Friday
Leaves Kinsgshouse at 9:30 a.m. to go to Glen Coe—journey through Glen Coe observed at length and in detail—arrives at Loch Leven—Ballachulish—slate

quarries—dines at Ferry House at Ballachulish—crosses on ferry—walks along Loch Linnhe to within a mile and half of Fort William—drinks contaminated water, becoming violently ill—arrives at Fort William, first to Mrs. Monroe's then to Mr. Livingstone's, inns (staying at latter).

3 September, Saturday
Has clothes washed. Writes letters—has been ill. Stays another night.

4 September, Sunday
Leaves inn a little after 8:00 a.m. after a hearty breakfast—walks through Glen Nevis and back—observing in detail—sits on a grave stone to write about the experience—pursues road to Fort Augustus—Highbridge (Spean Bridge) admiring bridge—arrives at Letterfinlay at 9:00 p.m. (staying at Letterfinlay Inn)—has tea and goes to bed.

FOURTH WEEK

5 September, Monday
Has big, odd breakfast at Letterfinlay and leaves at 11:00 a.m. for Fort Augustus. Passes Loch Lochy and Loch Oich, where he has a cup of whisky and hot water in a hovel, "the Gout rising." Reaches Fort Augustus at 4:00 p.m.—"very unwell"—sees the fort. Has checked into an inn, but may have spent night in prison of Fort Augustus.

6 September, Tuesday
Has breakfast with the Governor, having been clapped into prison, taken for a spy, letters confiscated—leaves Fort Augustus at 11:00. a.m.—on to Stratherrick—Whitebridge—Foyers—the General's Hut (staying at the General's Hut)—dines—sups—has "screamy night."

7 September, Wednesday
Walks back about a mile to see the Falls of Foyers—back to General's Hut—description of room there—walk along Loch Ness—two burnt huts—the burial ground—sight of Urquhart Castle across the loch—Inverness (staying at the New Inn).

8 September, Thursday
Leaves Inverness at 8:00 a.m. "in a return post Chaise . . . with a mad drunk Post Boy"—probably to Fort George and Culloden in the chaise—walks on Wade's road to 11th milestone, Moy Hall—20th milestone—Slugan Bridge—darkness—Aviemore (staying in Aviemore).

9 September, Friday
Leaves Aviemore at 8:00 a.m.—more milestone-by-milestone description—the 38th, the 39th, at the 40th, etc.—Kingussie—MacPherson's mansion—Pitmaine—Ruthven Barracks—notices mountains—Dalwhinnie (staying at place with "a good bed").

10 September, Saturday
Leaves Dalwhinnie at 9:00 in the morning—passes 60th milestone—turns off at Dalnacardach—over a bridge—heads down (through Trinafour) to Tummel Bridge—notices bank of the Tummel is very beautiful—ascends 3 miles over the top of a mountain—crosses bridge to Kenmore (staying in Kenmore).

11 September, Sunday
Sees Taymouth Castle, Park, and Woods. At 12:30 p.m. leaves Kenmore—on to Amulree—crosses the Bridge of Almond—over a "blasted Heath" 2 miles to (Methven). Arrives in Perth at 8:30, receives two disturbing letters from Southey—at 9:00 p.m. writes a letter to Southey (incorrectly dated the 10th) that includes the "Pains of Sleep" poem—hastens to return to Keswick—(staying in Perth)—at 4:00 a.m. the next morning takes a mail coach to Edinburgh.

12 September, Monday
Arrives in Edinburgh by noon—checks into the Black Bull, in Grassmarket—climbs crags below Arthur's Seat, in the evening—writes to his wife.

13 September, Tuesday
Edinburgh. Between yesterday and today has seen Holyrood House, the Abbey, Arthur's Seat, Calton Hill Observatory—found Scott's residence—picked up the clothes and other belongings he had sent ahead from Tarbet—spends a second night at the Black Bull—writes to Welles and Southey—has a dream that he is dying and composes his epitaph in his sleep—leaves Edinburgh by coach in the morning.

14 September, Wednesday
Arrives in Carlisle at midnight—probably stays on the coach to Penrith (had not been sure whether he would walk or ride).

15 September, Thursday
Arrives in Keswick by noon (having walked from Penrith, if he stayed on the coach, or walked from Carlisle if he did not). Will dine with Southey in the afternoon.

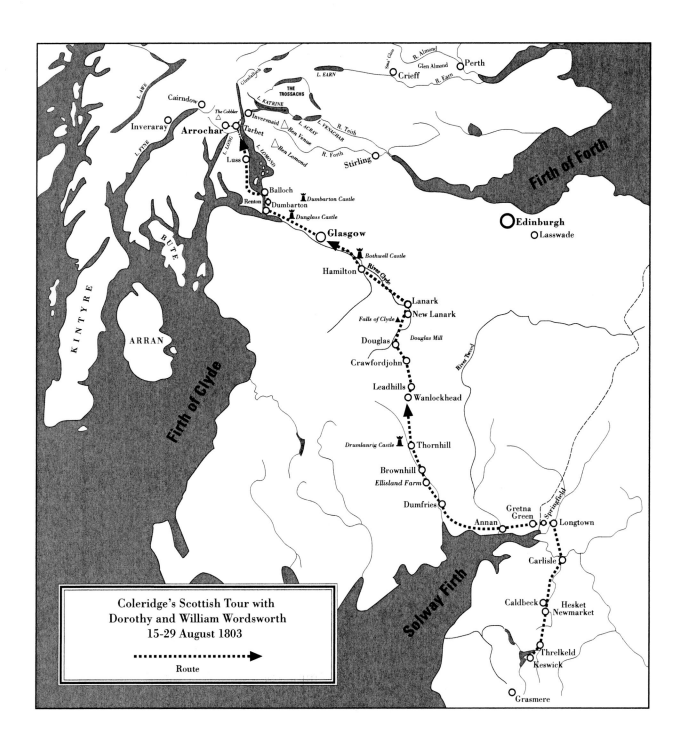

**Coleridge's Scottish Tour with
Dorothy and William Wordsworth
15–29 August 1803**

▪▪▪▪▪▪▪➤ Route

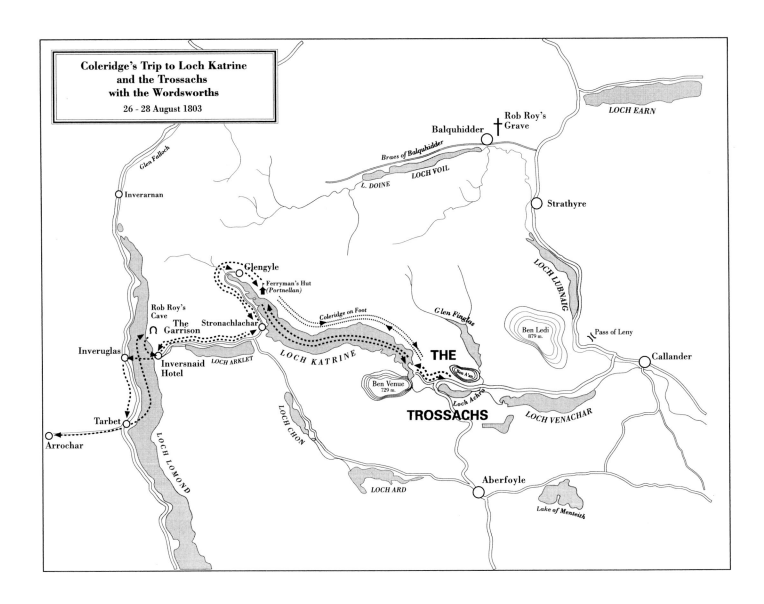

Coleridge's Trip to Loch Katrine
and the Trossachs
with the Wordsworths
26 - 28 August 1803

LOCH EARN

LOCH VOIL

L. DOINE

Braes of Balquhidder

Balquhidder

Rob Roy's
Grave

Strathyre

Glen Falloch

Inverarnan

LOCH LUBNAIG

Glengyle

Ferryman's Hut
(Portnellan)

Coleridge on Foot

Glen Finglas

Ben Ledi
879 m.

Pass of Leny

Rob Roy's
Cave

The
Garrison

Stronachlachar

LOCH KATRINE

THE

Ben A'an

Callander

Inveruglas

Inversnaid
Hotel

LOCH ARKLET

Ben Venue
729 m.

Loch Achro

TROSSACHS

LOCH VENACHAR

Tarbet

LOCH CHON

LOCH LOMOND

Arrochar

LOCH ARD

Aberfoyle

Lake of Menteith

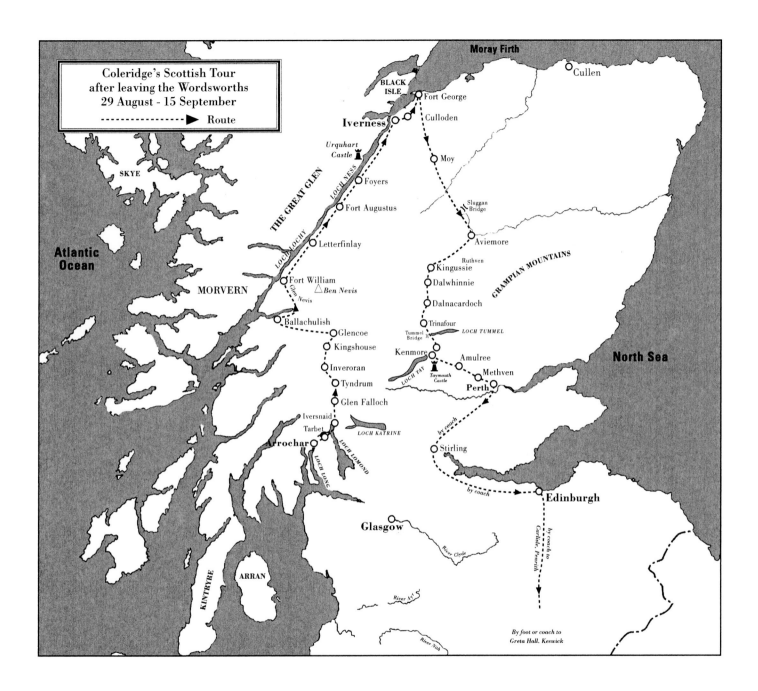

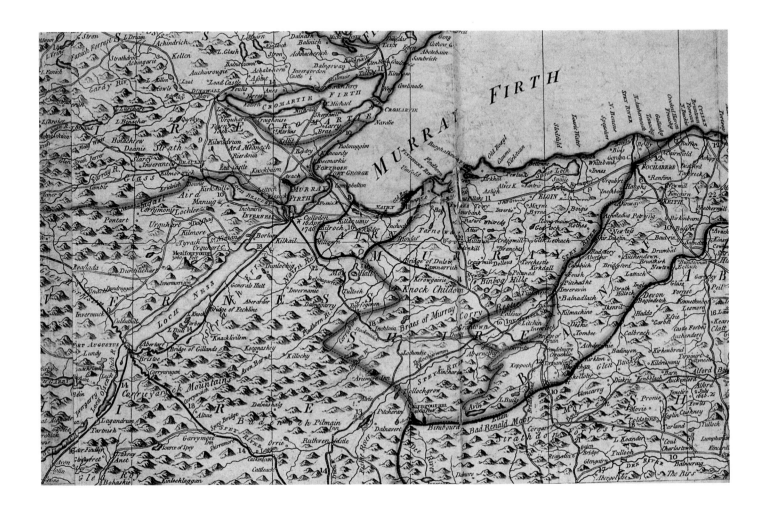

Detail of *A New and Correct Map of Scotland or North Britain with all the Post and Military Roads, Divisions &ca,* by Lieutant Campbell. London: R. Laurie and J. Whittle, 1799. In a *A New Universal Atlas*, T. Kitchen. Plate 10, showing northern Scotland from 1794 edition. Maps 40.f.9. The British Library.

PHOTOGRAPHIC
RETRACING OF THE TOUR

1.   Keswick. River Greta.

2. Keswick. Greta Hall.
"August 15, 1803, W. And D. Wordsworth, and S.T. Coleridge left Keswick, in the Jaunting Car, for Scotland . . ."

3. En route. The White Horse.
"up the steep Hill to Threlkeld—turned off at the White Horse, under Saddleback to Grisdale. . . ."

4. Winding road taken from the White Horse to Mungrisdale ("Grisdale").

5. Caldbeck Commons, on the way to Hesket Newmarket. Pony on the path.

6. Hesket Newmarket. Former public house on the market square.

"—At Hesket we stayed at Young Husband's, The Sign of the Queen's Head. . . ."

7. Caldbeck. The Howk, a limestone gorge with waterfall.
  "After tea we walked to Caldbeck to the Hough or fairy Breaks/"

8. Caldbeck. Ruined bobbin mill at the Howk.

9. Hesket Newmarket. Bridge crossed leaving town.

"—N.B. Between Heskett & Rose Castle two bridges infamously perilous—& no Guide Posts on a road that unusually needs them."

10. Bell Bridge, the second of the "infamously perilous bridges" crossed on the way to Rose Castle.

11. Rose Bridge, over the River Caldew.
"We come to the Bridge over the Caldew by Rose Castle. . . ."

12. Rose Castle.
"We are delighted with Rose Castle, the thickest green Fence to the garden, the two walls, the lower making a terrace/ the House, the Orchard crowding round it— The Chestnuts—"

13. Gateway to Rose Castle.
   "the masses of Ivy over the gateway, from one great root."

14. Sign post near Rose Castle.

15. Hawksdale Bridge.

"Come to Hawksdale Bridge—all above the Bridge very pretty, but all below it a place of ugliest desolation, flooded with stones & sand by the winter Torrents/ in the bed at the River, great Hogsheads of Stones, for what purpose I did not learn/"

16. (*left*) Longtown. The Graham Arms.

"—At ½ 8 in the evening arrived at Longtown, Graham Arms—"

facing page clockwise from top left

18. Carlisle. Present day Court House, in a tower Citadel, erected in 1810.

"At Carlisle I alarmed the whole Court, Judges, Counsellors, Tipstaves, Jurymen, Witnesses, & Spectators by hallooing to Wordsworth who was in a window on the other side of the Hall—Dinner!"

19. Carlisle. West Wall of the old City Walls.

"Walked on the wall—"

20. Carlisle Cathedral.

21. Carlisle. Market Cross, dating from 1682.

"—The divine pearly Whiteness of those rich fleecy Clouds, so deliciously shaded toward the top of their component fleecy parts—Think of this often."

17 The Graham Arms. View from within.

"Reason contents me."

22.   Entering Scotland. Bridge over the River Sark.
"Enter Scotland, on foot—over a Bridge . . ."

23. River Sark, seen from the bridge.
   "of the scanty River Sark, that winds like the convex edge of a
crescent of sand/ then rolls dark over its red brown stones, a peat-
moss River with a 1000 leisurely circles & eclipses of foam/"

24. Springfield. Row of cottages with a two-story building, a former public house, at the end.

"... so mounting a Hill come to the Village of Springfield, 12 years old .../ o what dreary melancholy Things are Villages built by great men/ cast-iron Hovels/ how ill does the Dirt & Misery combine with the formal regular shapes. Are they cells of Prisons? It is the feeling of a Jail. Here at the public House the marriage Ceremony is performed/"

25. Gretna Green. Gretna Hall Hotel, the "New Inn."
"Gretna Green about half a mile a handsome nice-looking 'New Inn' on your Right Hand down a Treeey Lane where the new married Elopers consummate/"

26. Gretna Green. Gretna Old Parish Church and Burial Ground.
"The Chapel & Burial Ground crowded with flat grave Stones, as high as from one's knee to one's Hip, commands a view of Solway Firth."

27.   Gretna Green. Marriage place at blacksmith's shop of Gretna
Hall Hotel, with Jim Jackson, available to preside over vows.

28. Dumfries. Bridge over River Nith.
"We arrived at Dumfries, in the evening, having previously baited the Horse, and dined at Annan—"

29. Ellisland Farm.
On the fourth day of their journey Coleridge and the Wordsworths were aware of passing Ellisland Farm, where Burns lived when he wrote "Tam o Shanter," "Auld Lang Syne," and "Mary in Heaven" while experimenting on farm methods, in 1788.

30. River Nith at Ellisland Farm.
"A hot ride up the pleasant Valley of Nith . . .

31. Brownhill, near Closeburn. Formerly an inn, now a private residence.
"—to a single House, called Brown Hill/ at which our Dinner & apartments gave me the first specimen of the Difference between English and Scotch Inns."

32. Drumlanrig Castle. Built for the 1st Duke of Queensbury.
"We come to Drumlanrigg, thro' a village, long, & all of thickest short single storied Cottages, to contrast with the huge monster . . ."

33. Drumlanrig Castle. Detail of ornamental top.
"crowned with pepper castors, straight before us.—Here I entered into a long reflection on the Duke of Queensburies Character/"

34. Mennock. Old village.
"[W]e proceed to Meinek Turnpike . . ."

35. Route through the Lowther Hills to mining country.

"then up the Coomb, in 9 long winding reaches. . . . Enchanting Coomb, its living smoothness & simplicity for the first 4 reaches, the purple heather on one side give it a character of gay *fineness/*."

36.   Wanlockhead. Sheep leaping through old village.

37.   Wanlockhead. Old School House.
   Children claiming to have studied Latin and Greek fled from Coleridge's examination, Dorothy recollected.

38.   Leadhills. Miners Library.
   "& to Lead Hills. . . . Left Leadhill, Sat. Aug. 20. We leave the good Inn, having had the particulars of the Library, & move on on a like Road. . . ."

39.   Crawfordjohn. Moor, with Duneaton Water running through.

40. Crawfordjohn. Road into the village.
   "to a village called Crawford John"

41. New Lanark. ("Lanark"). Mills on the River Clyde.
   "Huge Cotton Mills, 1000 with Rocky River, the Hills that form its banks, finely wooded deeply and variously ravined. . . ."

42. Lanark. Clydesdale Hotel.
   A plaque reads: "The Building, Formerly the New Inn, stands on the site of the Monastery of Grey Friars. William and Dorothy Wordsworth and Samuel Taylor Coleridge stayed here on 20th and 21st August 1803."

43. New Lanark. Falls of the Clyde. "Theatrical wall of rock."
  "[T]his precipice is part of that round theatrical wall of rock which
embraces the pool at the foot of the Cora Lynn on the left."

44. Falls of the Clyde. Spreading water.
"[B]etween the lower & higher fall . . . is a smooth slope of rock 30 yards in length perhaps, over which the water spreads itself thin & black, rocks just white enough from some unevennesses on this Slope to be a bond of connection between the two masses of white above it and below it/"

45. Falls of the Clyde. Corra Linn.
"Moving higher & winding till we climb up directly over the place where I first sate, we see the whole fall, the higher, the lower & the inter-slope, with only a fragment of the wall-rock & the pool—the whole at once, with the white conical Rock, with a cloak of Mosses, and bushes & fir Trees, growing out of them/"
"The Pool ample & almost round harmonizes very well with the broad *flight-of-stairs* fall/"

46 Corra Castle, above Corra Linn. Ruin.
   "& the old round Tower on the Top of all/"

47. Cartland Crags. View from the summit at the Cartland Hotel.

   "Reaches, short & quite land-locked, the rocks of each from 460 to 500 feet high, as high as any possible Effect could require: now one green Drapery of flowing woods from the summit to the very water."

48. Bothwell Castle. "Douglas Castle."
"Monday Noon, Aug. 22, left Hamilton for Glasgow, where we arrived at 4°clock, having seen Douglas Castle on the way— The Castle of massive red Freestone, surrounded with Rose beds, Shrubs & Climbers indigenous & planted/"

49. Abbey of Blantyre. Ruin opposite Bothwell Castle.
"over the Clyde the more perfectly impressive Abbey of Ballantyre/"

50. Glasgow. The Saracen Head at 209 Gallowgate, formerly an inn.

Like Boswell and Johnson before them, Coleridge and the Wordsworths stopped at the Saracen Head, dining and sleeping there on the night of 22 August.

51. Glasgow. Trongate. "At Glasgow, the hurry & Crowd of People & of Carts, marking a populous trading City, but no Coaches or Carriages!"

52. Glasgow Green, near People's Palace. The "drying grounds," with poles.
"At Glasgow I was most pleased by the two great Washing-Houses & Drying Grounds/"

53. Dumbarton. Dumbarton Rock.

"—The Governor's *new genteel* House between the two Heads of the Rock . . .— We walked at the bottom round the Rock, one side a most noble precipice indeed with two huge Rocks detached from it, one of them larger assuredly than Bowder Stone, & very like it/"

54. Renton. Birthplace of Tobias Smollett (1721—71), near Leven Water. Smollett Monument.

Coleridge translates the long inscription on the monument for Dorothy and tells her the Latin is "miserably bad."

53b. Bowder Stone. At Borrowdale, in the Lake District.

55.   Loch Lomond, with Ben Lomond.
   "Ben Lomond from the Lake rises up, & goes *bounding* down, its outline divided into six great Segments, scolloped like many Leaves, with 5 or 6 small Scollops in each great Segment, of the same Shape—"

56. Luss. Colquhoun Arms Hotel.

Dorothy: "On seeing the outside of the inn, we were glad that we were to have such pleasant quarters. It is a nice-looking white house, by the road-side. . . ."

57. Luss. Chimneys of cottages in the village.

"Observed the Fern-roofed Cottages . . . / the round Chimneys or stool-shaped of 4 sticks—on them a Slate and on the Slate a Stone—"

58.   Loch Lomond. Inchtavannach Island.
  "Mount Inchdevannoch, by a Path most judiciously winding up
this Mountain-Isle."

59.   Tarbet. Pier.
   "Took a couple of Fowls from our Inn, our hospitable Inn, at E.
Tarbet . . ."

60.   Inversnaid. Opposite side of Loch Lomond. Rob Roy's Cave.
  "[and] went with the Jacobin Traitor of a Boatman to Rob Roy's Cave. Such Caves as are always & of necessity where hugh masses of Stone in great numbers have fallen down on one another."

61.   Inversnaid. Ferry Crossing.
  "We returned half a mile to the Ferry."

62.   Inversnaid. The Garrison.
  "—so we ascended into moorland, with strong Views behind us of the three pyramidal Mountains of the opposite Coast of Benlomond these when all becomes Moorland Desolation, combine awfully with two lofty Houses, each with a smaller one attached to it— which we wondered how they came there, but afterwards, found they were a Garrison/"

63.   Loch Katrine.

"The first reach of the Lake, 2 miles perhaps in length, has four Islands, sweet Bays, & Island-like Promontories, one shaped like a Dolphin, another like a Sea-lion/"

64.   Glengyle, on Loch Katrine. Glengyle House. One of the "Gentlemen's Houses."

"We wound along over a Hill into a very interesting moorland till we came in sight of what I may call the Haft or Handle of the Lake, with two Farm Houses—here called Gentlemen's Houses/ . . . a little before we reached the second White House, a perfect Picture . . ./ so we went on, the white House 'green to the very door.'"

65.   Glengyle. Burial ground near Glengyle House.

"—Here Rob Roy died, we passed by his *Burial Ground*/ (each House has a square inclosure for Burying)—" Coleridge was misinformed about Rob Roy, who died and was buried at Balquhidder. The burial ground of Glengyle House was, however, devoted to Mac Gregors.

66.   Loch Achray and the Trossachs.

   "Still as I went on, the view varied & improved in distinctness/
...Till I arrived at the Foot in the Heart of the Trossachs/ I
exclaimed Galilæe vicisti—"

   After spending the night in a ferryman's hut in Portnellan,
Coleridge walked while the Wordsworths went by boat to the foot
of Loch Katrine to discover the Trossachs.

67. Portnellan, below Glengyle. The ferryman's house and another MacGregor burial ground, at the end of the promontory, were at Portnellan.

"I returned to the Ferryman's House—& soon after my Friends—& an Artist, of Edinburgh./ We had a merry meal in the Hovel black & varnished & glistering with peat smoak, the Fowls roosting in the Chimney amid the cloud of Smoke/" Coleridge, the artist, and William slept on hay in the barn. To Sara: "Dorothy had a bed in the Hovel which was varnished so rich with peat smoke, an apartment of highly polished oak would have been poor to it: it would have wanted the *metallic* Lustre of the smoke-varnished Rafters."

68.   Lock Katrine.
     To Sara: "This was the pleasantest Evening, I had spent, since my
Tour."

69.   Inversnaid. Inversnaid Waterfall.
   The party returned to Inversnaid "by the old Path by the Garrison to the Ferry House by Loch Lomond/ where now the Fall was in all *its fury*—"

70. Arrochar. Cobbler Hotel.

"On Monday we went to Arrochar, formerly a Gentleman's House on Loch Long/" Coleridge and the Wordsworths dined here before going their separate ways.

71. Cobbler Hotel. Gaelic inscription over the door.

It was on this very spot that John, chief of the Mac Farlanes had his original home. The massacre of Glen Fruin in 1603 when the Mac Farlanes and the Colquhouns of Luss fought their bloody battle was already history when this stone was engraved in 1697.

72. Mountain called the Cobbler, seen across Loch Long from Arrochar.

To Sara: "So on Monday I accompanied them to Arrochar, on purpose to see THE COB[B]LER, which had impressed me so much in Mr Wilkinson's Drawings—& there I parted with them, . . . having previously sent on all *my* Things to Edinburgh by a Glasgow Carrier who happened to be at E. Tarbet."

73. Tarbet. The harbor and pier, with boats.
  "returned myself to E. Tarbet—slept there. . . ."
  "Tuesday Morn. Aug. 30—Walked to the Shore opposite to the
Ferry, & having waited & shouted & made signals for near an hour
in vain, I wandered on—."

74. River Douglas. "Inveydougle."
"I gave the man 2 ˢ & he said I must drink a glass of Whisky with him, & carried me up the mouth of a River called Inveydougle . . ."

75. Coiregrogain Farm. River, foliage, distillery site.
"& there I found a Distillery all under & among Foliage . . ."

76. Coiregrogain farmhouse and equipment.
"which with its Hogs &c sufficient picturesque—"

77.   Bridge near farm and distillery site.
  "Crossed little Bridges, where streams came down over black
Rocks—"

78.   Company on the return track to Loch Lomond.

79. Pulpit Rock. The "Bull Stone."

"...on my descent I see to the Left a large single Rock, far away from the foot of the Mountain, in a green plot by itself—a little stream winds almost around it, overhung with Alder Bushes—it is cowl'd with Heath—all its side Bare/ the amplest side, viz, that facing the road, is 25 Strides in length, & I suppose at least 40 feet high/ it is 60 Strides round/ in shape it resembles the Gavel End of a House.... This is called, I find, the Bull Stone ... Two Bulls fighting said to have thrown down the Stone/—"

80. Garbel, in Glen Falloch. Ruined, but in the memory of local residents, once a fine home and farm.

"—A Cloud broke on the Hill a little above Garbel, the name of the Dram house where I stopt/ ... Here I determined to go to Glen Coe/. My Landlord asked me 8s for a Pony & Lad for 12 miles!—Good people nevertheless." Coleridge called Garbel a "Cottage Inn" when he wrote to Sara.

81. Glen Falloch. Falls of Falloch.

"I went with him [an intelligent Highlander who spoke low Scottish] into a field to my right, & visited a noble water-fall—during rain it must be a most noble one/ the Trees are old, & *army*, one on each side/ it is one great *Apron* with an oval Pool at the Bottom, but above it you look up thro' a rocky Stream with trees & bushes, & the Fall itself is marked by two *great Cauldrons* delved out in the black rock, down which it falls—into which cauldrons it boils & rebounds/"

82. Upper Glen Falloch.

"I am enjoying myself, having Nature with solitude & liberty; the liberty natural & solitary, the solitude natural & free!"—To Sara.

83.   Tyndrum. The Royal Hotel.
   "—Dined at Tyndrum/ walked a brisk pace under the inspiration of a Bottle of Burton Ale, from Tyndrum to Inveroonan/"

84.   Inveroran Hotel.
   "Waited an hour & a half for a dish of Tea/ the most civil promises all the while/ at Inverooran/ this a fair specimen of Highland Manners."

85.   Kingshouse. Kings House Hotel.
   "This Kingshouse from the rancid Moorland Peat smells like a dirty Macquerel with Bilge-water/ 9 miles every way from all Dwelling, vile Troop of Drovers, with fiddle & dancing, & drinking, kept it up all night, one clamour like a crew of Pirates that 'House on the wild Sea with wild usages.' When they broke up, one of the Household had the modesty to open my bedroom Door, & bring me in a Drover for a Bedfellow/ and I might have been forced to get up, if the Drover had not had some sense & good manners—"

86. Stream in Glen Coe.

   "Sept. 2. 1803. Friday Am—when at length I shall have procured abit of Breakfast, to go to Glencoe and thence whither?—84 miles to Inverness.— $\frac{1}{2}$ past 9 left that devoted Kingshouse, & in less than a mile entered Glencoe."

87.   Glen Coe. Mountains.
  "Mountains, Turrets, Steeples, Sugarloaves, & often Bulls' Brows,
Brows savager than those of Urus or Byson/"

88. Ballachulish. Slate quarry.

"So the country growing more and more cultivated, I came down on Loch Leven. . . ."

"—Pass a slate Quarry, with a brig close under it."

89. Ballachulish. Old Ferry House, now Ferry Bar of the Ballachulish Hotel.

"—Dined at the Ferry House at Ballychulish . . ."

90. Ballachulish. Ferry crossing. With new bridge, looking back to Ballachulish Hotel across Loch Linnhe.

"and—crossed the Ferry—"

91.   At the ferry crossing, looking back toward Glen Coe.
"& that *Pitadonish* mountain with the obscene name/ O horid!
The blessed Sun fell on it, above the green Hill, with the slate
Quarries now appearing at its feet/ between that green Hill & another high mountain this Maiden of Glencoe appears behind and
between them bleak, & sunny with scattered Clouds—"

92.   Ballachulish. View toward Mull.

93. Fort William. Glen Nevis and Ben Nevis. ("Glen Nevish" and "Ben Nevish.")

"—The Day continues glorious—enter Glen Nevish, a broadish Valley with a broad Shallow River, single Trees, Alders, & Sycamores, planted thick without interspace along its Banks—Ben Nevish to my Left, its height entirely lost to me, but its sides are nobly torrent-rifted—a belt of ragged Wood athwart it, half way, the *apparent* ascent—above the woods grey craggs stained with yellow green—8 great rifts, each no doubt forming tremendous Precipices to look down into—"

94. Glen Nevis. River.

"/at the end of the Coomb a low curve from Ben Nevish slides softly down into the Glen, and incloses the river, and its stony Bed now too big for it & trees or rather tall Bushes/"

95. Glen Nevis. The road.

"Here thro' the whole Glen, the road most, very, or damn'd bad/ Adam Smith? Pray, would the Regiment have been better employed drinking at their Quarters than in substituting those fine Roads for such as these?"

96.   Glen Nevis. Water, rocks.
   "For there are 2 falls, one on each side of the
Rock/ the further broad, this narrow & higher/
the hugh Stones above this fall, one adhering to
the Bank, a middle Stone, & the prolongation of
the rock, & the water of this fall runs in two
gutters one each side this middle ridge of
Stone/"

97. Glen Nevis. Road through arch of rock and tree.

"So having mounted a little & seen that there was not probably anything more to be noticed,

98.   Glen Nevis. Stream and trees.
   "& now my mind being as it were leisurely and off the stretch with
what delight did I look at a floatage of Shadows on the water, made
by the wavelets of the Stream, with what delight that most exquisite
net at the bottom/ sandy & pebbly river, all whose loops are wires of
sunshine, gold finer than silk. . . .—O we turn from novelties &
rarities to old Delights & simple Beauty!—"

99. Glen Nevis. Burial ground.

"I pass a Churchyard close by the road, fended from the Sea by a natural Wall of rock—..."

100. Glen Nevis. Burial ground.

"went *up* two of my steps, & sate down on a flat grave-stone, & wrote this. —Peace & Blessings be with us all!—With thee, my Sara!—"

101.   Spean Bridge. High Bridge, now a ruin.
  "Highbridge—refused Tea—Highland Inhospitality explained—the desolation dreamlike of the fine Road, of the ghost-like 'High Bridge' & its 2 arches, and ½—...O it is indeed a High Bridge. What can Sappho's Leap have been beyond this?—The building of the Bridge mixes so indistinguishably with the schistous slanting Strata, that form the Banks of the River."

102.	The Braes of Lochaber, a few miles above Spean Bridge.

"But what a joyous Sight of Cows & Calves, a lowing browsing Multitude, with milking Lasses chattering Erse/ church & 20 or more scattered Hovels on the Cultivated Hill, that climbs half way up the black Mountain Brays of Lochaber."

103. Letterfinlay. Former Letterfinlay Inn.

"Arrived at Letir Finlay, IX oclock/ all in bed—they got up—scarce any fire in; however made me a dish of Tea & I went to *bed*.—Two blankets & a little fern & yet many Fleas!"

104. Letterfinlay. Loch Lochy, opposite the inn.

"Loch Lochay very like the narrowest, & barest parts of Ulswater/ a Lake, in short, among bleak Hills."

105. Fort Augustus, as Benedictine Abbey.

To Sara: "I was writing to you from Fort Augustus, when the Governor & his wise Police Constable seized me & my Letter—Since then I have written to nobody."

106. Prison cell in Fort Augustus.

To Southey: "I have been a wild Journey—taken up for a spy & clapped into Fort Augustus—"

107. Stratherrick. Tarn with islands, on Wade's military road.
  "Pass a Tairn, almost surrounded by 5 bare-knobby Hills, with 4
Islands in it, covered with Bushes & Heather—"

108.   Road north from Stratherrick to Whitebridge and Foyers.
"Over the Hill a most extensive area of Heath & Moorland crowded to the right & left."

109.   Whitebridge. Bridge.
   A Wade bridge, this 1732 hump-backed single span structure crossing the River Fecklin was critical in connecting the military road
engineered by Caulfield, Wade's inspector General, to provide a
direct route from Fort Augustus to Inverness, both Hanoverian barrack forts.

110. Zig-zag road to Foyers.
"The road turns down into like a winding Staircase, & I face what was before at my back—"

111. River near zig-zag road.

112. Foyers. On Loch Ness. Foyers Hotel and General's Hut Bar.
"I wound up thro' a wood to the General's Hut where I was received with sufficient & increasing Civility—"

Said to be on or near the site of the General's Hut, General Wade's headquarters while he was supervising the building of roads and bridges, the present hotel celebrates a significant military past with its General's Hut Bar. Wade's headquarters functioned as an inn to travellers, including Boswell and Johnson, well after it served its original purpose.

113. Foyers. Falls of Foyers.
   "[T]he Fall at length grew into sublimity &
its own dimensions. . . . The vase-like Shape
of the fracture out of which it comes, as if one
side of a hugh vase had been chipped out, & this
stream flowed out at the rim/"

114. Lower Foyers. Woods.

"The road from the General's Hut goes between Birch Trees—"

115. Along Loch Ness, above the General's Hut. Ruined hut.

"About $\frac{3}{4}$ of a mile from the General's Hut, divided from the Lake by a Birch Coppice & a cornfield two burnt down Huts bearing every mark as if the owners had burnt them in heart's-spite-Joy before their Emigration—"

116. Along Loch Ness, above the ruined hut. Burial ground.

"a Horse, two Birchen Poles with 5 cross rafters with twists of Hazels & Rope—inclosing a few Sheaves of Oats, the poles dragging along the ground, their ends merely flattened.—This I stopped & examined by the Burial Ground of Stratherrick, 40 strides long, 35 broad—a grave dugged, 2 Spades in it, the bank of Earth, Thighbone & shin by it/ tis a wild burial place—contrast it with St Clement's in the Strand/ twice I walked round it, & stripped the seeds from a large Dock which I will plant at home in its memory."

117. Loch Ness. Urquhart Castle, on opposite shore.

"A Break in the Mountain Bank of the Loch Ness, the Interspace green & yellow, but mostly, yellow, with cultivated Ground—& at its foot washed by the Loch, on a rock-ground of its own a mass of Building, Tower, Castle, I know not what/"

118. Loch Ness. View toward Inverness.

"Now approaching the end of the Loch, many Juniper Trees on each side of my Road—The mountain across the Lake— one single Farm naked, clay Scars—with grey-blue Slate Screes, then a Break & a Dip."

119.   Inverness. River Ness and bridge.
    "When I come within view of Inverness, stop—take the view of the River—the Town of Inverness & Fort St George—" (Travel advice given to Coleridge by Dr. Hay Drummond at Kingshouse.)

120. Inverness. Columba Hotel, on the River Ness.

"—I was every way unfortunate— Dancing with Indian Yells to a late Hour at the new Inn in Inverness—"

121. Inverness. Steeple in Town Center.

122. Fort George, on the Moray Firth. Entrance.

Coleridge would "take a view of" Fort George if he followed Hay Drummond's advice.

123. Fort George. Parade, with soldiers of a Highland Regiment.

124. Culloden Moor. Section of the battlefield.

125.   On Wade's military road from Inverness to Moy.
"—6 miles from Inverness, the Country rude Moorland . . ."

126. Road to Moy.
  "after this the wildest of all wild moor-lands—"

127. Road to Moy.
  "The 9th mile Stone locks me in completely with high Heath-hills, a few Scotch Firs—the hills often black—and the whole Surface tossed about, rising, dipping, buldging & sinking—"

128. Moy. Moy Hall.
"11th milestone, a water & handsome House, Moy Hall, to my left—"

129. The "water" on which Moy Hall stands, in private grounds.

130. Sluggan Bridge, over the River Dulnain. After the twentieth milestone.

"Cross a high Bridge over River Slugan/ a pretty wooded bank/"

131. Woods near Sluggan Bridge.

"Long field & then a Hill-Bank of Birches—seen till my road comes among Firs, & at last thru' a *noble* Firwood— Remember that bough caught up by the wind, forced over the fork of the Tree, & there growing, its elbows on the side split & naked!—O what work the winds make with these Branches!"

132. Aviemore. Cairngorm Mountains seen from the town.

"I walked thro' a birch grove/ & so on to Aviemore—Left it, Friday morning. . . .—At length gain a view of mountains before me/"

133. Kingussie. Ruthven Barracks and Castle.

"—40th [milestone] a new or new-making Village, Kingussie—& a fine Ruin of a Castle to the Left—"

134. Kingussie. Pitmaine Lodge, now the Folk Museum.

"& so to Pitmaine—the first place where *whisky* was not—& Rum commenced—"

"To be sure, the Gardens at Pitmaine worthy of note/—a bank, a sloping down Bottom, a semi-ellipse of Trees, form the only inclosure; & many Trees in the Garden itself—"

136. Dalwhinnie.   Government-built
hotel.
  "a good bed, & left it Sat. Morn."

135.   Milestone, on the old military road
to Dalwhinnie.
  "—a wild & desolate Moorland, with
moorfowl, on the Dalwhynny . . ."

137.   Dalwhinnie Distillery.

138. Dalnacardoch. Former kingshouse with barracks, renovated for use as a private residence. Front entrance.

139. Dalnacardoch. Entrance from the stable yard.
"Dalna Cardach/"

140.   Dalnacardoch. Bridge crossed after leaving Dalnacardoch.
   "& turned off over the Bridge—" And onto the military road to
Tummel Bridge, by way of Trinafour.

141. Tummel Bridge. The 1773 bridge over the Tummel.
"Between the 73 &74th Stones a Bottom, with a stream, pleasantest Fields—& human white Houses. The Bank of the Tummel very
beautiful. . . ."

142. Kenmore. Eighteenth-century bridge to Kenmore.
"The darkness came on after I had crossed the Bridge by the Castle/

143.   Kenmore. Kenmore Hotel.

144.   Kenmore Hotel. Interior.

145. Kenmore. Taymouth Castle.
"—Taymouth Castle, Park, and Woods."

146. (below left) Kenmore. Gate to castle and park.
147. (below right) Kenmore. Gate at exit of park.
"Left Kenmore, Sunday M. ½ twelve, Sept. 10—for Perth—"

148. Amulree. Amulree Hotel, originally a kingshouse.
"sent out of my way to Amalrhee/

149. Perth. Bridge over the River Tay.
To Southey: "I arrived here half an hour ago—& have only read your Letters—scarce read them." (Sunday night, 11 September.)

150. Perth. View down Tay Street.

To Southey: "O dear friend! it is idle to talk of what I feel—I am stunned at present—& this beginning to write makes a beginning of living

151.	Perth. Salutation Hotel.

To Sara: "—I have not heard of Wordsworth; nor he of me. He will be wondering what can have become of me ....I must write no more / it is now 1 0 0 clock / & I go off in the mail at 4 in the Morning—....—O Sara! Dear Sara!—*try* for all good Things in the spirit of unsuspecting Love / for miseries gather upon us. I shall take this Letter with me to Edinburgh—& leave a space to announce my safe arrival, if so it please God—Good night, my sweet Children!"

152.	Perth. Tower of Church of St. John's.

The seriousness of Southey's news—the death of his child—prevails over Coleridge's time in Perth, and determines his plan to return to Keswick as speedily as possible.

153.	Dupplin Castle, near Perth. Rebuilt, on the site of the original castle, and now a private residence owned by the Dewar family.

Coleridge had learned from Hay Drummond that it was a mere "5 miles from Perth to Dupplin Castle."

154. Edinburgh. The Black Bull. Grassmarket.

To Thomas Wedgwood: "—To diversify this dusty Letter I will write in a Post-script an Epitaph, which I composed in my Sleep for myself, while dreaming that I was dying. . . . It was on Tuesday Night last at the Black Bull, Edinburgh—"

155. Edinburgh. Street scene in Grassmarket. Buildings below the Castle.

"—What a wonderful City Edinburgh is!—What alternation of Height & Depth!"

156. Edinburgh. Scott's residence at 39 Castle Street.

To Southey: "Walter Scott is at Laswade, 5 or 6 miles from Edinburgh—his House in Edinburgh is divinely situated—it looks up a street, a new magnificent street . . ."

157. Edinburgh Castle.

"full upon the Rock & the Castle, with it's zig-zag Walls like Painters' Lightning—."

158. Holyrood Abbey. Roofless chapel at Holyrood Palace.

The church per se had been destroyed during the Reformation; the roof collapsed in 1768, and it was in that condition when Coleridge viewed it.

158. Holyrood Palace.

"—Holy rood House palace & Abbey in front form an arch up to the Castle for a mile."

160. Edinburgh. Arthur's Seat.
To Southey: "I climbed last night to the Crags just below Arthur's Seat, itself a rude triangle-shaped bare Cliff, & looked down on the whole City & Firth."

161. View from crags below Arthur's Seat.
"—The smokes rising up from ten thousand houses, each smoke from some one family—it was an affecting sight to me!"

162.   Return to Grassmarket and the Black Bull.
To Southey: "No Conveyance left or leaves this place for Carlisle earlier than tomorrow morning—for which I have taken my place."

163.   Street in Grassmarket.
"The passing a day or two, quite unknown in a strange City, does a man's heart good—He rises 'a sadder and a wiser man.'"

164. Return to England. Cumbria. Mileage sign at the Salutation Inn at Threlkeld.

165. Keswick. Mountain view from home, Greta Hall.

THE TRAVEL LITERATURE

SCOTTISH NOTES
AND LETTERS

COLERIDGE'S NOTEBOOKS AND letters provide a radiant chronicle of his journey through Scotland. The notebooks themselves read like artists' sketchbooks, filled with quick verbal pictures and small line drawings. One can imagine Coleridge jotting and drawing even as he walked, lifting his eyes to a passing scene and dropping them to his small notebook, pencil in perpetual motion. Some images come in a flash, others seem methodically drafted. He scrutinizes nature, getting to the essence of a particular tree, or the contours of a mountain. He is excited to absorb and remember an object in the external world he is discovering: "O never, never let me forget the beautiful birch stems, like silver tarnished. . . ." It frustrates him that he cannot fix a scene with more than words and pencil: "O Christ, it maddens me that I am not a painter or that Painters are not I!" The looseness and irregularity of his punctuation, the total absence of it at times, the ubiquitous Coleridgean slash (or forward stroke)—all give the impression of hectic journalism. This quality is reinforced by an editor's ellipses, inserted to show that words have been lost, and with which, of course, Coleridge had nothing to do.

The letters reveal the more "correct" Coleridge. Written though they were under intense circumstances, they enjoy the advantage of being composed in a still place, most in a hotel room, and with the purpose of communicating thoughts and passions to a particular reader. Together with the notebooks, the letters constitute a stunning body of travel literature that takes the reader through the range of notes written on the go, with their vitality and spontaneity, to commentary composed with a backward look and time enough for

making judgments. Style runs from loose and personal, at times even confessional, to relatively formal and outgoing. The two poems Coleridge included in his letters, the long one that would become "To Sleep," and the short epitaph on his death, indicate clearly that he was still exercising his poetic faculties.

Coleridge used three very small notebooks on this journey, no single one of which was dedicated entirely to the Scottish tour, and all three now in the British Library. Anyone who has taken a strenuous journey and attempted to keep a journal must marvel at what and how Coleridge stored in virtual computer-chips of notebooks. One, "Notebook 6" (MS 47, 503), had a brown leather cover with a metal clasp (broken) and measured, both cover and pages, $4\frac{1}{2}$ by $3\frac{3}{4}$ inches. Of the 50 pages, numbered, by Coleridge or someone else, only some refer to the Scottish tour. All are written in pencil, and at this point, very difficult to read. (An advertisement for "metallic pencils" in one of his notebooks promised the merchant's product was of such a fine quality that "the Writing is Secure from Erasure"!)

"Notebook 7" (MS 47, 504) was of comparable size, also with a brown leather cover and metal clasp. Longer at 75 pages, this book is the most useful in that it covers almost all of the trip and is largely legible. Originally in pencil, some of the notes have been written over in ink. Coleridge used the inside of both the front and back covers as pages for his entries. The third journal, "Notebook 16" (MS 47, 513), was the largest, with a cover that measured $6\frac{1}{2}$ by $3\frac{3}{4}$ inches, and pages of $6\frac{1}{8}$ by $3\frac{3}{4}$. Like the others, it had a brown leather cover but was secured by a flap across the front that slipped into a belt. Obviously more expensive, it had a portfolio-like space for, perhaps, extra paper; a green lining; three channels for pencils; and a handsome binding. Of the 240 pages (numbered like the others) some were filled with notes from the Malta visit of 1804–1805.

Kathleen Coburn edited these notebooks for inclusion in the first volume of her major work, *The Notebooks of Samuel Taylor Coleridge* (4 double vols. New York: Pantheon Books, 1957; Bollingen Series L, Princeton University Press). Coburn's achievement in identifying the notebook entries that pertain to the 1803 tour and transcribing Coleridge's handwriting, often so faded, smudged, or hastily put down, commands the respect, and speaking for myself, amazement, of the scholarly visitor to Coleridge's notebooks. I have based my text on Coburn's edition, making only minor changes in punctuation to clarify meaning and eliminating some of the editing apparatus (varieties of brackets and numbering of entries). Where Coburn offered two or even three possible readings of a word that was unclear to her, I have made a judgment based on my examination of the original manuscripts. I have been fortunate in receiving guidance in settling on an appropriate way to present the notebooks to readers from the eminent Romantics editor Jack Stillinger. All headings are my own. The small symbol ~ replaces Coburn's numbering to indicate the beginning of a new entry. The collective body of entries on the 1803 tour have been called *Scottish Notes* to distinguish them from *Notebooks*.

The letters have been reprinted from *Collected Letters of Samuel Taylor Coleridge, Volume* II, *1801–1806*, edited by Earl Leslie Griggs (6 vols. Oxford: Clarendon Press. 1956–72). All brackets in my text are as they appeared in the Griggs edition. If the letters employ a slightly different editing style from the notebooks, it is not only because Griggs and Coburn had slightly different practices in general but also because Griggs had more clearly defined material to work with, for, to put it simply, Coleridge's handwriting is comparatively easy to read in his letters. One of these, Letter 2, to his wife, is not complete. The bottom of each page had been cut off, and five and a half lines had been heavily inked out. As he did in the notebooks Coleridge misspells or varies the spelling of place names (Edingburgh, for example), and his use of capital letters continues to be unsystematic. Still, the letters are coherent, engaging, often moving, always lively. The letter we do not have because, as he tells his wife in Letter 4, "I was writing to you from Fort Augustus when the Governor & his wise Police Constable seized me & my Letter—," provokes interesting conjecture. Would it have told precisely why he got into trouble? Missing, too, is the letter he directed his wife to address to him, with £5 enclosed, to the post office at Perth. What might Sara have said about his departure from William and Dorothy? These mysteries aside, the surviving letters of the Scottish tour make compelling reading as travel literature, fleshing out an itinerary that began with a scheme and ended with an accident.

Scottish Notes

Greta Hall, Keswick to Gretna Green, Scotland

~Monday, Morning, 20 minutes after 11, August 15, 1803, W. And D. Wordsworth, and S. T. Coleridge left Keswick, in the Jaunting Car, for Scotland, up the steep Hill to Threlkeld—turned off at the White Horse, under Saddleback to Grisdale[1] . . . road/ so on to Carrock, and Heskett Newmarket.[2] Dined . . . Eggs, Chicken . . . , &c Arrived about half past 4. After tea we walked to Caldbeck to the Hough or fairy Breaks/[3] —In addition to my former remarks on this place note[4] that the upper waterfall within a yard of it [was] parted into two by a great black Block of Rock covered with . . . angles & concave Scollops, is that of a Pulpit, & Reading Desk, only suppose them solid instead of hollow/ The Pulpit's Front is bare of water, which pours down on each side of it in two streams of unequal legs—both whirl, but the short Leg more copiously, falling—the reading Desk cloathes it with a thin surplice of white water. Close by the rock which helps to form the recess ⟨⟩ on the left as you look up the Brook is a little quiet Spout//What a self-same Thing a Waterfall if you like/ if you look at it stedfastly, what fits & starts and convulsive Twitches of Motion//

The Ash hanging in an inclined Plane, like a sloping Plank Bridge, across the Brook half a stone throw from the waterfall// the Hayfield close on my right, on the Hill above me, its limestone wall by my right hand/

Seat of limestone, in the limestone Bank of the Dell Brook, coming out from the rock, like a thick Slate, or London Flag Stone/ —above it some 4 or 5 feet a low ruined Garden wall, overgrown with gooseberry Trees, which formed a thick bushy *Shed* over the seat—& above these a double-blossomed Cherry Tree in its barren Pomp, stretching out beyond the Shed, & dropping its flashing Blossoms into the River/ —at Hesket we stayed at Young Husband's, The Sign of the Queen's Head[5] where I was before—a striking & noble-looking Girl, with a flat face, but yet with large features & large eyes a noble one. Out of the parlour window looking across the market place & over the market House, a group of Ashes, of which the hithermost hath its

[1] "Mungrisdale" on today's maps.

[2] Hesket Newmarket has a town cross at its center, a little market square opposite the inn in which Coleridge and the Wordsworths stayed. The town became a "new" market in 1751.

[3] In Caldbeck, named for the cold beck, the River Caldew, that runs through it, the remains of mills, driven by water, tell the tale of a once active mill town. A ruined bobbin mill, carefully preserved, lies on the path to the waterfall in a deep gorge referred to as the Howk (Coleridge's "Hough"). A Lake District National Park Authority plaque reads: "A Magical Gorge. The limestone gorge in which the mill sits is a very special place. Its water-sculptured features have attracted romantic names such as 'Fairy Kettle' and 'Fairy Kirk.' The rich vegetation of the gorge is typical of a limestone woodland and it includes rare ferns, such as the Shield Fern." Of additional interest to Colridgeans visiting Caldbeck is St. Kentigern's churchyard where the beautiful Maid of Buttermere, Mary Harrison, *née* Robinson, is buried.

[4] Coleridge had visited Caldbeck and the Howk in October, 1800, noticing "prodigious quantities of [a] huge-leaf Plant on the banks of the water" and "Fairies' parlors and fine Cathedral seats overhung by rocks—in the parlour two window-holes." On this occasion he crawled into the caves (the "windows") near the waterfall. (See *Notebooks*, 1, 828)

[5] The house, now a private residence, represents only part of the original Queen's Head. The public house, as an

inn, extended to neighboring houses. A plaque acknowledges the visit of a later celebrity, forgetting Coleridge and the Wordsworths. Charles Dickens and his friend Wilkie Collins stayed here in September 1857 while on a journey to Cumberland. The landlord's name at that time was Joseph Porter. The high point of their visit was a climb up Carrock Fell during which Collins sprained his ankle. Dickens and the landlord, who had gone along as a guide, returned the disabled Collins to the Queen's Head in a dog cart. The two writers collaborated on an amusing travel account of their Cumberland visit entitled "The Lazy Tour of Two Idle Apprentices," serialized in the weekly journal *Household Words*. The first chapter (3 October 1857, XVI, pp. 315–17) offers a description of the interior of the Queen's Head that is worth comparing to Coleridge's: "The ceiling of [the] drawing-room was so crossed and re-crossed by beams of unequal lengths, radiating from a centre in a corner, that it looked like a broken starfish." A "snug fire-side and a couple of well-curtained windows, looking out upon the wild country behind the house" were noted as well as the nick-nacks, engravings, Staffordshire china, musical instruments, and books (Fielding, Smollett, Addison and Steele), the authors praising the "evidence of taste, however homely, that went beyond the beautiful cleanliness and trimness of the house," and contrasting this to the gloom and loneliness of the village itself.

<hr>

[6] Carrock Fell, a low mountain near the Mungrisdale road, with its "brethren" in the Skiddaw Fells range, primarily Skiddaw itself and Blencathra (or Saddleback, as it was called in Coleridge's time).
[7] Now the residence of the Bishop of Carlisle.

topmost Twig exactly like a Rook or Magpie perching on the topmost Twig. N.B. The manifest magnitude which this Twig attained by its assimilation to a familiar Form, the size of which had been exempted by its old acquaintance, Queen Imagination, from all changes of perspective.

The sanded stone floor with the spitting Pot full of Sand Dust, two Pictures of young Master & Miss with their round Birds' Eyes & parlour Dress, he with a paroquet on his hand, horizontal, the other hand pushed forward just below it—she with a rose in her uplifted perpend. hand, the other hand grasping it to support it in that Posture. The whole Room struck me as Cleanliness quarreling with Tobacco Ghosts.

~Tuesday Morning, Aug. 16. left Heskett at 9 °clock/ our whole Expence 0,,18,,10. —a fine view behind us from the first Hill— and a pleasant country of Hills & Woods and Dells, & valleys—in the manner of the Yorkshire Dales—/ Rose Castle & the valley thro' which the road leads delightful with richly wooded Hills & a peep of the Caldew, rich fields—the whole rich & green, & bounded on the South by the Carrock & its Brethren[6]—N.B. Between Heskett & Rose Castle two Bridges infamously perilous—& no Guide Posts on a road that usually needs them. Lay stress on this.—We come to the Bridge over the Caldew by Rose Castle,[7] look S.W. up the bed of the River, glittering down a gentle Slope about 400 yards—thinly wooded with low woods single Trees—on its Banks—then a large Bank of Wood, & Carrock over beyond it/ but 30 yards from the Bridge to my left hand as I look up the river, the most glorious Tree a Beech Elm, I believe, that I have seen this many a year. It is on a green platform, a small nook formed by the river, the high woody Bank, & the Bridge, all which are a harmony of shade & Coolness.—

We are delighted with Rose Castle, the thickset green Fence to the garden, the two walls, the lower making a terrace/ the House, the Orchard crowding round it—The Chesnuts—the masses of Ivy over the gateway, from one great root. This stands on the other side of the wall to my left as I face the gateway—Go in, the ivy over the Coach House, belonging [to] the same mass—the horns of the dark old mulberry Tree among it—the Swallows & their Shadows on the Castle-House walls—the green shaven Bank, like the roof of a House between the main Building & the Castle, properly so called/ the great 30′ Nets on this Castle, to cover the fruit Trees/ —all, all perfect— Cottage Comfort & ancestral Dignity!—

Come to Hawksdale Bridge—all above the Bridge very pretty, but all below it a plain of ugliest desolation, flooded with stones & sand by the winter Torrents/ in the bed of the River, great Hogsheads of Stones, for what purpose I did not learn/on the other side of the River a Sodom & Gomorrah Cotton Manufactory—so on to Dalston/ nothing very impressive in the first View of Carlisle.

~Butterfly let loose, how very high, how madly, how purposeless/ it pushes the air under it & runs up the Stairs of Air./ 2 Butterflies, an Image of the restless Fondness of two young Lovers. Goose—/ would be a noble Bird if it did not remind us of the Swan = Wyndham : : Burke.[8]

~Longtown—a neat town of Brick—Graham arms, reason contents me[9]— cross street pillar in the middle.

~Stockings 4 pair
Breeches
Waistcoat 1
Shirt 1
Neckcloths 3
Cravats

~Glasgow[10]
Dunbarton   15
Luss   12
Ballockferry 7
Drumond   9
Kippen   8
Sterling   13
Falkirk   11   36 from F[alkirk] to B[allockferry]
15 Dunbarton
Luss   12
Ballockferry 7
Drumond—   9
Luss back again   12
              15

~At Carlisle, dined—at $\frac{1}{2}$ past 8 in the evening arrived at Longtown, Graham Arms—left it, Wednesday 9 °clock, 17.
    At Carlisle I alarmed the whole Court, Judges, Counsellors, Tipstaves, Jurymen, Witnesses, & Spectators by hallooing to Wordsworth who was in a window on the other side of the Hall—*Dinner!*[11]
    Walked on the wall—the divine pearly Whiteness of those rich fleecy

[8]The invidious syllogistic comparison is of William Windham, M.P. (1750–1810) to his predecessor, Edmund Burke. Coleridge did not think well of Windham's support of Pitt or of his style as a speaker, which was angry in tone and goose-like in vocal quality.
[9]The motto of the Grahams of Netherby, Cumberland, found on their coat of arms.
[10]The route implied here was not the actual itinerary of the tour, though perhaps one Coleridge toyed with.
[11]John Hatfield, a.k.a Hadfield, had gained tabloid celebrity as an imposter, a bigamist, a womanizer, a swindler, and an ex-convict before the court and jury in Carlisle, seeking to make him pay for cumulative infractions, cited his crime of forgery, a capital offence. In a sensational trial at the town hall during the 1803 August assizes, the fascinating rogue was indicted on two counts of forgery and one count of defrauding the Post Office by franking letters under the name of a Member of Parliament. He was convicted and sentenced to death. Coleridge arrived in Carlisle with the Wordsworths on 16 August, the day after the trial itself ended but in time to make a conspicuous appearance at Hatfield's sentencing. By the time Dorothy and William passed through Carlisle again at the end of their Scottish journey, Hatfield had been hanged.
    The conduct that most outraged the Lake District was Hatfield's betrayal of a beautiful and virtuous country girl, Mary Robinson. Hatfield, born in Cheshire in 1759 and married with children, had passed himself off in Keswick society as

Alexander Augustus Hope, M.P. for Linlithgowshire, Lieutenant Colonel of the 14th Regiment of Foot, brother of the 3rd Earl of Hopetoun. His charm and silver tongue, his interest in fishing, and his accounts of being wounded while fighting America, made him attractive to both men and women; he carried out his masquerade with savoir-faire. Colonel Hope, as he was called at the Queen's Head, where he stayed in Kewsick, occasionally took side trips for leisure and sport. On one excursion he spent three weeks in the village of Grasmere, where he was noticed toying with the affections of one of the good local girls. On another he rode nine miles from Keswick to the town of Buttermere, to fish for char. Here at the Fish Inn he met and eventually won over Mary Robinson, the owner's daughter who worked there and had enjoyed a widespread reputation, since she was fourteen, of natural country beauty. They were married in the Lorton church on 2 October 1802, then hastened to Scotland for a honeymoon. News of the marriage quickly reached Keswick and sent a wave of indignation through the Lake District. At the time of his marriage to Mary, "Colonel Hope" was engaged to the wealthy ward of Colonel Nathaniel Montgomery Moore, M.P., a tourist in Keswick. The young lady had already bought her wedding clothes when "Colonel Hope" took off for Buttermere. Shamelessly, the day before he married the Beauty of Buttermere he wrote to Colonel Moore asking him to cash a draft for £30, drawn on the account of Mr. John Gregory Crump. When Hatfield signed Crump's draft and posted his letter as Alexander Augustus Hope, M.P., he committed the particular crime for which he was tried in Carlisle.

Coleridge had played a significant hand in exposing Hatfield nationally through five articles he wrote for the London *Morning Post* which were run almost immediately in other papers. The first of

Clouds, so deliciously shaded toward the top of their component fleecy parts—Think of this often.

Then visited Hatfield,[12] impelled by Miss Wordsworth—*vain*, a hypocrite/ It is not by mere Thought, I can understand this man/

~Enter Scotland, on foot—over a Bridge of the scanty River Sark, that winds like the convex edge of a crescent of sand/ then rolls dark over its red brown Stones, a peat-moss River with a 1000 leisurely circles & ellipses of foam/ —flows by a Hill, of a red clay Bank/ the lines of the *Hillage* playful & like the ramparts at Hamburgh/ so mounting a Hill come to the Village of Springfield, 12 years old/ then there was but one clay house. Sir William Maxwell,[13] of Spring. [leased] ground, a penny a foot to build on,[14] as a grouped row, & to every House four Acres/ some at 20, some at 30 s. the acre/ most of them weavers/ o what dreary melancholy Things are Villages built by great men/ cast-iron

two pieces entitled "Romantic Marriage" came out on Monday, 11 October 1802 and created a ready audience for the second, which appeared on 22 October. On 5 November a one-paragraph piece entitled "The Fraudulent Marriage" appeared, giving an account of the contents of a dressing-box Hatfield left behind with Mary after he fled the area, in the double bottom of which she found indisputable evidence of bigamy—letters addressed to him from his wife and children. Two pieces entitled "The Keswick Imposter," appearing on 20 November and 31 December, completed Coleridge's damning portrait of Hatfield. (See *Recollections*, App. 1, pp. 219–20 and Molly Lefebure, *Samuel Taylor Coleridge: A Bondage of Opium*, App. 2, pp. 496–99 for fuller discussion of the Hatfield case.)
[12] In jail, of course, though what was the reason for the visit? To give Hatfield an opportunity to meet the journalist who exposed him? To gain some insight into what made him tick as material for further publication? Dorothy's account of the visit sheds little light: "I stood at the door of the gaoler's house, where he was;

William entered the house, and Coleridge saw him; I fell into conversation with a debtor, who told me in a dry way that he was 'far-over-learned,' and another man observed to William that we might learn from Hatfield's fate 'not to meddle with pen and ink' " (*Recollections*, p. 40).
[13] Son of Patrick Maxwell, of Springkell, Sir William Maxwell founded Springfield in 1791. The place took its name from the farm on which it stood. (Springkell was the seat of the Maxwells, in Dumfriesshire, on Kirtle Water.)
[14] The memoir of a local "parson," Robert Elliott (b. 1784), offers this recollection: "The village of Springfield is built on a lease of ninety-nine years by the payment of annual rent of 3s.4d. It is part of the Springfield estate, all of which is now the property of Sir Patrick Maxwell, Bart., and where he resides. It consists of one street; the houses are nearly all one story high, except in the inn where the marriages were celebrated. Every house had an extent of forty-feet in front, with a garden behind, and the privilege of cutting peat or turf for fuel" (*The Gretna Green Memoirs*, p. 34).

Hovels/ how ill does the Dirt & Misery combine with the formal regular shapes. Are they cells of Prisons? It is the feeling of a Jail. Here at the public House the marriage Ceremony is performed/[15] Gretna Green, about half a mile, a handsome nice-looking "New Inn"[16] on your Right Hand down a Treeey Lane[17] where the new married Elopers consummate/ The Chapel & Burial Ground[18] crowded with flat grave Stones, as high as from one's knee to one's Hip, commands a view of Solway Firth, & the flat land between/ & the mountains beyond/—

On the Road from Gretna Green, immediately, & close in & about the Village a good number of Trees—but yet all so dreary/ A public House with a gaudy Daub of *Hope* "to crown returning Hope"—no Beer!—What then? Whisky, Gin, & Rum—cries a pale squalid Girl at the Door, a true Offspring of Whiskey-Gin-&-Rum-drinking Parents. At Springfield I was led into reflections on the contrast between the Providence of God & the *Providence* of man/ the latter while it gives is sure to *prevent*; man's providence provides *Moulds*, hard iron moulds; but God's gives the growing Principle/ We arrived at Dumfries, in the evening, having previously baited the Horse, and dined at Annan—

To Dumfries, following the River Nith to Mennock,
across the Lowther Hills through Mining Country to Crawfordjohn,
following the River Clyde to Lanark

~Thursday Morning, August 18, ½ past 11 we left Dumfries, W. and Dorothy Wordsworth having spent the morning in visiting Burns's House &

[15] The Marriage House of Springfield was a small, two-story building at the end of the street. It did a brisk business in runaway marriages, located as it was on a principal coaching route from Carlisle. Elliott recalls: "The old wedding inn at Springfield, so long kept by the worthy old Mrs. Johnston, is now in the possession of Alexander Beattie, the Sawney so often spoken of, he was a long time hostler there and 'a braw chiel he is, and keeps a gude hoose tu'" (*Gretna Green Memoirs*, p. 35).
[16] Another inn, this one in Gretna Green, a half mile from Springfield, attracted countless English runaway couples,

especially from about 1738 to 1856. The influx came as a consequence of a change in English law. In 1754 Lord Hardwick introduced a bill to prohibit the clandestine or runaway marriages that were taking place in profusion under corrupt circumstances at a state prison in London called The Fleet. The new English Marriage Law required banns (a publicly announced engagement), a license, and a marriage in a church. Desperate couples thereafter fled to Scotland, where the new marriage law did not apply. In Gretna Green and Springfield, immediately across the Scottish border, an eloping couple might

be secretly married in a ceremony conducted by a self-proclaimed parson (who might actually be a pub keeper, a tollgate operator, a postman, a smuggler, a weaver, or any secular body at hand) performed in the presence of two witnesses, which, according to Scottish law, was all that was required to constitute a legal marriage. David Lang (1755–1827), a smuggler on the Solway Coast who escaped his ship and settled in Springfield would have been the "priest" performing marriages at the time Coleridge visited. Robert Elliot, whose memoirs record dramatic situations like that of an angry father charging onto the scene in pursuit of his young daughter, only to find he was too late and she had become her forbidden lover's wife, was one of the more refined "parsons" in the Gretna parish.   The Gretna Hall Hotel, as Coleridge's "New Inn" is called today, was built as a manor house in 1710 and later became a coaching inn. Literature for this upscale hotel claims that "within its halls during the last century [the 18th] no less than 1,134 runaway marriages have taken place, not all of them with parental approval." Gretna Hall remains a popular venue for weddings. In the adjacent blacksmith's shop marriage vows are exchanged over the anvil with a kilted gentleman named Jim Jackson, who is disposed to poetic expression, presiding over the non-religious ceremony. Photographers and pipers are always on hand.

[17] Some tall trees still stand close to the building, but more shrubs than trees flank the lane today.
[18] After visiting Gretna Green Old Parish Church, built 1710, Dorothy recalled: "There is a pleasant view from the churchyard over Solway Firth to the Cumberland mountains," though she found Gretna Green itself "a dreary place; the stone houses dirty and miserable, with broken windows" (*Recollections*, p. 41).

[19] Robert Burns lived in a house on what is now called Burns Street until his death in 1796, when he was buried in a modest grave in a corner of St. Michael's Churchyard. (His body was to be moved to a showy mausoleum elsewhere in the churchyard in 1815.) It is interesting to consider that although Coleridge did not visit the Burns home and grave, ostensibly because he was not well, he had admitted Burns into his own poetic consciousness. Burns died admired but impoverished. Coleridge contributed a poem entitled "To a Friend who had declared his intention of writing no more poetry" to be included in a volume to raise funds for Burns's children and widow. (See Anya Taylor, *Bacchus in Romantic England: Writers and Drink, 1780–1830*, p. 37.)

[20] The farm called Gallow Hill, near Scarborough, in Yorkshire, had special significance for Coleridge as the place where he received sympathetic and tender attention from Sara Hutchinson, the woman with whom he was now obsessively in love. Tom Hutchinson, brother of Sara and Mary Hutchinson (now Mrs. William Wordsworth) managed Gallow Farm as a tenant farmer. Coleridge spent some ten days there in the summer of 1801, with Sara and Mary. He had hoped to gain some relief from his gout and aching joints by taking the sea water at nearby Scarborough, but the greatest balm for him turned out to be Sara's warmth, which proved to be, paradoxically, an incurable infection.

[21] This fast spreading weed with a yellow rayed flower is more commonly known as ragweed or wortweed.

[22] English travellers seemed to arrive in Scotland with a preconception of bare feet as a disagreeable cultural characteristic. Stoddart warns his readers: "An Englishman is apt to be surprised, and somewhat disgusted, at observing all the lower class of women . . . trudging through the streets, and entering the houses, with bare feet. We have associated such appearance with ideas of poverty, and a want of cleanliness; we are displeased to see women in neat gowns and caps, and perhaps, in laced cloaks and bonnets, without shoes or stockings, or, what is still more disagreeable, with stockings which have no feet" (*Remarks*, I, p. 34).

Grave[19]—and W. having called *to & on* Rogers—A hot ride up the pleasant Valley of Nith, which strongly reminded me of Gallow Hill/[20] every feature greatly magnified—to a single public House, called Brown Hill/ at which our Dinner & apartments gave me the first specimen of the Difference between English and Scotch Inns. We have had a great difficulty started about beds, & I cut the knot, by offering, if any body came, to sleep on the chairs in the Parlour—We must expect many of these Inconveniences during the Tour, we wanting three beds for 3 persons.

~*Feckless* in an Inn, & wants dignity & courage/ and with no want of Courage wants kindness & stateliness & gentlemanly Dignity.

~I went to sleep, after dinner, Aug. 18th, & reflected how little there was in this World that could compensate for the loss or diminishment of the Love of such as truly love us/ and what bad Calculators Vanity & Selfishness prove to be in the long Run—

~The Groundsel[21] every where in the Hedges, instead of the Fox Glove, Lychnis, & 50 other *Englishmen*.—Say what you will, "the naked feet"[22] is disgusting more so in Scotland than in Germany, from the *tawdry* or *squalid* appearance of the bare-footed// In Germany there is a uniform Dress in the Class that go bare-footed & they always have their Shoes in their Hands or on their Heads/ In Scotland Cabin Gowns, white Petticoat, all tawdry fine, & naked Legs, & naked Splaid-feet, & gouty ancles.

~Friday, August 19. left Brownhill & along by the Nith, this an interesting Valley, the Nith a rough rocky stream, the rocks like those on a low but savage sea coast/ the Hills now thickly, now thinly wooded, now with single Trees, & now bare/ here & there a Cottage on them, but all single storied.— We come to Drumlanrigg, thro' a village, long, & all of thickset short single storied Cottages, to contrast with the huge monster crowned with pepper castors, straight before us.—Here I entered into a long reflection on the Duke of Queensburies Character/[23] The bank of the Nith continues very interesting—/ We proceed to Meinek Turnpike,[24] then up the Coomb, in 9 long winding reaches, . . . of Meinek/ so to Wanlock head, & to Lead Hills,[25] Enchanting Coomb, its living smoothness & simplicity for the first 4 reaches, the purple heather on one side gives it a character of gay *fineness*/ D.W.

[23] William Douglas, 4th Duke of Queensbury (1725–1810) was notorious for his gambling debts. As well, he violated the environment, stripping forests and cutting down ancient trees around Neidpath Castle, visited by William and Dorothy later on this 1803 tour (on 18 September). William's "Sonnet, Composed at——Castle" (Neidpath Castle) targets "Old Q," as he was known:

> Degenerate Douglass! thou unworthy
>   Lord
> Whom mere despite of heart could so
>   far please,
> And love of havoc (for with such
>   disease
> Fame taxes him) that he could send
>   forth word
> To level with the dust a noble horde,
> A brotherhood of venerable trees,
> Leaving an ancient Dome and Towers
>   like these
> Beggar'd and outraged!
>   (ll. 1–8, in *Recollections*, p. 201)

The extravagance of Drumlanrig Castle that caused Coleridge to reflect on Douglas's wanton ways is mitigated today by a happy circumstance—the grounds are rich in trees, especially some aged Sycamores.

[24] In the old village of Mennock, a handful of buildings, including a smithy's and a defunct bridge, remain as reminders of the time when a nearby intersection of busy roads merited a tollhouse, which no longer stands, having burned down twenty to thirty years ago, according to local history. The road to Wanlockhead and Leadhills bore heavy traffic in coal carts, the rattling of which bothered

Dorothy. Coleridge and the Wordsworths visited the intelligent, well-travelled bachelor who occupied the turnpike house and operated the turnpike gate, and Coleridge, for some inexplicable reason saw fit to present him with a copy of a pamphlet called "The Crisis of the Sugar Colonies" which he was carrying with him for an equally inexplicable reason.

Published in 1802, the pamphlet was written by James Stephen (1758–1832), Master in Chancery. Stephen ardently opposed slavery and both spoke and wrote against it. Having briefly visited Barbados, he had first-hand knowledge of how the slaves were treated in the sugar colonies. Coleridge held comparably strong anti-slavery convictions, actively campaigned against the slave trade, and advocated the boycott of sugar and rum. In a piece entitled "On the Slave Trade" for *The Watchman* (No. IV. Friday, March 25, 1796) he argued, "If only one tenth part among you who profess yourselves Christians; if one half only of the Petitioners; instead of bustling about with ostentatious sensibility, were to leave off—not all the West-India commodities—but only Sugar and Rum, the one useless and the other pernicious—all this misery might be stopped." The line of thinking that had gained currency among some abolitionists was that in abstaining from the use of sugar and rum British citizens would save the lives of slaves on the sugar plantations. One advocate, William Fox, had worked out a probability formula: "A family that uses 5lb. of sugar per week, with the proportion of rum, will, by abstaining from consumption 21 months, prevent the slavery or murder of one

fellow creature; eight such families in $19\frac{1}{2}$ years prevent the slavery or murder of 100, and 38,000 would totally prevent the Slave Trade to supply our islands" (*An Address to the People of Great Britain, on the Propriety* of Abstaining from West India Sugar and Rum. (Pamphlet, in its 26th ed. in 1793. See *The Collected Works of Samuel Taylor Coleridge. The Watchman*, p. 138n).

[25] Wanlockhead, the highest village in Scotland, and Leadhills, both in the Lowther Hills between Dumfriesshire and Lanarkshire, were coal and lead mining towns with progressive programs for enriching the lives of miners. The mines of Wanlockhead were owned by the Duke of Queensbury. The village provided literacy through a Reading Society as well as a library, established in 1756, encouraged by the success of the Miners' Library in nearby Leadhills. Miners' children received schooling. "The village had a schoolmaster by 1750. Education in the village followed the highly successful Scottish pattern of giving encouragement to those boys who showed signs of a high ability by preparing them for entry to university and, by the end of the eighteenth century, the village had achieved local renown on account of the singularly keen interests of its menfolk.... During the first half of the nineteenth century the Rev Thomas Hastings, for forty years minister here assisted in the education of more than forty boys who entered the professions as surgeons, lawyers, teachers, ministers and clerks" (*All about Wanlockhead: A Brief History of Scotland's Highest Village.* Wanlockhead: Wanlockhead Museum Trust, 1989, p. 16). Coleridge encountered young lads from the village without shoes and stockings who said they were studying Latin (Virgil) and Greek (Homer). "When Coleridge began to inquire further, off they ran, poor things! I suppose afraid of being examined," Dorothy noted (*Recollections*, p. 48).

137

[26] They left at nine o'clock, according to Dorothy. They had been staying at the house of Mrs. Otto, which had been recommended to them "with encomiums" (p. 51), rather than the "decent-looking"Hopetoun Arms, named after Lord Hopetoun, who owned the village and the lead mines.

[27] Founded in 1741, the Leadhills Miners' Library is the oldest subscription library in Britain. Also called the Allan Ramsay Library to honor the poet (son of a mine overseer) born in Leadhills in 1686, who had become a bookseller in Edinburgh by the time the Leadhills Miners' Reading Society and the library were founded, the library, supplemented by a school, stood for the value of education. Indeed, the children of miners were being well educated.

Dorothy recounts the threesome's experiences in the mountain mining villages, in *Recollections*, pp. 48–54. They had an amusing reaction to a Watt steam engine: "When we drew nearer we saw, coming out of the side of the building, a large machine or lever, in appearance like a great forge-hammer, as we supposed for raising water out of the mines. It heaved upwards once in half a minute with a slow motion, and seemed to rest to take breath at the bottom, its motion being accompanied with a sound between a groan and 'jike.' There would have been something in this object very striking in any place, as it was impossible not to invest the machine with some faculty of intellect; it seemed to have made the first step from brute matter to life and purpose, showing its progress by great power. William made a remark to this effect, and Coleridge observed that it was a giant with one idea" (p. 50).

[28] On the advice of travellers they met along the way the Coleridge-Wordsworth party scrapped their plan to proceed on the "new road" and took instead a route up the hill that would, after winding around, lead them to the valley and village

~Left Leadhill,[26] Saturd. Aug. 20. We leave the good Inn, having had the particulars of the Library,[27] & move on on a like Road thro' a like Country, now not differing from the inside of moorish mountains in general, where the Hills ∨ ̸ and the bottom is now just large enough for the road & the stream, running side by side—now admitting a little green boggy valley for the Stream/ & now the road climbs on the side of the Hill a 100 yards leaving the stream on one's right beneath it in its green ellipse of grassiness—a cottage

at the end of this 〈A 7 B〉 A a gavel end wall upstanding, in ruin, the other part inhabited, 7 trees, three of them blighted and one thin thing among Potatoes—green turf fence. . . .

. . . moor/ to a village called Crawford John,[28] still over moorland till we reach the Turnpike, & . . . came to Douglas [Mill]. . . . [29]

Dined, & passed on, 9 miles, to Lanark . . . with the River Clyde to [our] Left for the greater part . . . way/ the grounsel Probably. Crossed over into. . . .

~ Clear tints upon the edge of the fell Moss, scraps of land in the down/ corn—children weeping—turnips—bit of grass land—Solway Firth on the left dull plantation of firs— . . . Or . . . the Wind.

~   I see thee daily weaker grow
          Thy spirits take a fainter flow
          Twas my distress that brought thee low
                    My Mary![30]

of Crawfordjohn, from which place they could proceed to their destination, Douglas Mill. Before they arrived in the village they realized their cart's wheel needed mending and asked a middle-aged man dressed in black like a minister, "who spoke like one who had been accustomed to dictate," if there was a blacksmith in the village. The fellow told them they didn't need a blacksmith; the job fell on William, who obeyed the dictator's instructions and repaired the wheel. The same chap led them through fields of corn and potatoes, "and Coleridge and he had a scientific conversation concerning the uses and

properties of lime and other human manures." For the journey from Crawfordjohn to Douglas Mill see *Recollections* pp. 55–57.

[29] Douglas Mill no longer stands, either as a place or as an inn. The mill was powered by Park Burn, which ran into Douglas Water. Nearby were Castlemains, the occasional residence of Lord Douglas-Home, and Millbank, with the former gamekeeper's house. These remain andgive today's visitor a good sense of the environs.

[30] The lines, the first two of which Coleridge puts in reverse order, are from the second stanza of a poem entitled "To

~Imperfection of Drawings in the tricks of Height & Magnitude when there are proportions in the same picture. From my Window Sketch/ The high mountains. . . .

~River Sark,[31] a single arch'd brid[g]e into Scotland, a green open half common field with Cattle. Springfield upon the hill in front Bosworth a rod farther. Here was light flowered field with tufts of furze beyond G G., miserable thatch'd clay huts bare, fells behind. Prospect in forward still dreary, St. Patricks Kirk on the left, no steeple but built in the shape of a cross with something like a small cupola with a bell—with a porch to the North West—red Window shutters—

  Village gone to decay in. . . . —low cottage in front naked—narrow winding Valley—One—with gate—Woman—descent a small hut to the left/ 2 huge stacks on very small square mound enclosure—thatched stone hut —pair horses—cows—hay taken from moor mown—lower down—farm turnips from six corn fields thatch'd barn one bare hut potatoes are . . . sources of Clyde. above the farm—Yevon Water 11 mile of new roads Yevon vale—alders rocky stream—hut with five enclosures/ We pay 1/ . . . chose the ferry . . . —cross the Clyde—tiny stream. Dor. Slow on —Tweed our Annon. Poor Clyde fell & broke his neck. Annon first River on Solway Firth—falls at Lanark—break neck. Tweed longest river. Tweed/ Annon/ Clyde for our . . . . town— Leadhills—Crawford, Many corn fields one or two stunted ashes near house/ no enclosures dog/ cows go home to dine—little haystacks or large cocks, sheaves of ripe corn . . . but the one plain of smooth appearance. Sheep dog next something like Exmoor—Huts of . . . low newer & thatch'd when . . . leave Clyde turning to the left wind of the river of amber or less green green grasses—some brown with scanty heath patches of corn as before.

  River Day realm of David Ogilvy, Airley,[32] being desirous to preserve the game on his estates in Feof in Perthshire hopes no person will shoot there this season and begs that none of his friends will ask leave to do so—

  To be let by public roup the farm, &c within the house of Mr Dow upon Tuesday—the articles of the roup will be seen in the hands of James Hay and the Shepherd upon the premises will shew the marches.

  Lands To let by private bargain and entered to at the term of Martinmas

to him, and his care, becoming a kind of second mother. Coleridge admired Cowper's poetry and spoke of him, William Hazlitt reports, "as the best modern poet" (*William Hazlitt: Selected Writings,* p. 62). Cowper's long conversational poem "The Task" influenced both Coleridge and Wordsworth.

[31] In this and the following paragraph Coleridge recapitulates the journey from entering Scotland to visiting the Falls of the Clyde at Lanark and takes account of places that lie ahead on the tour. "G G." is for Gretna Green. Bosworth has disappeared from maps. Rivers are on his mind: the Rivers Sark, Annan, and Clyde figure in the stretch of their journey already accomplished. Dorothy and William would follow the River Tweed in the latter part of their journey. Yevon Water (Leven Water) and Yevon vale (Leven Vale) are above Glasgow and Dumbarton and have reference to the poem "Ode to Leven-Water," by Tobias Smollett (1721–71) as well as to the site of the monument of Smollett in his home town of Renton which the three would visit on 24 August. Crossing the River Clyde is a detail Dorothy does not mention, perhaps because she was not as nimble as Coleridge would have liked, as he suggests in the fragment "Dor. Slow on." Coleridge muses at the hazards of getting a look at the Falls of the Clyde ("falls at Lanark-break neck") after making a joke about the Clyde, personified: "Poor Clyde fell & broke his neck."

[32] This and the following two paragraphs appear to be posts and advertisements, very likely in a newspaper. A "public roup" is an auction. "16 Scots acres" would have amounted to considerably more than the same number of English acres, the English acre being 4,840 square yards and the Scottish 6,150.4.

Mary," by William Cowper (1731–1800), published in 1803, but written in 1773, for Mrs. Mary Unwir, with whom Cowper lived, in the country, following a period

of insanity, the chief symptom of which was hypochondria. Cowper suffered from mental illness and depression throughout his adult life. Mrs. Unwir was devoted

[33] Bagenal Beauchamp Harvey (b. 1762) was an Irish barrister, from the County of Wexford, educated at Trinity College, who became commander of Wexford insurgents (the United Irishmen) in 1798. During a particularly bloody and confusing battle he and his aide-de-camp took to a neighboring hill and remained there as spectators of the fight. He was subsequently deposed as commander in chief of the insurgents and made president of the provisional government that had been established at the beginning of the Insurrection. In another battle, on 21 June, Wexford was lost to the king's troops. Harvey, a friend, and the friend's wife fled to one of the Saltee Islands, off the coast of Ireland, and hid in a cave disguised as peasants. They were discovered, and Harvey was executed on a bridge in Wexford on 28 June 1798. His head was put on a spike at the courthouse. His body, which had been thrown into the river, was recognized by friends and given a proper burial. Wales being virtually opposite the county of Wexford across the St. George's Channel, a wary Welshman might have suspected Harvey's presence on Welsh turf after his flight from the king's army; and as Harvey did in fact resort to a disguise, a dancing master might have drawn suspicion. But this seems a stretch, and Coleridge was most likely having fun with the facts, though why Bagenal Beauchamp Harvey should enter his thoughts in Scotland remains just another mystery of how this poet's mind ranged as he moved from place to place.

[34] These mills, in New Lanark, where one enters the grounds of the Falls of the Clyde today, are the setting of a remarkable socialistic labor community put into effect by Robert Owen (1771–1858), who purchased the mills with two partners in 1799, married the daughter of the former proprietor, and settled in New Lanark. He set about shaping social and industrial changes based on the values of

next—lands let are not on lease—for the particulars enquire at the Proprietor—then two [portions] for the two—consisting of 16 Scots acres or thereby—for thereabouts—peculiarly adapted for setting down villas on lands at 49 £ mony 16 bowls of wheat 11 bowls barley.

~   A Man
Happily made, but most unhappily thwarted,
And oft there came on him—&c
And sudden Thoughts that riv'd his heart asunder
By the road-side, the while he gaz'd at flowers.

~They knew that Jesus was a great man, but guessed not that he was God. That it was a mountain, nor could be ignorant, but they dwelt too near to behold its Summit.

~Mere Flash!—B. (knocks him down) do you not know, that the Flash always is seen before the Bullet is felt?

~Welshman who thought the Dancing Master must be Bagnel Harvey[33]— Now this being Bagnel Harvey, & B. H. being a bloody, desperate fellow, we had better *shoot* him first. This for my Book of Logic—Petitio Principii.

~The Rocks in the middle of the Torrent protecting two beautiful Ash Trees, safe tho' unquiet in the Blast of the Torrent—

Lanark, Falls of the Clyde, and onward toward Glasgow

~Huge Cotton Mills,[34] 1000 with Rocky River, the Hills that form its banks, finely wooded deeply and variously ravined, and gullied, perpendicular, transverse, horizontal, no inclosures consequently, no Styles—the Men & women in their Sunday finery straggle like Cattle, each in his own path/[35]

cooperative living that would later earn him the reputation of utopian socialist and reformer. As manager of the textile mills he improved the output and earnings of the industry as a well as the working conditions and lives of the workers.

[35] Visitors to the falls had to find their own routes around the hills or along the water, unless they hired a guide, as William and Dorothy did. Today well marked paths, steps, and viewing platforms make the visit safe though less awesome. The Falls of the Clyde have changed significantly, with far less water

Thus as you move on you behold the grand red precipices glooming thro' the Trees—a clump of Trees at the end of a wood on my left had a fine effect/ This precipice is part of that round theatrical wall of rock which embraces the pool at the foot of the Cora Lynn on the left/ The general colour of this wall a dim white with patches of green, & patches & streaks of red & yellow/ The half farthest from the Falls pushes out young Elms from its clefts, & a little Coppice of young elms grow at its *Feet*—/ The Pool ample & almost round harmonizes very well with the broad *flight-of-stairs* fall/ The water runs in a slant direction, & the *Screen* of rock close beside it on the right is beautifully fringed with trees, which shade & *lattice* the third part of the lower fall, & half of the higher/ Between the lower & higher fall (the higher *seeming* here about $\frac{1}{3}$ as large as the lower) is a smooth slope of rock 30 yards in length perhaps, over which the water spreads itself thin & black, rocks just white enough from some unevennesses on this Slope to be a bond of connection between the two masses of white above it and below it/ On the left of the fall, right above this Slope, is a red path, which has a good effect, & about a 100 yards from this path, the whole interspace filled with Trees, overhanging the Wall-rock are three firs which had a very fine effect/ First they made a new feature, and a striking one, secondly their straightness & tallness gave perhaps some dim association of the human form, at least, they did certainly impress on my mind a distinct breezelet of Fear/ & lastly, the Trees with which this whole semicircle of wall-rock is crowned, are so various, that this variety acted upon you without acting so obtrusively as to offend/ —O that I had seen this in the evening a thumbsbreadth from Sunset, the solemn motions of the Trees, is on such nights harmonious with the dimmer shape & deeper colour.—

As I write this, I turn my head, & close by me I see a Birch, so placed as among a number of Trees it alone is in full sunshine, & the Shadows of its Leaves playing on its silver Bark, an image that delighted my Boyhood, when I had no waterfalls to see/ Moving higher & winding till we climb up directly over the place where I first sate, we see the whole fall, the higher, the lower & the interslope, with only a fragment of the wall-rock & the pool—the whole at once, with the white conical Rock, with a cloak of Mosses, and bushes & fir Trees, growing out of them/ & the cold round Tower on the Top of all/ The little Girl sent to *dog* & guide us,[36] yawning with stretching Limbs, a droll dissonance with Dorothy's Raptures./ So we go to the top of all, & look down on both a noble precipitation, its ⌒ still observed—the rocks & the breadth in the Water/ the lower fall has two Wheels, the first grey-green, the lower, & larger, white & loose with the delicate shade as of diluted Black, among it & upon it. The path of the River above the fall, still

shooting from the dramatic heights. Since 1927 a hydro-electric plant has harnessed water from the falls for cheap electrical power, so that one finds a tilting weir above Bonnington Linn and the power station itself below Corra Linn in that very setting that inspired awe in the Romantics and compelled Turner to paint it. They are still stunning, on a different scale, and are incorporated into a nature preserve in the care of the National Trust for Scotland.

[36] Dorothy found this child pleasing. "My guide, a sensible little girl, answered my questions very prettily. She was eight years old, read in the 'Collection,' a book which all the Scotch children whom I have questioned read in. I found it was a collection of hymns…" (p. 59).

[37] "Another romantic feature was the doo-cote on the island at Bonnington Linn. Towards the end of the eighteenth century this was converted to a 'fog house' which was completely lined with moss, including the bench seats. . . . To get to this island a narrow iron bridge was built though it must be assumed that the doo-cote had some other access before this" (Brochure: *Falls of Clyde*. Scottish Wildlife Trust, n.d.).

[38] Dorothy recounts: "We came to a pleasure-house, of which the little girl had the key; she said it was called the Fog-house, because it was lined with 'fog,' namely moss. On the outside it resembled some of the huts in the prints belonging to Captain Cook's Voyages, and within was like a hay-stack scooped out. It was circular, with a dome-like roof, a seat all round fixed to the wall, and a table in the middle,—seat, wall, roof, and table all covered with moss in the neatest manner possible. It was as snug as a bird's nest . ." (*Recollections*, p. 64).

[39] Coleridge here compares the upper fall, Bonnington Linn, to the lower and more dramatic fall, Corra Linn.

[40] Tourists in Lanark are no longer encouraged to visit the Cartland Crags. Access to the gorge is now ambiguous and one is warned that trekking through it would be extremely dangerous. From an unmarked, risky route at the top of the crags, near the Cartland Bridge Hotel, it is possible to glimpse the cliffs and trees and to hear the water. Almost twenty   years after Coleridge visited, the Cartland Bridge, designed by Thomas Telford in 1822, was built over the Mouse Water at a point where the gorge is 130 feet deep. Wallace's Cave is just below this bridge. The early tourist, however, found a guided excursion along the river with its deep cliffs, all covered with trees, thrilling, as Coleridge attests in the account of his adventure. Stoddart offers a sharp picture of how rocky haunts along Mouse Water struck Romantic travellers: "These can

thro' the unroofed Antichamber or Passage of rock, sometimes naked & sometimes bushy/ —so we come to the Moss House[37] exactly like a Hay-stack scooped out/ lath & the moss apparently beaten into it/ for it is smooth bruised, not cut smooth—a curious table of moss, like an Axis on a Tripod/ or rather stem with 3 branches Ⲧ grows out of the ground/ —Then the round bason, a little hole at the bottom where it rises, & a little hole on the Marge where it escapes.[38] Close Half a mile from Cora Lynn is another Fall/[39] the course of the river between the two thro' a Passage of Rocks, with occasional Bays & Coves—till we reach & overhang the Fall—a strait Line to a curve ∿ but the long Fall below it is awful indeed/ O for evening & solitude/ such Cathedral Steeples, broken Arches/ so overboughed/ such sounds, such shapes, such motions above the Fall, the banks of the river fall at once into mild & cultivated green Hills/ & fields/ —Sunday Morning, Aug 21.

~See the shapes below me, in 3 yards of water/ smooth water in a vault, smooth water close to the smooth rock—a hollow, unquiet, & changeful between the waters/ water with glassy wrinkles, water with a thousand wrinkles all lengthways, water all puckered & all over dimples, over smooth rock rough with tiny roughnesses, the boiling foam below this fall.

~Carland Crags[40]—O Asra, wherever I am, & am impressed, my heart akes for you, & I know a deal of the heart of man, that I otherwise should not know.

~Reaches, short & quite land-locked, the rocks of each from 460 to 500 feet high, as high as any possible Effect could require: now one green Drapery of flowing woods from the summit to the very water; now blank, naked, and

only be approached by wading in the channel, or scrambling along the edge of the bank, which is sometimes beset with tangling shrubs, and sometimes formed by naked shelving rocks, while the lofty cliffs shooting to a height, as it is said, of 400 feet, and winding like a labyrinth, involve the whole in obscurity, and form gloomy, and apparently impenetrable recesses . . . . [T]he features here possess a . . . savage grandeur, from the superior height of the cliffs, the more frequent and abrupt turns made by the river, the rocks rent as it were by an earthquake, and appearing, at times, like massy pillars naked to the top, at others, wholly shrouded by dark coppices, and ancient pines. Every thing seems to show the hand of desolation, and untameable wildness; and so dreary a spot is a fit haunt for its only inmates, the fox, the badger, wild cats, and birds of prey" (*Remarks*, 1, p. 162).

staring; now half clad, now in patches:—the Rocks now retiring in Bays &c; & now bulging out in Buttresses;—now in Giant Stairs, now in needle points, now in huge Towers with Chimneys on the Top.—The single Trees on the very Edge of the Top, Birch and Ash, O how lovely!—Pity there is any water or that it is not clear/ —now the lower Half wood and the higher bare; now the higher wooded & the lower bare/ and sometimes one great huge Spreading Tree, all branches, and no Trunk, starts out of a starting Rock, & over-canopies half the Stream; sometimes top & bottom thick wooded & the middle bare; sometimes the nakedness running transverse or curvingly or ⌒ a whole Reach together/ & once a huge bulging ragged 1000-angled Crag on whose endless surface one might read hieroglyphics, whole naked but greeted at the edge of its summit by branching Trees, Ashes, & Birches & Hazels & one great Oak in a center all shooting out their branches far far over the Bulge of the Crag; but the Oak seeming to canopy the stream in the Bottom and at the foot of this great semicircular Convexity of naked Rock one tall slender Ash Tree with no branches save only at its very Top.

Larches & Firs a Repetition of units in time rather than an Assemblage in Space/ units without union consequently without Greatness, no character of relationship, no neighbourhood which Fir trees would gain, no motion/ nor all this till tamed down by exceeding number & the exclusion of all things to be compared with.

The Country by the Clyde tossing, playful, surface patchy with an odd mixture of fertility & barrenness—the Hills often delved with Gullies/ —but the last hour of the ride to Hamilton changed into large square Corn fields upon Hills of more ordinary outline./

~Arrived at Hamilton,[41] Sunday Night, 9 °clock/ walked next morning to Barrancluch/ a wild Terrace Garden over the *Avon*, Terrace above Terrace, 5 Terraces—the opposite Bank of the River clothed richly with Trees—/— Observed here the Dragon Scales of the Bark of old Sycamores—Yew Trees cut out into all Shapes contrasted with the wild Beauty of the opposite Bank, Monday Morning, Aug. 22 1803.

N.B. The mirror of Steel placed/ at the Top of the Room opposite the window that looks out on that vast waterfall with all its Rocks & Trees[42]—

~Monday Noon, Aug. 22, left Hamiltoun for Glasgow, where we arrived at 4 °clock, having seen Douglas Castle[43] on the way—The Castle of massive red Freestone, surrounded with Rose beds, Shrubs & Climbers indigenous

[41] At Hamilton they had hoped to visit Hamilton Palace, particularly intent upon viewing one of the famous paintings that hung in the picture gallery, *Daniel in the Lion's Den*, by Rubens. They were turned away from the palace, however, and went instead to visit Baroncleugh (Barncluith, or Baron's Cleugh), an ancient terraced garden in the dell of the River Avon. Hamilton Palace no longer stands, having been demolished in the 1920s because of subsidence in the land, which was over a coal mining area. The Rubens painting is now in the National Gallery of Art, Washington, D.C.

[42] A hall of mirrors had been erected on a pavilion at the Falls of the Clyde to provide an enhanced view of the spectacle of Corra Linn, the greater fall. The hall had only one mirror when it was first built by Sir James Carmichael of Bonnington in 1708, but more mirrors were added later.
[43] Bothwell Castle, as it is called today, stands high upon a bluff overlooking the River Clyde, still a formidable, if ruined, structure of red stone, with some walls more than six feet thick. It was the stronghold of the Scots through their many sieges with England from the early fourteenth century. For a brief period it was occupied by the English, but its possession by the Black Douglases first, and Red Douglases later branded it Douglas Castle for some. Dorothy had a grasp of the castle's history: "In this fortress the chief of the English nobility were confined after the Battle of Bannockburn [1314]. If a man is to be a prisoner, he scarcely could have a more pleasant place to solace his captivity . . ." (*Recollections*, p. 72). Lord Douglas's mansion stood close enough to the castle to upset Dorothy, who found that a "modern mansion" detracted from the sense of history the castle inspired. The mansion is no longer there.

[44] It is puzzling why Coleridge considered Blantyre Priory "more perfectly impressive," since it is quite imperfectly viewed from Bothwell Castle. Though it is just across the River Clyde, this thirteenth-century priory is a considerably reduced ruin, at the top of a perpendicular rock, more like a wall, and very little of it can be seen. Dorothy's recollection of how the three experienced the Priory of Blantyre may explain Coleridge's preference. "We sat upon a bench under the high trees, and had beautiful views of the different reaches of the river above and below. On the opposite bank, which is finely wooded with elms and other trees, are the remains of an ancient priory, built upon a rock: and rock and ruin are so blended together that it is impossible to separate the one from the other. Nothing can be more beautiful than the little remnants of this holy place. . . . It can scarcely be conceived what a grace the castle and priory impart to each other . . ." (*Recollections*, p. 72).

[45] In Glasgow Green, near the present People's Palace, traces of the "bleaching grounds," as they were also called, may still be seen. Poles on which the wash would have been hung to dry, and bleached, in this public laundry area have been preserved.

[46] The party had arrived in Glasgow on Monday 22 August, and were annoyed by noisy carts, dirt, congestion, and the fact that they and their car were being stared at, "the children often sent a hooting after us." They found their way to an inn recommended to William by an ostler in Hamilton, the Saracen's Head, which still stands, at 209 Gallowgate (near the Barras, a few blocks from Glasgow Cross). After dining, William and Dorothy went to the post office to pick up their mail and afterwards walked about the streets, observing Trongate and New Town. The next day (a "cold morning") they walked to the bleaching ground, near

& planted/ over the Clyde the more perfectly impressive Abbey of Ballantyre/[44]

At Glasgow, the hurry & Crowd of People & of Carts, marking a populous trading City, but no Coaches or Carriages!—

Here I stood beside an asthmatic Town-Cryer, a ludicrous Combination // a woman-Shaver, & a man with his lathered Chin most amorously Ogling her as she had him by the Nose.

At Glasgow I was most pleased by the two great Washing-Houses & Drying Grounds/[45] –Four Square Cloysters, with an open Square, & the Cauldron in the Middle/ Each Woman pays a $\frac{1}{2}^{ny}$ for her Tub & $\frac{1}{2}$, sometimes in scarce times 1^d for a Tub of hot water/ a penny to the Watcher—so that the poorest person who can get Cloathes to wash may earn their living, whereas in other cities those only can do it who can pay for Lodgings with Fire & Washing utensils &c—I suppose there might be 120 women in each House/—

~A perpetual repetition of Suspensions of the Habeas Corpus Act compared to a man who *always* kept an oil Skin Cover over his new Hat./

~The still rising Desire still baffling the bitter Experience, the bitter Experience still following the gratified Desire.

Glasgow to Loch Lomond

~From Glasgow which we left Tuesday Afternoon Aug. 23,[46] thro' a country not partic. interesting till we came to the Top of the Hill 5 miles from Dunbarton[47] where is a Prospect which every Traveller must remember/ on the

the River Clyde. It rained while they were there, and after they left, it rained so much harder (and William and Dorothy were so tired), they put off visiting the High Church, though they noticed the shops, the piazza of the Exchange, and "the largest coffee-room I ever saw" (the Tontine Hotel and seventy-two foot long coffee room). "Dined, and left Glasgow at about three o'clock, in a heavy rain, and headed up the Clyde toward Dumbarton." See *Recollections*, pp. 73–76.

[47] This earlier spelling of Dumbarton is closer to the origin of the name Dun Bretane (the Fort of the Britons), referring to the enormous rock on the River Clyde fifteen miles northwest of Glasgow. The Hill of Dun, at 208 feet, would have provided the panorama Coleridge refers to here, and the ruin he notes near Bowling was Dunglass Castle, on a protrusion of rock into the Clyde at Bowling. Dorothy's recollection fills in some of Coleridge's gaps: "[W]hen we

left Lord Ballantyre's House & Plantations, the . . . Village & ruin of Bowling End on the opposite Bank with a curve of wild Mountain land behind it/ and

on beyond, in the centre of the view, a majestic single Rock, between a ∧ and a ⌒ in shape/ the Clyde now almost Sea, & Sloops thick upon it.

~Shadows over Corn & Woods like the motion of the Air in Sails/

~Enormous Rock—one Patch of lank weeds moving in the mass—

~First view in a field of Loch Lomond—Wednesday 24 Aug. 1803—most like the view from Mr Clarkson's,[48] but inferior—but about a short mile onward you see it as you mount a little ascent of the road under the boughs of Trees that stretch all across the road as under the Arch of Bridge, the water, the Island as a low Ridge of Mountain, & then [Ben] Lomond towering behind that! most lovely & most simple—

The Lake ceased to interest me till within 2 mile of Luss a wooded Cliff all green rises up, & bare Ben Lomond in a like Ridge rises up behind it/ —Here too I saw for the first Time a Larch wound round with Ivy, from the Top of the Stem to the Bottom/

Another curious Larch by the side of a farm House bending like an Arbor across the whole Road.

Yet another right opposite to the first Inn at Luss, close by a Shed, & having for its neighbour a gigantic Sycamore/ This Larch is spread into an Arbour perfectly round, like the Expansion of an Oak, with its limbs twisted in among this round Spread of Boughs in the wildest Shapes, Knees, & Elbows, & Crosses, & Loops, & figures of 8.

~We arrived at Luss, Wedn. Aug. 24[49]—Afternoon from Dunbarton/ at Dunbarton Tuesday Afternoon from Glasgow—A glorious view at High Tide

& under interesting Accidents from Dunbarton Rock[50]—⌒⌒—of the mouth of the Clyde & the Mountains beside it & beyond it & of the Towns,

came to the top of the hill, it opened upon us most magnificently. We saw the Clyde, now a stately sea-river, winding away mile after mile, spotted with boats and ships, each side of the river hilly, the right populous with single houses and villages—Dunglass Castle upon a promontory, the whole view terminated by the rock of Dumbarton, at five or six miles distance, which stands by itself,

without any hills near it, like a sea-rock" (*Recollections*, p. 76).

"Lord Ballantyre's House" would have been Erskine House, the seat of Lord Blantyre. Dunglass Castle is now on the grounds of an ESSO oil terminal and kept under strict security.

[48] Thomas Clarkson (1760–1835) was, with his wife Catherine, a friend of both the Wordsworths and the Coleridges. The Clarksons lived in Eusemere, near Pooley Bridge, at the northern end of the lake called Ullswater, the view of which Coleridge now compares to Loch Lomond.

[49] They stayed at an inn that had been a gentleman's house, probably the still hospitable and popular Colquhoun Arms Hotel. On entering Luss Dorothy announced, "We were now entering into the Highlands. I believe Luss is the place where we were told that country begins. . ."(*Recollections*, p. 83). She was in fact articulating the view accepted through the eighteenth century to the Romantic period and beyond that Luss marked the entry point to the Highlands from the west (as Dunkeld did from the east). To the reader of his guide book Stoddart pointed out: "The Highlands are usually distinguished from the Lowlands by the use of the Gaelic, and Scottish languages. According to this rule, Luss might be called the portal of the Highlands, as the former of those tongues is used to the north of it, and the latter to the south. Here also begins the more general use of the plaid, with all its accompaniments. I need scarcely mention the great picturesqueness of this dress . . ." (*Remarks*, I, p. 228). Coleridge had not been feeling well on arrival and therefore did not go out for a stroll through the village as William and Dorothy did.

[50] Dumbarton Rock, rising to a height of 200 feet out of the water at the meeting of the rivers Clyde and Leven, has a kindof double hump, giving the appearance of two enormous rocks conjoined. An

important fortress of basalt dating from Roman times, and accurately depicted by Coleridge's little line drawing, Dumbarton Rock was, by the time Coleridge and the Wordsworths climbed it, endowed with much history and a fair share of lore. The Governor's House at which Coleridge sneers, was built in 1735 along with the surrounding battery, and stands upon a significant portion of a sprawling medieval castle. George's Fort now commanded Dumbarton. A French prison attested to the fort's strategic importance during the Napoleonic wars. The thirty-six-year-old trout Coleridge mentions would have been kept (if it actually existed) in a deep natural well near the French prison.

51 In the Lake District of England, in Borrowdale, a huge rock known as Bowder Stone distinguished itself as a curiosity to tourists and residents alike not only for its size but for the accident of its having fallen from a nearby crag and landed on its edge, giving it the appearance of being delicately balanced. Coleridge uses Bowder Stone as a standard of measurement here.

52 The cottages in the present village of Luss, designated a preservation village, and used as the setting for a popular Scottish television series, *Take the High Road*, retain this affect.

53 The mountain (3,192 feet) that dominates Loch Lomond.

54 Of the several small islands in Loch Lomond opposite and below Luss, the one that attracted the three English travellers most was Inchtavannach, one high peak of which afforded a pleasing view of the other islands and beyond, looking south to Dumbarton Rock. What they observed from the island struck them as "outlandish," according to Dorothy, who in her amazement claimed, "[W]e might have believed ourselves in North America" (*Recollections*, p. 87).

Greenock, Port Glasgow &c on its Bank, Shipping &c &c/ —the Governor's *new genteel* House between the two Heads of the Rock/ Wallace's Sword, & the Trout in the Well 36 years of age/ black, & 18 inches long—we walked at the bottom round the Rock, one side a most noble precipice indeed with two huge Rocks detached from it, one of them larger assuredly than Bowder Stone, & very like it/[51]

~Thursday Morning, 25th—side of the Loch Lomond—Observed the Fern-roofed Cottages,[52] the fern stalk of glossy Polish ending in $\frac{1}{2}$ an inch of Black lie like Tiles on the bedde Form beneath/ the round Chimneys or *stool*—shaped of 4 sticks—on them a Slate and on the Slate a Stone—Ben Lomond[53] from the Lake rises up, & goes *bounding* down, its outline divided into six great Segments, scolloped like many Leaves, with 5 or 6 small Scollops in each great Segment, of the same Shape—

Mount Inchdevannoch,[54] by a Path most judiciously winding up this Mountain-Isle & everywhere shewing to our right the delicious Islands/ one close by us in contrasted & perfect Flatness, another *so* close to us, a hilly Isle, that the water in two points disappears & the Intermediate Water forms a compleat little Lake/ the endless variety of Shapes, of Bays, of Tongues—the varying Lights/ on the various shores, some sandy, some rocky, some green with Grass, some dark-green with forest Trees/ The most striking, & a

frequent, Form of Bay, is the Hook ‿/ Look at that black-green Isle in shape like the Sword-fish inclosed within a circular Island of melted-silver-white Sunshine/—. The broad low Hills at the bottom of the Lake are in fine keeping with the Island Character, & where they sink in a long gentle under curve of an Ellipse you see the two points of Dunbarton Rocks—/ On the point of the Hook of the flat Island a Hut most delightfully placed—The last Island, which I see (there are four running across the Lake in one line)—the second & third small & fish Shape—the third, sword fish, the second Dolphin shaped—the first & fourth, very large—you look over the first to Dunbarton

Rock, & the fourth vaults in those plunging Lines, &
connects itself with the mountain, whose Tongue of Land almost meets it, of the same bounding, plunging, vaulting Line of Descent.—

~What? tho' the World praise me, I have no dear Heart that loves my Verses—I never hear them in snatches from a beloved Voice, fitted to some sweet occasion, of natural Prospect, in Winds at Night—

~Landed on the Island,[55] where the Bark Hut is (*not* the Hut Island)—went into the Hut where the Woodmen sleep—Straw beds inclosed by thick Sticks, one raised off the ground like a Bed-stock—and in the middle the Fire place—Stone with the crooked Stick to hang the Pot on—the smutty wooden Crock—The Woodman's roof-shaped Hut, with 2 straight gavel ends, & slanting Door/ Clay, sods, & Brush wood/ one gavel end supported by two silver Birches—the wooden Hammer (for ripping) on the ground by the Straw Beds/ (Note the Bark Rick, the deep Orange with the tarnished Silver, with masses of Sunshine & Shade on it.)

~A solid Cube of Stone on the Gavel Top of a Cottage, with two Dials on the two sides that were visible. The same Cottage Roof with the Roof of the outside that joined it overgrown with Brambles, Grass, & weeds, resembled even to identity the side of a Hill.

~The Head of the Lake as seen from Luss & a mile or more above it, is very

simple—Point——& Ben Vorlich run down   & Ben Lomond runs down between them[56]—/ & beyond all Ben Loy runs like a broken wall, closing the Prospect—

~   Upon a rock beneath a Tree
                     Its shadow on the sandy shore
                     Its Image in the glassy Lake/

~As we ascend, the Lake becomes very like Ulswater, with a character of Crommock/ Benlomond is indeed a Thing betwixt Melbreak, & Place fell—higher still the Lake gains a character of its own, Nesses running down into the Lake on each side, at certain distance appearing to run in behind each other, at other distances to meet & close up the Lake/[57] —& now they seem opposite, & the Lake runs up endlessly between them/ the road & the mountains close by my left hand—wild, & steep, but not particularly interesting & every where we want the 'Statesmen's' Houses, & sweet spots of Cumberland Cultivation/ but every where there is a distressing Sense of local unrememberableness. On the Descent of the Hill close upon Tarbet, we had to our left a view of the wild broken Cliff, called the Cobler,[58] looking

[55] They had gained the island on a "strong boat" with two rowers and a boatman.

After enjoying the prospects, in all directions, from Inchtavannach, they had the boatman row them to a neighboring island (Inchconnachan) for a closer look at a bark hut they had noticed and afterwards spent some time walking about, discovering several woodsmen's huts which impressed them. "They were built in the form of a cone from the ground, like savages' huts, the door being just large enough for a man to enter with stooping" (p. 88). For a full account of the island visits, see *Recollections*, pp. 86–89.

[56] Ben Vorlich, Ben Lui ("Loy"), and Ben Lomond, all over 3,000 feet, have the effect of enclosure.

[57] Ullswater and Crummock are both lakes; Melbreak and Place Fell are both crags, the former near Crummock Water and the latter near Ullswater. All, of course, are in Coleridge's Cumberland. Nesses are projections of land into the lake.

[58] The Cobbler, as it is called familiarly (Ben Arthur formally), had been anxiously anticipated by the travellers. Dorothy records their collective pleasure in discovering this 2,891-foot mountain with its distinctive outline at the top of a cobbler seated at his stool at work: "When we were within about half a mile of Tarbet, at a sudden turning looking to the left, we saw a very craggy-topped mountain amongst other smooth ones; the rocks on the summit distinct in shape as if they were buildings raised up by man, or uncouth images of some strange creature. We called out in one voice, 'That's what we wanted!' alluding to the frame-like uniformity of the side-screens of the lake for the last five or six miles. As we conjectured, this singular mountain was the famous Cobbler, near Arrochar" (*Recollections*, p. 90). They were to have an even better view of the Cobbler from the inn at Arrochar, looking across Loch Long. Coleridge's spelling, with one "b" was an early spelling, oddly enough, not adopted by Dorothy.

in over a smooth Ridge.—I knew it instantly, from recollection of Mr Wilkinson's Drawing/[59]

Two Children, in the rain, under one cloak, their arms round each other, their two faces, a pair!—the drapery, &c, very picturesque.—A Fisherman's Hut/ the Oar, the one end on the ground, leaning on the Cottage, the broad end rising a few Inches above the little Chimney—an image for a poet—The view from the parlor Window at E. Tarbet[60]—& all the walk for more than 2 miles above so deludingly like Ulswater by Patterdale & Glenridden.[61] (alas! too few Houses, too little motion)—the most striking feature an ascending Terrace of cultivated Fields with frequent interruption of wooded bushy rocks, a steep Mountain above, a perpendicular Precipice below it/ —both the Mountain & precipice bushy—

In a nook formed by the Turn of a Brook a stone's Throw from a Cottage a whole forest of Raspberries—only old people in the Cottage—

~Friday, August 26th [62]—Took a couple of Fowls from our Inn, our hospitable Inn, at E. Tarbet, went with the Jacobin Traitor of a Boatman[63] to Rob

[59] A Quaker friend who lived in Yanwath, on the banks of the River Eamont, near Penrith, Thomas Wilkinson (1751–1863) had visited Scotland in 1787 and written an account of his travels which he shared with his friends, including Coleridge and the Wordsworths, in manuscript form. Whether the drawing in question here or the drawings mentioned below, in Letter 1, are ones he created himself or brought back from his travels is not clear. In 1824, Wilkinson's work was finally published as a book, *Tours of the British Mountains, with Descriptive Poems of Lowther, and Eamont Vale*. The published work does not contain illustrations. It does, however, offer a lively verbal picture of Wilkinson's experience of the Cobbler. "Some people imagine the figure of an old man mending shoes: I could imagine no such thing. Had I been for creating, I should have fancied the gigantic figure of a hooded nun: but, altogether, it has most the appearance of the ruins of some ancient castle" (p. 42). (His remark that he had not "been for creating" hints that the drawing Coleridge saw and remembered had not been done by Wilkinson himself.) Unlike most travellers, Wilkinson was not content to stand back and admire: he felt compelled to climb to the summit of the Cobbler, changing his position there to enjoy the views in all directions—of the valleys, the neighboring mountains, and the lakes—and imagining the presence of the MacFarlanes, knights of Loch Sloy, as they acted upon their motto, "We will guard this Loch" (p. 44), or marched in armor across the mountain tops.

[60] The "E" (for east) seems to be a Coleridgean idiosyncrasy; neither the early maps nor present-day ones use this designation for Tarbet, a generic Gaelic term for an isthmus or crossing place over water. The present hotel at Tarbet, in the Scottish baronial style, is at the site of the inn that probably provided a night's rest for Coleridge and the Wordsworths. The family who operated this inn, the parlour window of which provided a memorable view for Coleridge, spoke only Gaelic and could not understand the inquiries and requests of the English travellers, Dorothy recollected. Moreover, the dining and ambience left much to be desired. "Nothing but salt meat and eggs for dinner—no potatoes; the house smelt strongly of herrings, which were hung to dry over the kitchen fire" (*Recollections*, p.90).

[61] Patterdale and Glenridding are both villages close to the head of Ullswater.

[62] The party got a late start, leaving between 10:00 and 11:00 in the morning. They hired a boatman to take them across Loch Lomond to Inversnaid, stopping first just above Inversnaid to visit Rob Roy's Cave, guided by a small Highland woman. After landing at the Inversnaid ferry house they paused to view the splendid waterfall, and then, with a Highland woman for a guide, climbed up a hill that lead to the Garrison, and following the same path proceeded to Loch Katrine, reaching it at Stronachlachar. Coleridge and Dorothy paused there to eat some of the food they had brought with them while William explored the route up the loch. At the head of the loch, in Glengyle, they received and accepted an invitation from the gentleman of the Macfarlane home, "a white house," to rest there and "be accommodated with such beds as they had" (*Recollections*, p. 97). See also, pp. 91–98.

[63] After keeping them waiting, "and many clumsy preparations," the boatman subjected his English passengers—as well as a Highland woman and the boatman's helper—to a precarious and cramped ride in a small, leaky boat until he could transfer them to a larger, more suitable boat. Wordsworth dropped their food in the water, but was able to retrieve it. "The fowls were no worse, but some sugar, ground coffee, and pepper-cake seemed to be entirely spoiled" (*Recollections*, p. 92).

Coleridge had originally written "Jacobite" in pencil in his notebook— a term that would have given his epithet for the boatman a sharper edge. Nothing could be more despicable in Rob Roy country than a traitor to the Jacobites.

Roy's Cave. Such Caves as are always & of necessity where huge masses of Stone in great numbers have fallen down on one another; but the Masses, the Bushes & Trees, & the half-wooded Precipice above, all all most impressive/ We returned half a mile to the Ferry—a cottage with a few Fields among Trees by a wild Waterfall[64]—so we ascended into moorland, with strong Views behind us of the three pyramidal Mountains of the opposite Coast of Benlomond. These when all becomes Moorland Desolation, combine awfully with two lofty Houses, each with a smaller one attached to it—which we wondered how they came there, but afterwards, found they were a Garrison/[65] we move on about 3 miles to a little Lake, like Burnmoor Tarn, & in about two miles to a sheepfold at the edge of Loch Ketterin/ a fine body of water in an elbow bend, but the mountains were all too dreary and not very impressive in their Forms or Combinations—There was wood on them, but a total want of cultivated Land & happy Cottages/. We wound along over a Hill into a very interesting moorland till we came in sight of what I may call the Haft or Handle of the Lake, with two Farm Houses—here called Gentlemen's Houses/ —This first reach of the Lake, 2 miles perhaps in length, has four Islands, sweet Bays, & Island-like Promontories, one shaped like a Dolphin, another like a Sea-lion/ & still as we moved along, there formed new pictures, sometimes shutting out, sometimes admitting a Peep, sometimes pouring in a full view of the large mass of water./ But our Road, our wild moorland Path thro' the most luxuriant Heaths, the purple, the white, the pale purple, the deep crimson, or rose-color Purple/ thro 'a mountain Pass, like a Giant Gate-way—while on each side the Mountain Sides were cloathed wildly with willow Trees, in ravines or around bulging Rocks—& the Edges of the Mountains wildly

broken/ . The Rocks, by which we passed, under the brow of one of which I sate, beside an old blasted Tree, seemed the very link by which Nature connected Wood & Stone/ The Rock Substance was not distinguishable in grain, cracks, & colors from old scathed Trees, Age- or Lightning-burnt/ Right opposite to me the willowy Mountains with the broken wild craggy summits, & half way up one very large blasted Tree, white & leafless/ —Here too I heard with a deep feeling the swelling unequal noise of mountain Water from the streams in the Ravines/ We now found that our Expedition to the Trossacks was rashly undertaken/ we were at least 9 miles from the Trossacks, no Public House there or here/ it was almost too late to return, & if we did, the Loch Lomond Ferry Boat uncertain. We proceeded to the first House in the first Reach, &

[64] The Inversnaid Waterfall and its environs inspired William Wordsworth's "To a Highland Girl" as well as, in the twentieth century, Gerard Manley Hopkins's poem "Inversnaid."
[65] Built by order of the Hanoverian government soon after the rebellion of 1715, the Garrison was situated on an elevated site that afforded a prospect over two critical passes. Rob Roy and his men are said to have abducted some of the quarriers and masons working on the building of this garrison, which was completed in 1719. "The building was quite a substantial affair, comprising two barrack blocks facing each other across a walled courtyard. . . . During the second Jacobite rebellion of 1745, the garrison was partially destroyed by Rob Roy MacGregor's eldest son, James MacGregor" (Mike Trubridge, *The Inversnaid Hotel and its Surroundings*; Perth: M.F Wells [Hotels] Ltd., 1992, p. 23).

[66] A bannock is a round, flat cake, softer and thicker than an oatcake; it may be made of either barley meal or oatmeal and is cooked on a griddle.

[67] This was a strenuous day, rewarded by reaching the longed for Trossachs. After a good breakfast of cheese, barley cakes, butter, freshly baked oat cakes, and bread, as well as some good conversation about the French, Rob Roy, and the sheep farm, they walked three miles down the opposite side of Loch Katrine (from which they'd come up to Glengyle) to a place where they had been told there was a ferry boat and someone who would row them down the loch to the Trossachs. They spent time in the ferryman's hut, "the first genuine Highland hut we had been in," warming up near the fireplace and enjoying the generous and solicitous attention of the ferryman's wife. The hut was located near the water and the burial ground of some of the MacGregors. Coleridge, "afraid of the cold in the boat," chose to walk rather than ride with the Wordsworths. William, on the other hand, "wrapped himself in the boatman's plaid" and slept in the bottom of the boat part of the way. When they all met in the Trossachs, where Lady Perth had built huts to protect visitors from the elements, "Coleridge hailed us with a shout of triumph from the door of one of them, exulting in the glory of Scotland." After fully rejoicing in what they found in the Trossachs, they returned to the ferryman's hut, the Wordsworths in the boat, Coleridge on foot. Coleridge arrived first and had coffee waiting for the others when they got there. Coleridge and William and a vacationing drawing master from Edinburgh whom they had met in the Trossachs slept that night on hay in the barn, while Dorothy had a bed in the Highland hut. In all, this seems to have been one of the happiest and most satisfying experiences of the journey with the Wordsworths. See *Recollections*, pp. 98–107.

threw ourselves upon the Hospitality of the Gentleman, who after some Demur with Wordsworth did offer us a Bed/ & his Wife, a sweet & matronly Woman, made Tea for us most hospitably. Best possible Butter, white Cheese, Tea, & Barley Bannocks[66]—

~Saturday Morning, Aug. 27th [67]

Mr James McAlpin, Mr Andrew McFarlan,[68] Glengyle—left the House—a little before we reached the second White House, a perfect *Picture* from the two Hooks, one of a promontory, & another of an Island, seeming a *promontory*, within another larger Hook/ and in the foreground a fisherman's Hut with the Oars—/ so we went on, the white House *"green to the very door"*[69]—Here Rob Roy died,[70] we passed by *his Burial Ground*/ (each House has a square inclosure for Burying)—

The path now lead[s] up, then along the breast of the mountain. Hazels, Ashes, Birches, above us to the Height, with starting Cliffs, of the *wood-fibre* Stone—below the eye made its way thro' tangles & little openings down a steep of Hazels & wood down upon the Summit of a flat wood in upon the ever-sounding Lake/ the Mountain from many distances looking in upon my right Hand/ Benlomond—& behind those 3 pyramidal mountains in mist— opposite the ferry on Loch Lomond/

N.B. Gregor MacGregor the Ferryman—$3\frac{1}{2}$ miles from the head of the Lake/

[68] James McAlpin was Mr. Macfarlane's wife's brother.
[69] Coleridge recalls Wordsworth's "Lines Written a Few Miles above Tintern Abbey":

Once again I see
These hedge-rows, hardly hedge-rows, little lines
Of sportive wood run wild; these pastoral farms
Green to the very door. . . .

(ll. 15–18)

The lone white house found in Glengyle with "G. Mac G 1704" on its lintel today is very likely the Macfarlane home of Coleridge's narrative. Known as Glengyle House, it is privately owned. It stands on the site of the building in which Rob Roy was born in 1671.
[70] The information given to Coleridge and the Wordsworths by local figures was incorrect. Rob Roy was buried in a graveyard in Balquhidder, near where he spent the last active years of his life and died. However, there was a small square burial ground for Clan Gregor near the Macfarlane house and another a few miles down the Loch at Portnellan, where the ferryman's hut was. The latter has been moved slightly, and is now at the end of a causeway into the water.

~Sat. 27. Sund. 28. Mond. 29.

Sat. 27. We came to the Ferry House, where W. & D. took boat—I declined it—lost my road, clambered among woods almost to the top of the Fells—but regained it in about a mile/ —the road a most delightful one, all along by the Side of the Lake, now open, now inclosed, now a broad road, now a brown pathway thro' a green Lane./ About 2 miles from the Ferry, the views of the Foot of the Loch begin to be highly interesting & the Lake itself always highly so from the multitude & fine Shape of its Bays—But here as I leaned against an ash Tree, I saw such a visionary Scene!—One promontory from the Right ran down into the Lake like a stretched out Arm bent downwards with a *bend* as if to support something, then a long Island midway the Lake/ then from the left another promontory much resembling the former, but varying in the Steepness of its Segments/ Again from the Right a high Headland falling down steep & high as far as the Tower/ & in the far distance & exact Center of the View a small Sugar Loaf Hill—all these in exquisite Harmony, every ridge branch out, every intervening Distance softened by the rainy Air/ —Still as I went on, the view varied & improved in distinctness/ Promontories that could not be distinguished from Islands/ Island mistaken for Promontory/ —till I arrived at the Foot in the Heart of the Trossacks/[71] I exclaimed Galilæe vicisti—If the Lake of Keswick were to push up a mile into Borrodale, and interweave itself among the Mountains—& if those mountains were built up still more detachedly in a universal harmonious *Dislocation* of all its component Cliffs—those Cliffs all wooded—variously wooded/ young wood chiefly from *stumps* of huge Trees/ weeping Birches surmounting steep Precipices, as large as the largest weeping Willows/ But I must see it again!—I returned to the Ferryman's House—& soon after my Friends—& an Artist, of Edinburgh./[72] We had a merry meal in the Hovel black & varnished & glistering with peat smoak, the Fowls roosting in the Chimney amid the cloud of Smoke/ we slept in the Barn upon the Hay/ My Friend O me! what a word to give permanence to the mistake of a Life![73] & the Artist had a sort of Hay Bed with Blankets spread on the Ground/ but I preferred the Hay Rick, & was right/ the Brook ran as if running under my Hay pillow!—Next morning we went in the Boat to the End of the Lake./ & so on by the old Path by the Garrison to the Ferry House by Loch Lomond/ where now the Fall was in all *its fury*—& formed with the Ferry Cottage, & the sweet Highland Lass a nice picture/ the Boat gone to the Preaching, & we stayed all day in the comfortless Hovel, comfortless, but the two little Lasses did every thing with *such* Sweetness, and one of them, 14, with such native Elegance/ O she was a divine Creature![74]

[71] "I believe the word Trossachs signifies 'many hills:' it is a name given to all the eminences at the foot of Loch Ketterine, and about half a mile beyond," Dorothy explains (p. 104). The word is Gaelic meaning "the bristled country" and refers to the physical features of this wooded glen which extends from Loch Achray to Loch Katrine and slightly up the northeast side of Katrine.

[72] As mentioned, in the Trossachs the party had met a drawing master from Edinburgh who was on holiday making a pedestrian tour all the way to John o' Groats, at the northern extremity of Scotland. He came back with the Wordsworths to the ferryman's hut and spent a merry evening with them there and slept with the men in the barn. Curiously, neither Coleridge nor Dorothy recorded his name.

[73] This remark was inserted into the notebook as Coleridge was reviewing it at a much later date, in 1812, after a bitter falling out with William. (See Introduction.)

[74] Dorothy was also captivated by the two girls they met as they descended the hill from the Garrison and headed toward the ferry house at Inversnaid: "One of the girls was exceedingly beautiful; and the figures of both of them, in grey plaids falling to their feet, their faces only being uncovered, excited our attention before we spoke to them; but they answered us so sweetly that we were quite delighted, at the same time that they stared at us with an innocent look of wonder. I think I never heard the English language sound more sweetly than from the mouth of the elder of these girls, while she stood at the gate answering our inquiries, her face flushed with rain; her pronunciation was clear and distinct: without difficulty, yet slow, like that of a foreign speech" (*Recollections*, p. 109). The attention of these girls, the dinner they received in the ferry house, the condition of the house, the drying of their wet clothes, the arrival

of their ferry (filled with folk in their Sabbath best, returning from a "preaching"), and their return to Tarbet are all appealingly portrayed in *Recollections*, pp. 109–114.

The image of the fourteen-year-old "divine Creature" had such a strong impact upon William that not long after he returned from Scotland he produced the poem "To a Highland Girl, upon Loch Lomond," which begins:

Sweet Highland Girl, a very shower
Of beauty is thy earthly dower!
Twice seven consenting years have shed
Their utmost bounty on thy head.

His poem ends with the confidence that the girl's image will remain with him to his old age:

Nor am I loth, though pleased at heart,
Sweet Highland Girl, from thee to part;
For I, methinks, till I grow old,
As fair before me shall behold
As I do now, the Cabin small,
The Lake, the Bay, the Waterfall,
And thee, sweet Spirit of them all.
    (in *Recollections* pp. 112–14)

It was his good fortune to grow old and remember: "This delightful creature & her demeanour are particularly described in my Sister's Journal. The sort of prophecy with which the verses conclude has through God's goodness been realized, and now, approaching the close of my 73rd year I have a most vivid remembrance of her and the beautiful objects with which she was surrounded" (*Fenwick Notes*, p. 26).

Incidentally, it appears the Edinburgh artist was still with the Coleridge-Wordsworth party when they arrived at Inversnaid. Dorothy writes: "Conceive what a busy house it was—all our wet clothes to be dried, dinner prepared and set down for us four strangers, and a second cooking for the family . . ." (*Recollections*, p. 110).

The Sight of the Boat full of Highland Men & Women and Children, from the Preaching, exquisitely fine/ —we soon reached E. Tarbet—all the while had Rain./ Never, never let me forget that small Herd boy,[75] in his Tartan Plaid, dim-seen on the hilly field, & long heard ere seen, a melancholy *Voice*, calling to his Cattle!/ —nor the beautiful Harmony of the Heath, the dancing Fern, & the ever-moving Birches—/ —That of itself enough to make Scotland visitable, its fields of Heath, those not subject to yearly Burning, giving a sort of feeling of Shot silk and ribbon *Finery*, in the *apotheosis* of Finery.

From Arrochar onto Separate Ways

~On Monday we went to Arrochar,[76] formerly a Gentleman's House on Lake Long/ the view of the Cobler interesting no doubt,[77] but I was disappointed with the place!—Here I left Wordsworth & D. (*utinam nonq. vidissem!*) [Would that I had never met them!] returned myself to E. Tarbet—slept there—& now (alas *now* it is June 5, 1812)[78]

Tuesday, Aug. 30, 1803—am to make my own way alone to Edingburgh— O Esteesee![79] that thou hadst from thy 22nd year indeed made *thy own* way & *alone!*

~The Rain drops on the Lake to an army of Spirits, or Faeries, on a wilderness of white Sand/ Multitude + Joyance, motion or a moving/

[75] "While we were walking forward, the road leading us over the top of a brow, we stopped suddenly at the sound of a half-articulate Gaelic hooting from the field close to us. It came from a little boy, whom we could see on the hill between us and the lake, wrapped up in a grey plaid. He was probably calling home to the cattle for the night. His appearance was in the highest degree moving to the imagination . . ." (*Recollections*, p. 114).
[76] The "Gentleman's House" on Loch Long is the present Cobbler Hotel, built originally by John, 19th Chief of Clan McFarlane and called Inverioch Castle or House, in 1697. The estates of McFarlane (Macfarlane) were sold in 1784 to Ferguson of Raith, whose factor, William Douglas, lived at the house. The house

was added on to in 1799 by the Duke of Argyll, who had leased the lands of Arrochar that had originally belonged to Clan McFarlane. As testimony to the history of the house a Gaelic inscription on a stone over the main entrance reads: "It was on this very spot that John, chief of the McFarlanes had his original home. The massacre of Glen Fruin in 1603 when the McFarlanes and the Colquhouns of Luss fought their bloody battle was already history when this stone was engraved in 1697."
[77] See notes 58–59 above.
[78] The date Coleridge went back to his Scottish tour notes, in the spirit of bitterness, after the betrayal of Wordsworth and their 1810–12 quarrel. (See Introduction.)
[79] Coleridge sometimes created a word out of his initials, S.T.C., and called himself that.

~My words & actions imaged on his mind, distorted & snaky as the Boatman's Oar reflected in the Lake/—

~The Cross—the Butter Hill—Ben Bean—and Benvaloch/ the 4 mountains opposite the Inverslade Ferry.[80]

~Tuesday Morn. Aug. 30—Walked to the Shore opposite to the Ferry, & having waited & shouted & made signals for near an hour in vain, I wandered on—/ & seeing a Boat on the Shore, went to the Cottage—which I found to be a small Slaughter House, engaged the Men to go with me—went & obtained my watch—returned—I gave the man 2^s & he said I must drink a glass of Whisky with him, & carried me up the mouth of a River called Inveydougle[81] & there I found a Distillery all under & among Foliage, which with its Hogs &c sufficient picturesque—tho' as offensive to my sense of smelling, is perhaps melancholy in its moral relation—/[82] —Passed on—the Mountain close by my side, high & green with ferns, Grasses, & young Trees—Trees scattered here & there, and often a handsome full grown Birch on the Edge of the Top of a naked Precipice// Crossed little Bridges, where streams came down over black Rocks—with many Views of that species of Scenery which is always so interesting—where Naked Rocks stand above each other some perpendicular & smooth & grey from a yard high to 20 fathom with green *Ledges* interspersed, some so narrow that a single sheep goes cautiously, some so broad that a small flock might graze there, or an industrious Chinese raise a crop of Corn/ —Holly Trees wedging the solid Rock/ Large Birch Tree filling up the hollow of the Arch of the Bridge—/ passed by Bays & Promontories, some wooded, some craggy & heath-rich, some cultivated, often a Boat heaving in the secure Bay, & now the road ascending a Hill led me to the last Reach of Loch Lomond, which resembles a majestic River, distinguished from it by the Ledger-like Lines of Foams, & its own lakish *Sound* of Water,—the head is crowned by 3 ridges of Mountains, the highest not very high, but bare & black & of very various outline; and such as in rainy or misty weather would be sublime—in this reach too is one of those *Terraces* before described—& there is another between this & the Ferry—the road up & down another Hill, on my descent I see to the Left a large single Rock, far away from the foot of the Mountain, in a green plot by itself—a little stream winds almost around it, overhung with Alder Bushes—it is cowl'd with Heath—all its sides Bare/ the amplest side, viz,that facing the road, is 25 Strides in length, & I suppose at least 40 feet high/ it is 60 Strides round/ in shape it resembles

[80] Opposite Inversnaid at the ferry crossing Coleridge would have seen A Chrois, Ben Vane, and Ben Vorlich, three of the mountains spanning the eastern range. Local historian Norman Douglas, F.S.A., of Arrochar conjectures that Butter Hill is Ben Arthur (the Cobbler). "On the East side of Ben Arthur, there is a Burn [that] flows down into Loch Long. This Burn is known locally as The SOOR (Sour) MILK BURN because when in spate the cascade resembles a flood of milk. Sour Milk is of course Butter Milk, and I have often heard visitors to our area describe the site as Buttermilk Burn. I feel quite strongly that Ben Arthur is the Butter Hill that Coleridge is writing about" (Letter to the author, 18 July 1998).

[81] The river has been called by many names: River Douglas, Inverdougle, Inveruglas, and Inveruglas Water. Following the river Coleridge would have come to Coiregrogain, where in 1803 he found a distillery, perhaps a part of the farm which still stands there. The bridges and trees he describes in the passage follow the river. Coleridge's interest in the distillery may have grown from his awareness that the distilling process in the Highlands was superior to that in the Lowlands. Stoddart noted that: "A line has long since been drawn, by the legislature, between the Highland, and Lowland districts, the former of which was allowed to distil spirits, for its own consumption, at a lower rate than the latter, and whiskey being best produced by a slow process and in small stills, the Highlanders were enabled to make it better than their neighbours, by being permitted to make it cheaper" (*Remarks*, I, p. 95).

[82] Stoddart pointed out, in his discussion of taxation of distilleries in Scotland, that "the moral and physical effects, produced by the habit of drinking these liquors, are matters of much moment" (*Remarks*, I, p. 94).

[83] True to Coleridge's description in shape and size, the stone is also called Pulpit Rock. A recess large enough for a preacher to stand in has been cut into the stone at an elevated level; from this "pulpit" the preacher could address his congregation, who stood in a clearing in front of the stone. Very likely "the Boat full of Highland Men & Women and Children, from the Preaching" Coleridge admires above had gathered at Pulpit Rock and were returning from this open-air church.

[84] Slightly less than two miles above the Bull Stone, following the road along the loch, Loch Lomond narrows to become River Falloch, giving Glen Falloch its name.

[85] Garbel was a farm in Glen Falloch, remembered by local people as having a beautiful house. In its present state it is a ruin, a Belgian entrepreneur having demolished it with the intent of developing a lodge and then abandoning the plan. It is about a quarter of a mile below the Inverarnan Inn, though it cannot be seen from the road. Garabel Hill may have given the house its name.

[86] Coleridge had mistakenly written 1801 for the year.

[87] The Falls of Falloch, about two miles above Inverarnan Inn, four miles below Crainlarich, still attract tourists willing to digress from the road.

the Gavel End of a House, rudely

This is called, I find, the Bull Stone/[83] "Cry to the Guid Man to come up, the Gentleman wants to *crack* wi' 'im."/ Two Bulls fighting said to have thrown down the Stone/ —The river is a fine one/[84] and [on] one side of it an O shaped Pond, Falloch—i.e. White Lake, of 200 yards or so, in length, & one all wooded hill; standing by itself close by its Bank, which I mention because half a mile on it forms a beautiful feature in a fine river view, as you look backward down toward Loch Lomond, upon Ben Lomond & the ridges of Hills intervening—I stop at a farm House, & meet the kindest reception/ From E. Tarbet 7 + 9 miles up the Lake & up Glenfalloch but 3 Farms—One Farmer has within a very trifle one whole Parish, a farm of 1100 £ per annum, in this *wild* Country—/ Preaching four times a year at the great Bull Stone, by the desire of the Inhabitants/ this is one among the many proofs that natural Objects do *impress* the minds of the Inhabitants who are familiarized to them, tho' they do not use epithets of Delight or Admiration/ —A Cloud broke on the Hill a little above Garbel,[85] the name of the Dram house where I stopt/ broke in the day time, & swept away two whole Villages, all but one strong Slate House, which however it filled with stones & gutted of its furniture/ the Houses came floating down, standing upright, & the poultry, & Cats on the House tops, mewing, clucking, crowing—& Beds floated by with Dogs yowling on them/ the people all away—Here I determined to go to Glen Coe/. My Landlord asked me 8 s for Pony & Lad for 12 miles!—Good people nevertheless. Comment on this—Had a wretched Night—& with an aching head, eye, face, ear, tooth, left Garbel Wednesday Morning, $\frac{1}{4}$ past 9, August 31, 1803[86]—& pursued my way up Glenfalloch toward Tyndrum, the Glen narrowing, the river becoming more & more wild & rocky, running & roaming among Alders & coppice Woods, the Hills landlocking the Glen with less than half a mile interspace, in Hills not very high, but much broken, & their wildness a ragged wildness.—I now passed over a Bridge with a stream dashing down over rocks, & under table Rock on which the foam of Monday's Storm was lying yet—this I learnt was Fiona glen or the Glen of Fingal/ met with three good Highlanders, two understood & talked Gaelic, the third, an intelligent man, spoke low Scottish only—I went with him into a field to my right, & visited a noble waterfall[87]—during rain it must be a most noble one/ the Trees are old, & *army*, one on each side/ it is one great *Apron* with an oval Pool at the Bottom, but above it you look up thro' a rocky Stream with trees & bushes, & the Fall itself is marked by two *great Cauldrons* delved out in the black rock, down which it falls—into which cauldrons it boils & rebounds/ this is on the River of *Glenfalloch*, which word signifies the *Hidden Glen*—I talked much with the Scotchman—the oppressions of the Landlord—& he used these beautiful words—"It kills one's affections for one's Country, the Hardships of Life, coming by change, & wi' injustice."—The Hills on each side of me are low, for I myself am on very high Ground—they are almost cragless, an intermixture of beds of purple Heath, slumbring in its Beauty, & beds of green fern, always alive & fluttering—but to my right the Hill breaks, & lets in upon the view a trian-

gular Mountain of fine outline. And in the break a little Stream with glimmering Waterbreaks & cowering Alders/ wild Sheep-folds in the Hills but before me Ben More[88] or the Huge Mountain/ One of the highest in the highlands, shaped like a haystack, which dallies with the Clouds, that now touch, now hide, now leave it/

~Among the Beauties of the Highlands in Aug. & Sept. let me not forget the Fumitory[89] with its white flower on the Hovels & Barns/ & the Potatoe fields with white Blossoms—appearing to my eye the loveliest & richest flower of Gardens—

~About two miles from the Glen of Fingal,[90] Glenfalloch—how altered its character altogether—I had been lost in reverie—and on awaking found myself with low Hilly Ridges to my Left, for the road itself was now very high indeed/ but behind me, before me, & close by my right (just over a narrow Bottom in which were a cluster'd Cottage, & near it one slate House) high, separating mountains, pyramids, Cones, ridges, which one might stride across, some running straight on, some curving into arcs of circles, & forming Basons & hollows—a Break of an inverted Triangle shape, & a naked Sugar loaf looks in from a distant country—Ben Lomond behind

me in that shape— a vast multitude of Sheep, alas! the very first time, I ever looked at Sheep, with melancholy & indignant feelings!—[91]

~Waited an hour & a half for a dish of Tea/ the most civil promises all the while/ at Inverooran/[92] this a fair specimen of Highland Manners.

~Took shelter under a bridge[93] in a tremendous storm on a rock by the side

[88] At 3,852 feet Ben More was indeed the highest in this area, but Ben Nevis, which Coleridge would be seeing within days, would be the Highland superior at 4,406 feet.

[89] A climbing plant, with multi-divided leaves and small tubular flowers. A weed, it grows in fields and empty places but may be cultivated to grow as ornamental vines. Figuratively speaking, it spreads as fast as smoke, hence its name, from the Latin *fumus*.

[90] About one and a half miles northeast of the Falls of Falloch and Glen Falloch is Fionn Ghleann, the stream named Fionn running through it.

[91] Coleridge may have been responding sympathetically to the effects of the Highland clearances, which began *c*.1782 and involved replacing Highland cattle by the introduction of sheep, a change that resulted in extensive displacement of rural Highlanders and the loss of a deeply rooted way of life.

[92] Travelling northward from Tyndrum on General Wade's road, Coleridge would have come to Inveroran Inn, three miles from Bridge of Orchy, and still an operating hotel. Dorothy and William stayed here, after an uncomfortable night at Kingshouse, and found it comparatively hospitable, though short on service and good food: "When we arrived at the huts, one of them proved to be an inn, a thatched house without a sign-board. We were kindly received, had a fire lighted in the parlour, and were in such good humour that we seemed to have a thousand comforts about us; but we had need of a little patience in addition to this good humour before breakfast was brought, and at last it proved a disappointment: the butter not eatable, the barley-cakes fusty, the oat-bread so hard I could not chew it, and there were only four eggs in the house, which they had boiled as hard as stones" (*Recollections*, p.157).

[93] Very likely the military bridge over the River Orchy at Bridge of Orchy.

[94] The tragi-comedy *Count Benyowsky; or the Conspiracy of Kamtschatksa*, by the German dramatist August von Kotzebue (1761–1819) had been translated into English by W. Render in 1798, though Coleridge may have read it in the original German.

[95] The Earl of Kinnoul owned land in Perthshire, and his name was given to a parish adjacent to the town of Perth. The name Kinnoul had association not only with Perth but with nearby Dupplin Castle, which at the time Thomas Pennant visited in 1769 was the residence of the Earl of Kinnoul. Both Perth and Dupplin Castle lay ahead for Coleridge.

The entry concerning "Benyowski" and this one on "E. Of Kinneal" are not in sequence with the other entries; they occur at the end of Coleridge's notebook on the last folio page and are especially demanding as manuscript.

[96] The route described in this entry is the one Coleridge learned from the gentleman he met at Kingshouse, Dr. Hay Drummond. He did not, in the end, follow the exact route. After Inverness he did not choose one of the military roads running from Fort George to Bridge of Dulsie to Granton. Instead he took Wade's road from Inverness to Moy, called the Moy Road on some old maps. Also, logistically, going from Fascaly to Taymouth (Kenmore) to Dunkeld does not make sense. Coleridge took the route from Dalnacardoch to Tummel Bridge via Trinidad, then on to Kenmore, afterwards making his way to Perth by way of Amurlee and Glen Almond.

Here, as elsewhere, Coleridge spells some place names as he heard them pronounced, writing Balahuhlilsh for Ballachulish.

Like the entries on "Benyowsky" and "Kinneal," this one was written on the last folio page of the notebook and was thus not part of a sequence of entries.

[97] He took the one to Tyndrum, the military road.

of the stream that overflowed it—till this I expect swoln by the Rains, forced him once again into the Storm/

~A character of complete *Ingratitude*—Stephano in Benyowsky[94]—Likewise . . . you not known. . . . a character whose tender mind was so haunted by the causeless hatred unjustly. . . . A. did a real injury & a very-great one to B. in order to make his Hatred more natural, less dæmonish, whereon B. ceases to hate hm/ soothed by the power of *forgiving* A. & of feeling himself the superior—E. of Kinneal.

~Glencoe to Balahuhlish/ —to Fort William, my Ferry then at Mr Munro's—The Rev. Dr Hay Drummond six miles up Glen Nevish/ on way on Loch Lochy to Loch Oich/ to Fort Augustus to the Fall of Foyers—pass the Falls & go to a House called the General's Hut—on the Banks of Lochness./ From Fort Augustus, 7 miles, ascend to a Black Moor, to a Hut called Noch Lomoch/ apply for a guide for the Falls & Cavern of Foyers/ —the same guide that Dr D. had, exquisite Alpin scenery from Falls to Inverness thro' Birch & Oak Woods—When I come within view of Inverness, stop—take the view of the River—the Town of Inverness & Fort St George—From Inverness to Fort George/ by the Bridge of Dulse—Grantown, Aviemore/ Pitmaine/ Dalwhinny/ Dalnacardach/ Blair/ across the Tummel by Fascaly to Taymouth/ to Dunkeld/ Dunkeld to Perth/ —5 miles from Perth to Dupplin Castle/ Dr H. D. Hadleigh, Suffolk[96]

~ I come to a Double Road, one to Shirley[97]—the other to Tyndrum/ And for about a mile the moors & hills are less interesting but soon regain their former size—dined at Tyndrum/ walked a brisk pace under the inspiration of a Bottle of Burton Ale,[98] from Tyndrum to Inverooran/[99] a fine Road tho' a perfectly houseless Moorland, the mountains on each side,[100] behind, before, most noble—tho' green/ & I seemed to think that these high green mountains, so furrowed, delved, & wrinkled with Torrents are still wilder than craggy Mountains/ the Mountains were all detached, a great Beauty!—One I

[98] Burton Ale was so named because it came from the major breweries of Burton-upon-Trent in Staffordshire, England.

[99] Inveroran. See note 92 above.

[100] Beinn Breac-liath on his left and Beinn Odhar on his right would have been the first ones he passed after he left Tyndrum.

shall never forget/ in shape resembling a Schoolboy's Top, or rather presenting to the eye two sides of a spherical Triangle/ as I looked back, on my left, at the extremity of this side of the Triangle, a curving wall of green Highland, & over it from the distance a ⌃ mountain. At the extremity of the other side another mountain from the distance,[101] but of wild & fantastic outline/ but the Mountain itself, the spheric Triangle, so very vast, so high, so worn & marked/—The same road to Inverooran, the same to Kingshouse,[102] 18 miles of beautiful Road, such as you may see in Noblemen's pleasure Grounds, thro' a wide wide Moor, with rocky rivers—mountains of all shapes, scarr'd & lay'd open, but none Craggy—the rain all the way, except now & then a Blow off that discovered all the forms of the mountains & that I had lost nothing else/ add to these large moorland Pools with bushy Islets— and *one goat*—& you have the whole, I saw from Tyndrum & Inverooran/ to Kingshouse—*The whole Road from E. Tarbet to Ballachulish!*— ~Septem. 1 1803—I have walked from Inverooran to Kingshouse—nothing, they tell me, will *grow here*/ it is so high. They have tried it—they burn Peat & Turf here/ but have no Bellows. The weather so Misty & rainy that I have small heart to visit Glencoe this Aftenoon.

~This Kingshouse from the rancid Moorland Peat smells like a dirty Macquerel with Bilge-water/ 9 miles every way from all Dwelling, vile Troop of Drovers,[103] with fiddle & dancing, & drinking, kept it up all night, one clamour like a crew of Pirates that "House on the wild Sea with wild usages." When they broke up, one of the Household had the modesty to open my bedroom Door, & bring me in a Drover for a Bedfellow/ and I might have been forced to get up, if the Drover had not had some sense & good manners—

barracks-like appearance she wrote: "Never did I see such a miserable, such a wretched place,—long rooms with ranges of beds, no other furniture except benches, or perhaps one or two crazy chairs, the floors, far dirtier than an ordinary house could be if it were never washed" (p. 153). Another female traveller, guide book author Sarah Murray, stopped at Kingshouse during the same era, and did not mince her words in reporting on the conditions there: "Few beings, but drovers, take up their quarters at this house; not wholly because of its desolate situation, but because it is very dirty. It is one of the houses government provides; therefore, as those who keep it have it rent free, it ought to be made more comfortable for travellers" (*Companion and Useful Guide*, II, p. 372). After arriving Murray had a small meal and "secured my pig-hole to sleep in" (p. 373), then want off to visit Glen Coe, returning later in the evening, after dark, to Kingshouse. "King's House was full of people, and I made my way to my sty through columns of smoke. This sty was a square room, of about eight feet, with one window and a chimney in it, and a small bedstead nailed in the angle behind the door. . . . I soon ate my bit of supper, half choked with smoke, and in danger of getting cold by an open window, the damp from rain pouring in, and my petticoats tucked to my knees for fear of dirt, which was half an inch thick on the floor . . . (pp. 379–80). As the Kings House Hotel, the inn today offers a considerably more appealing tariff to its visitors.

[101] The combination of Bienn Dòrain and Beinn an Dothaìdh.
[102] Kingshouse was strategically located on the military road running from Tyndrum to Glen Coe. Although built in the seventeenth century, it was used after the Battle of Culloden (1746) as a barracks to house soldiers of King George III. On her arrival there with her brother William on 3 September, Dorothy noted: "The house looked respectable at a distance—a large square building, cased in blue slates to defend it from storms,—but when we came close to it the outside forewarned us of the poverty and misery within" (*Recollections*, p. 153). Responding to the

[103] Because Kinsghouse was situated on the drove road between Skye and Falkirk, in the direction of Edinburgh, as well as on the main route between Glasgow and Fort William, it made a good stopover for cattlemen and their herds, from the days when cattle were the primary industry in Scotland to (obviously) Coleridge's visit.

104 By today's road it is ninety miles.

105 Helm Crag dominates the village and glen of Grasmere, home of Wordsworth in the Lake District, as Buachaille Etive Mor (3,353 feet) stands as a sentinel to Glen Coe as well as Glen Etive.

106 Analogous to "the ancient woman seated on Helm Crag," an image from a poem by Wordsworth called "Joanna" (from his series "Poems on the Naming of Places") and the Cobbler, the kneeling saint is in the folk tradition of finding figures in the configuration of mountain peaks.

~Sept. 2 1803. Friday Morning AM—when at length I shall have procured a bit of Breakfast, to go to Glencoe and thence whither?—84 miles to Inverness.[104]—$\frac{1}{2}$ past 9 left that devoted Kingshouse, & in less than a mile entered Glencoe, the white mists (white with interspaces of diluted Black) floating away from the Mountains, & thinning off along their Breasts—gathering again—again thinning—all in motion—giving phantoms of motion even to the Hills—the first Hill, the Helm Crag & Centry of the Glen,[105] on my right, rises up into a naked sharp ⌂—craggy in the rude shape a Church & steeple—then flows down in a green ⌣ curve to the Moorland Stream at its feet. O the green shining Spots on the Hills thro' the openings & rents of the Mist—O those other rich white mists seen thro' the thinning of the nearer mist! & blue Sky, here & there, in the *low* Heaven!/ —Near the Top of this Centry Hill one figure of a Saint kneeling,[106] very wild & distinct—

~In my road from Tayndrum of a large number of young Trees in the valley below me, by the Burn—but they seemed as if they had no Business there/ no abiding place at least, as if they were met there, on a Moorland *Fair-Day*—so too in Glencoe, on the mountain walls, for so they are, brown-green with moss, bright green with stream-hiding Grass, & pinky in streaks where the Rainrills flowed or are flowing—here too I glimpsed Trees here & there/ but they looked like Apparitions—

~The first six miles of Glencoe a winding glen, on my right a bulgy rifted continuous mountain, but the mists lay heavy & thick on its Top, but the rifts & Caverns were dark as Darkness—to my left the lower & grassy Half of the Mountains was continuous, save only that they were rifted, often to the foundation, but the rifts in general were narrow—tho' a few wide enough to contain furious Waterfalls—the higher & craggy Half rose up into separate Mountains, Turrets, Steeples, Sugarloaves, & often Bulls' Brows, Brows savager than those of Urus or Byson/ one *cone*, of great Height, was connected with a rude triangle-shaped Mountain, of equal Height, by a semicircular Bason, or wall of rock in behind ⌒—after two hours walk I came in sight of a Cottage, two or three green enclosures, so green within stone walls, & a lake/ & about a furlong before I reached it, an enormous *Facing* of Mountain ⌒—the highest—almost $\frac{1}{3}$rd of the whole height of the mountain—a perfectly perpendicular smooth precipice with a huge Cavity in

a cylinder —This whole Mountain more like Grasmere or
Crummock[107] than any thing I have hitherto seen, tis the noblest too that I
have seen/ it is ledge & precipice as I have elsewhere described—only no
bushes or Trees—and only that the precipices are separate from each other
seemingly not by their own protrusion but by channels of delving Storms—
some traversing the Mountain, but by far the greater number running straight
down/—At its feet are two sets of Housage with their inclosures, & a small
dead Tairn out of which rushes a madcap of a River/ the next mountain to it,
with a Torrent between, is green & ragged with Trees—but at the summit of

the interspace, somewhat retiring, is a most remarkable naked rock
—resembling a house with two gavel ends fronting you, the one nearest

Grasmere , (Here I was rather alarmed by a Highland Bull, who tore up
the ground &c.) the other next the green mountain, round and resembling a
Porch—& now straight before me within a slingthrow, the Vale is closed by
a green mountain—& I am to commence a new reach of the Glen. —This
new reach brought in view another Lake at its termination/ it pleased me
much—the surface of the Mountain close by my right hand is playful, & its
craggy half is bulgy & brown with moss & pinky with Screes/ close by my
left hand the arch of the vale is crowded with 9 sugar-loaf green Hills, 2 only
quite Hills by themselves/ say 3 Hills, one with 7 heads—over these a noble
pyramidal Mountain, and another pyramidal mountain, but this was green, &
presented its whole side to us/ the other was craggier & pinkier, & stood
edgeways—an ocean of mist there retiring behind the Grasmere & its green-
er neighbor with her 10 rain channels floating down it (tho' now no water—
I speak only of the imaginary motion of its curvatures) like 10 pink Ribbons.
As I now stand, something more than half of the green Pyramid's side past,
the road ascending, I stood, turned round, & the view that had been *upon* my
Back, as it were—so finely do the mountains on my left—as I *now* stand—&
Grasmere close up the reach, so tight, so narrow/ for Grasmere seems now
to run across the vale/ it & its pink-ribbon'd neighbour of equal height—a
descent & retirement of various outline, with an enormous Notch, then the
Pyramid Edgways—& two houses at its feet/ —the 3 Hills, 1 with 8 Tops,
now cuddle in close at the feet of *Grasmere's Sister*—
   The *green* Pyramid whose broadside I am almost bisecting, sinks softly

[107] Grasmere is Helm Crag, the
dominating mountain, or fell, in
Grasmere. Crummock stands for
Buttermere, another of the fells in the
Lake District, which has a lake in its cleft
called Crummock Water. Throughout this
long entry on Glen Coe Grasmere refers
to Helm Crag or the mountain in Glen
Coe that reminds Coleridge of Helm
Crag, probably the Pap of Glencoe, the
name of which he does not discover until
looking back at it from Ballachulish, at
which time he is surprised by its "obscene
name."

[108] Mr. And Mrs. Oliff were neighbors of William and Dorothy whose home and field were close to the Keswick road between Dove Cottage, at Town End, and the inn called The Swan. The Oliff farm was called Hollens (or Hollins) because of the holly trees that grew in abundance there.

[109] William and Dorothy, having had an accident with their cart and horse as they walked along Loch Leven, were forced to stop at the slate quarry for help from the blacksmith there. "The village where the blacksmith lived was before us—a few huts under the mountains, and, as it seemed, at the head of the loch; but it runs further up to the left, being narrowed by a hill above the village, near which, at the edge of the water, was a slate quarry . . ." (*Recollections*, p. 147). While the blacksmith worked on the cart with William, Dorothy chatted with local women by the fireside and discovered that the superintendent of the slate quarries and his wife came from Cumberland and Westmorland, the same part of England the Wordsworths called home.

Evidence of what must have been a thriving industry may still be seen in the village of Ballachulish, where a blasted out mountain side betrays traces of mining techniques. Dorothy noted: "I forgot to mention that while the blacksmith was repairing the car, we walked to the slate-quarry, where we saw again some of the kind creatures who had helped us in our difficulties the night before. The hovel under which they split their slates stood upon an out-jutting rock, a part of the quarry rising immediately out of the water, and commanded a fine prospect down the loch below Ballachulish, and upwards towards the grand mountains, and the other horn of the vale where the lake was concealed" (p. 150).

[110] The ferry house was originally a stopping place for drovers, and as traffic in Highland cattle thinned and coaching and foot traffic increased, the ferry house

then rises again into another pyramidal, but far far lower where it deeps, there starts up a bare mountain—I might touch it with my stick if I were on that green ridge/ of a rich red brown—quite bare/ in shape resembling

the Doric Portal of S Paul's in Covent Garden ⌃ an obtuse triangle!— In this reach Oats, Potatoes (O that one tiny strange Hovel of Boughs of Trees, & its tiny Plantation of Potatoes) and Alder bushes innumerable! it is a sweet Reach, no doubt.

So the country growing more and more cultivated, I came down on Loch Leven, a Sea Lake, with a green Hill at its head, & a House under it/ with *Mr. Olives' very own garden walls*[108] on the side of the Hill/ —on the side of the Lake what seemed many houses after the solitude of the last 30 miles—the Hills woody—at the foot of the Lake or what seems so, high mountains with one deep gap or valley, thro' which, I guess, the road goes. The road is here a fine one again/ in Glencoe the Torrents had torn it up.

Crossing at Ballachulish, following the Line of the Forts North

~Three peat Islands, in file, near the opposite shore of the Lake, an uninteresting ruin of a Chapel on the largest—the Smell of the Sea water refreshing to me & the long rul'd lines of Foam always a thing to look on—Pass a slate Quarry,[109] with a brig close under it & in about a quarter of a mile (or a half a mile) turn round, & look back on a green field with Alders—/ then 3 Slate Buildings—/—a green Ascent —the Quarries, with rich metallic silvery Blue/ a green ascent & climbing Ridge above the Quarry—& looking over this ridge a Mountain, bare or only dark brown with moss, of a very shape more like

Brandel How, as seen at Portinscale/ ⌒ —Dined at the Ferry House at Ballychulish,[110] and—crossed the Ferry—& that *Pitadonish*

accommodated the general run of travellers to and from Fort William as well. Keats and Brown stopped here in 1818 while on their pedestrian tour of Scotland. Ferry boats plied the loch until the early twentieth century, when a bridge

was built, replacing the ferries and altering the significance of the ferry house. Once called the Drovers Inn, the old ferry house is now the Ferry Bar and attached to a much newer, larger and more stylish Ballachulish Hotel.

mountain with the obscene name/[111] O horrid! the blessed Sun full on it, above the green Hill, with the slate Quarries now appearing at its feet/ between that green Hill & another huge mountain this Maiden of Glencoe appears behind between them bleak, & sunny with scattered Clouds—

After having crossed the Ferry walked on, on a delightful road, high Hills on my right most richly wooded, all wood save where huge Rocks with Heath flowers, burst out of the Hill,—Trees too on my Left, with the Sea dashing its Spray among their Leaves—so for a mile & a half, or more, when I turned, looked back, & saw O what a sight!—the 2 Mountains running in & forming

an obtuse ⋁ and they, & the mountains in between & behind them covered with illumined Clouds, & so very yellowly & richly lighted up by the Sunbeams stealing down from under the Clouds.—O this does indeed surpass Porlock[112]—O that the Hovels looked comfortable. Sea truly, the roar & the waves & Feeling are of the Sea,[113] but far as my eye can reach, it is all embosomed—& all the mountains separate, how various in their forms. (The curiosity attributed to the Americans incident to all rude & thin-scattered People)[114]—Glen running up by my right, a furlong in length.—& the red cloudlike Edging in one straight Line on the distant Shore/ —& here just as I came in sight of a nice House, sheltered from the Sea by Trees, which I thought I should pass—my road turns off, & O Sorrow! I quit it!—My Blessings go with it—& all its deep murmurs!—In a Dell with Hills on each side, & in a mile regained the sight of the Sea, crossing the Bridge of a River creeping under alder Bushes on both Banks—

The road again by the Sea—a narrow Lake—the Mountains its other Bank, have their Tops in one even Line of lead-color'd Cloud, they are deeply gullied, straight down & aslant—Here I saw a field of Potatoes, within an inclosure of Turf, waving like Fern, a stone wall seaward, the Sea not a foot from the Stone Wall./

The road now continues by the Sea lake side—Mountains on the opposite Shore, rocks & woods, or woody rocks, by my right hand, & sometimes over my head/ now Darkness came on and I saw only that I was in the same scenery—so on *briskly* till within a mile & $\frac{1}{2}$ of Fort William, when I unfortunately drank/ instant Fatigue—pains in my Thighs/ arrive at Fort William—Mr Monro's—to Mr Livingstone's—hysterical weeping—&c &c—[115]

~Spent Saturday, Sept. 3rd—having my stockings & shirt washed, & writing—on Saturday night threatened with another Attack of Gout in my

[111] Sgnorr na Ciche, or Pap of Glencoe.

[112] The little harbor town called Porlock, in Somerset, on the Bristol Channel comes to Coleridge's mind not for the harbor alone but for Porlock Hill (1,378 feet) and for the remembrances its stirs of his days of living in Nether Stowey. But Porlock probably comes to the minds of Coleridge's readers because of the famous interruption by the "person who had come on business from Porlock" who broke the poet's reverie, leaving him, and posterity, with a poem we are told is only a fragment–"Kubla Khan."

[113] Coleridge has been walking along Loch Linnhe, a fresh water loch that opens into the sea. He will follow Loch Linnhe all the way to Fort William.

[114] Sarah Murray remarks on the same American curiosity, drawing upon Ben Franklin's claim about his compatriots that "their curiosity about strangers and travellers, took [the] place of every other consideration; that they would not stir an inch till that curiosity was satisfied" (*Companion and Useful Guide*, II, p. 347).

[115] He would not have drunk from Loch Linnhe but from one of many streams he crossed, the water of which may have been contaminated by cattle. The entire dreadful consequence of this unfortunate quenching of thirst is described in his letter to his wife (Letter 2).

Stomach, & frightened into diverting by a violent Stimulus, which kept me half-awake the whole Night—

~Sunday Morning, Sept. 4, a little after 8, after a hearty breakfast, my whole charges only 5„10—for six meals & 2 gills of whisky, & my bed—I walk off, first for Glen Nevish, then to return all the way, & begin anew my road to Fort Augustus—/ It is a lovely morning, but will it continue?—I pass a Church yard close by the road, fended from the Sea by a natural Wall of rock—went *up* two of my steps, & sate down on a flat grave-stone, & wrote this.—Peace & Blessing be with us all!—With thee, my Sara!—

Passed a Cottage, not only the Roof but all the walls overgrown like a Hill with weeds & grass—Why not a Crop of Peas on the Roof—& Sallad on the walls.—The Day continues glorious—enter Glen Nevish, a broadish Valley with a broad Shallow River, single Trees, Alders, & Sycamores, planted thick without interspace along its Banks—Ben Nevish to my Left, its height entirely lost to me, but its sides are nobly torrent-rifted—a belt of ragged Wood athwart it, half way, the *apparent* ascent—above the woods grey craggs stained with yellow green—8 great rifts, each no doubt forming tremendous Precipices to look down into—the mountain at the head of this Reach of the Glen shoots out in ridges from a lower wall of mountain turning into gavel ends, & roof-shaped ridges/ two narrow Coombes with steep Sides, a very fine gavel end wooded & a steep wall not so high as the sides/ at the end of the Coomb a low curve from Ben Nevish slides softly down into the Glen, and incloses the river, and its stony Bed now too big for it & trees or rather tall Bushes/ this curve runs slant across the second Gavel where the second reach of the Vale begins—In twilight or mist and Storm I could fancy it a huge Elephant, the four larger Rifts its legs, & its proboscis curving round/

Here thro' the whole Glen, the road most, very, or damn'd bad/ Adam Smith?[116] Pray, would the Regiment have been better employed drinking at their Quarters than in substituting those fine Roads for such as these?—I had not well described the head of the first Reach/ from a lower ridge of

[116] The great Scottish economist Adam Smith (1723–90) urged the improvement of lands as one of the proper ways to use capital in his major work *Inquiry into the Nature and Causes of the Wealth of Nations* (1776). He made the point that productive labor, which was not necessarily the same as useful labor, was essential to the economic growth of a nation. Coleridge, believing this to be a Wade road, suggests that the regiments charged with improving the preexisting roads (probably drovers' roads) through Glen Nevis, may have been productive but not useful.

mountain, of wild & concave outline ⌒⌒⌒ there shoots a roof-shaped mountain with a noble gavel end, say rather the front of a Tent—two thirds from the Top downward finely wooded—on each side of it a twisting Gully of water, over each gully a rude mass of mountain, that in the first reach of the Glen lower, that on the second far higher than the Tent/ this resembling more than aught else two sides of an unequal Triangle, but rounded at the Top—the surface rough & shelvy, tho' green—ragged too with Trees. The river of Nevish is a poor Likeness of our Greta.[117]

I had scarcely written the words when the River improved most surprisingly, huge masses of pinky Rock forming its side & narrowing its Channel & lo! as I turn with its Turn an enormous single Rock, higher than the high Banks, in the very middle of the River, filling up one half of the whole channel, leaving $\frac{1}{4}$th on each side/ (the River is on my left hand)—on the $\frac{1}{4}$th under the further Bank it flows deep & as calm as the pool of a waterfall can do, for two or 3 yards beyond the Rock on that side, seen under Boughs of Birch Trees, arching from the Bank to the Birch Bushes & Heath on the Rock, a fine fall/ on the other side close under me as I shall pass it the River flows rough & shallow over stones, the Bank naked, but fine young Birch Trees on the Rock; on its side, 2 yards from the Top, all along its whole side.—So it *appeared*/ but as I moved on ten or 20 yards, I found that there were but 3 Trees, 2 growing out of the cleft & as it seemed one root/ & here too I found a break in the Bank, where another stream flows into the Nevish/ a large Stream, and the Break *so exactly* corresponds in size to the rock, that one cannot help thinking, that some dread Torrent at the first bursting forth of this Stream must have shouldered away the opposing Bank, & pushed it in its madness just up the Stream/

I cross this Stream by a Bridge half of rock, half of an Alder Tree, whose

one bough curves over— ⟿ the rock over which the clear water, so clear its very foam seems scarce to lose its transparency, resembles undrest Lights so exactly in color & curvature that the likeness must excuse the ungainness—/ —I come to the great Rock/ Now I could easily get on it, by the Trees that grow on this Bank & bend over to it, so that the end of their Boughs hang over it—There are 3 Trees on the rock, all Birches, & then just where these leave off, three on the Bank, two Birches & one Ash/ This occasioned the Delusion/ but the Ash is farther from the Stone, a Thing for itself, hangs over a pool of water, in a bason of its own, from rain or flood/ Divided by a great Stone from the grand fall of Water, its root and bason in the same Line with the Head of the Fall/ for there are 2 falls, one on each side the Rock/ the further broad, this narrow & higher/ the hugh Stones above this

[117] The river called Greta runs through Keswick, and Coleridge's residence, Greta Hall, takes its name from the river.

fall, one adhering to the Bank, a middle Stone, & the prolongation of the rock, & the Water of this fall runs in two gutters one each side this middle ridge of Stone/ I must get from one to the other, & so on the Rock to see the other waterfall, & the black jagged precipitous Wall of its Pool; but lo! behind me a part of a naked serrated Cone of Rock behind that green wooded Gavel or

Tent/ smaller far & lower 🐾 shewing all one side, its apex, & no more, the rest intercepted by the Gavel. The broader fall among the sublimest I have ever seen/ it divides itself, I might say, it distinguishes itself into 3 falls, the one nearest the Great rock shoots out & leaves a large Cavern underneath where a man might stand & but for the *dashing in under* of the other part of the Fall shelter himself from a Storm under the ceiling of Foam—the 2 other parts are divided only at the very head by a tall pink rock, the one nearest the Shoot drives aslant the third which falls down in an opposite direction, and tho' they touch, preserve their Individuality/ the Slanter covering all but the higher part of the third ∨ —the pink rocks seen every now & then at the bottom thro' the white Foam most *lovely!*—The Cone behind the Gavel, I saw it all/ it was only a Jag of a noble rock rising up into a perfect acute Angled ∧ behind the Gavel/ or rather it is one of two cones in file rising up behind this ∧, & yet another rises behind that Triangle & that Gavel/ —first the Green Gavel, then, far lower than, but exactly like it in shape, a slender rocky Gavel, then higher perhaps even than the green Gavel this sharper & more perfect Gavel, then behind that a ridge having 2 sister Cones! This is to my right—to my left the river, & the *ledge-precipicy* side of the Proboscis of the Elephant/ with savage Trees, all straight, & by that extreme straightness harmonizing with the perpendicularity of the little precipices, of which the great precipice is made up/ before me 2 huts, & beyond them two ridges of savage mountain, tho' not without Trees—

The Head of Glen Nevish how simple for a Painter/ & in how many words & how laboriously, in what dim similitudes & slow & dragging Circumlocutions must I give it—so give it that they who knew that place best would least recognize it in my description/ the whole reach forms an Oval/ but a huge rocky Hill rising up from the river to the breast of the Mountain chokes it up at the Top/ above & beyond this the great wall of this segment of the oval makes 2 very deep segments, 2 inverted arches, and between one solid upright bridge of mountain/ in the further Inverted Arch, appears from behind, almost about to fill up the arch a bleak Bridge of mountain, shorter, thicker, less a striding ridge than that which intervenes between the 2 Segments/ the mountain at my back, first falling *down*, then shoots off, like a Fall that meets a rock half way, into a steep but not precipitous Hill, rough with loose stones & overgrown with Birches—So having mounted a little & seen that there was not probably anything more to be noticed, I turned back—& now my mind being as it were leisurely and off the stretch, with what delight did I look at a floatage of Shadows on the water, made by the wavelets of the Stream, with what delight that most exquisite net at the bottom/ sandy + pebbly river, all whose loops are wires of sunshine, gold finer than silk, beside yon Stone the Breeze seems to have blown them into a Heap, a rich mass of light, light spreading from the loop holes into the interstices/ —O we turn from novelties & rarities to old Delights & simple Beauty!—

On the whole I can scarcely say that Glen Nevish is worth all the fatigue of travelling thro' it—As you must return the same way every step/ the Mountains, both Ben Nevish & those Helvellin-shaped ones by and near the Green gavel, are far better & more impressively seen on the Road to Fort Augustus/ in the Glen itself, from its narrowness, the mountains *needs* look very low—. —On the main Road again, passed the Black Castle,[118] to my Left—a huge patch of Snow low down on the baldness of Ben Nevish—/ Dreary Moorlands, with distant mountains, but nought impressive except those close to my right, Ben Nevish to wit.

Highbridge—refused Tea—Highland Inhospitality explained—the desolation dreamlike of the fine Road, of the ghost-like "High Bridge" & its 2 arches, & $\frac{L}{2}$ [119]—the Mountain ridges so backlike, odd & void of connection or harmonizing Principle. The mountains in perhaps 8 main lines, all pushing toward the Bridge Bank but each so savage, & broken, 4 ridges, the next 7 or

8, semicircle Basons or Coves ⌒⌒⌒⌒⌒ O it is indeed a High Bridge. What can Sappho's Leap have been beyond this?—The building of the Bridge mixes so indistinguishably with the schistous slanting Strata, that form the Banks of the River. The Sunshine half on the Bank/ the lower Half shadow/ with so marked a Line/ & the noise of the Rapid above—for under the Bridge & for 200 yards above the River is calm, wrinkly indeed, in watery puckers & folds, with detachments of broken foam between the *so already split Slate*/ O for words to explain how Slate & Limestone lie! Verily it is a savage dreamlike, unlively Place, & the River on the Left hand of the Bridge after it has passed its savage black & grey Slate Banks—wild & mean, where a man falling would break his neck without Dignity—then it is fine to see the moorland River melt away in metallic Scoria—much as I have been among mountains—still this is new/

A moorland with 2 mute flocks of Sheep in sight, & one or more in *sound, guarded round* by M[ountains] not walled, the M[ountains] are too separate & individual—before me, on my road to F. Aug. it is indeed more of *one*

[118] Inverlochy Castle.

[119] The town today is called Spean Bridge. The intact bridge Coleridge describes is High Bridge, now largely in ruins, but in its day spectacular, with its three arches, constructed of rubble stone, completed in 1736 under General Wade and important as a connection of the Great Glen road from Fort William to Inverness over the River Spean. A monument placed near the bridge by the 1745 Association reads: "ACTION AT HIGH BRIDGE. Near this spot on August 16, 1745, the first action of the 'Forty-five' took place. Donald MacDonnell of Timradris with eleven men and a piper from Kepploch's clan, by making use of the now demolished High Bridge Inn and surrounding trees to conceal the smallness of their number, succeeded in preventing two companies of The 1st Royal Regiment of Foot (later The Royal Scots) from crossing the High Bridge over the River Spean. This force consisting of about eighty five men, had been sent from Fort Augustus to reinforce the garrison at Fort William."

mass, delved, rifted, channel'd, wrinkled, & with a dipping, leaping, tipsy outline/ but behind me, & to my left as I turn to look behind, I count 29 great lines of motion or direction, the 14, 15, 16 so semicircled & hollowed, that I might have made 30 out of the 3/ all indeed subdivisible enough!—Up to my right—as I now stand toward F. William that distant & their long ridge so variously segmented/ Silly words I am vexed with you—a File of Sheep among Heath, perfect Ribboning—It is an *intuition*. The Moor now tossed up & about into Hills, & these Hills inclosed, with Corn, or Potatoes in Blossom. All this to my Left— & a Lake beyond,[120] & a peep of another, & 5 heads of mountains/ with a continuous ridge  before them, close in the whole/ —But what a joyous Sight of Cows & Calves, a lowing browsing Multitude, with milking Lasses chattering Erse/[121] church & 20 or more scattered Hovels on the Cultivated Hill, that climbs half way up the black Mountain Brays of Lochaber.[122] Between the Lake & the Peep of the Lake a mountain of very various, but all superficial & gentle segments, runs down in between almost as gently as a man would lie on a bed, so imperceptibly declining from an Horizontal Line into a Slope/ — Those who hold it undignified to illustrate Nature by Art—how little would the truly dignified say so—how else can we bring the forms of Nature within our voluntary memory!—The first Business is to subjugate them to our Intellect & voluntary memory—then comes their Dignity by Sensation of Magnitude, Forms & Passions connected therewith. Come to a Devonshire *Cleve*—a Bridge, a deep down River playful, rifted, Hills— ramparts over them—/

  Brays of Lochaber—

~Arrived at Letir Finlay,[123] IX oclock/ all in bed—they got up—scarce any fire in; however made me a dish of Tea & I went to *bed*.—Two blankets & a little fern & yet many Fleas! —Slept however till 10 next morning/ no more Tea in the House—3 Eggs beat up, 2 glasses of Whisky, sugar, & $\frac{2}{3}$rds of a Pint of boiling water I found an excellent Substitute/ Left this house of Poverty (the Apartments large & sufficiently commodious) Monday, 11 °clock, Sept. 5—for Fort Augustus. Loch Lochay very like the narrowest, & barest parts of Ulswater/ a Lake, in short, among bleak Hills. The first two miles from Leter Finlay the Road torn up & covered by flood torrents of stones from the stream.

  Hill that hangs above the road seldom indeed more than (40 in one place, 100) yards together & always corresponding with some Torrent or water

[120] Loch Lochy.
[121] The young women were speaking Gaelic.

[122] Lochaber is a stretch of land in Invernesshire consisting of mountains, glens, and moors, on both sides of Loch Lochy, which Coleridge would have experienced as he walked northward.

[123] At Letterfinlay, on Loch Lochy, fourteen miles northeast of Fort William, stands a single house close to the water's edge that had been an inn serving travellers on the road north. Sarah Murray found it an appealing place: "At the door of the inn is a small green patch, bordered by birch and alders; rushes, bushes, and shrubs creeping down to the water. On this fairy green I had the chaise turned that I might face the grand scenery of the lake . . ." (*Companion and Useful Guide*, II, p. 377). In 1818, on 3 August, Keats and his friend Charles Brown checked into Letterfinlay Inn to rest after climbing Ben Nevis. It was here Keats wrote a long letter to his brother Tom that included a humorous poem about Ben Nevis (personified) as well as a sonnet written as he sat perched on a precipice at the top of the mountain (see *Walking North*, pp. 203–09).

course on the Hill above—In making these fine Roads this should have been fore-seen & (if possible) obviated.

Nature has in 2 or 3 places obviated it by a Bank/ Road still between Mountains lower than those of Loch Lochy till I come to Loch Oich, a more chearful Lake with some comfortable-looking Mansions on it, & opposite a tongue of Land on Left Bank of the Lake (suppose you sailing up to Fort Augustus) a very fine Ruin of a Castle[124] among Trees, upon a precipitous Rock-bank, but the Mountains, now mere Hills/ & scurfy with Trees & Bushes. —Went into a Hovel at the foot of Loch Oich, & drank a cup of Whisky & hot water, the Gout rising—4 stout men purely lazy! the Women at work/ in about a mile from this, on a savage piece of uncultivated ground on the other side of the wall on the left hand of the Road (to wit, as I face Fort Aug.), 8 miserable Huts, a neighbourhood! The best of which would have disgraced a Beaver, or republic of Termites. & out of their low slanting Door *come with a dip five* tall men, wearing on their backs & limbs cloathes-masks of the present Century!—a little way on, another Cluster of Turf Huts with Peat Roofs, wretched as the former, on the right hand of the Road—4 Huts. Do not forget the little black Dancing Master at Highbridge.

Fort Augustus/ 4 °clock, afternoon, Sept. 5th—very unwell & could eat only the Broth at Dinner/ a most interesting View from the back door of the Inn/[125] to the left the River, & beyond it a cluster of Wood, the Bridge, or ridge of Rock intercepting the Lake, heads of high Mountains behind each other seen over the ridge/ On my right orchard gardens with one Cottage in one of them, a smooth large Field/ the Fort Augustus, an ample & handsome mass of Building, the lake, and its noble mountain right-hand Bank—Height 3 pencils & $\frac{1}{2}$—breadth 3 penc./ opens before & behind, with bottle-notches in the shutters—/ higher half large Bottle—lower Half Drawers—the same at Back/—[126]

~Tuesday Morning, Sept. 6. 11 °clock, Left Fort Augustus, having break-fasted with the Governor,[127] ascended a very steep, high Hill, found myself in thwarting Coombes with brook & birch woods—on a second ascent found a sixpence, the first in my Life.

[124] Invergarry Castle, seat of the chiefs of the MacDonells of Glengarry, destroyed in 1746 by the Duke of Cumberland, Commander of the King's Army in Scotland.
[125] The inn in which Coleridge spent his first night faced onto the River Oich.

[126] Coleridge measures the size and dimensions of the old fort as an artist might, by holding up a pencil of a standard size. The design for the fort, by Captain John Romer, Engineer, reproduced in *The Great Glen & General Wade's Roads* (text by Gilbert J. Summers,

Jarrod and Sons, 1986), shows a "Fore Front of the Main Gate" facing onto the land and at the rear of the fort two galley ports facing Loch Ness. The Governor's House was on the grounds, within the walls of the fort. The prison was built into the structure of the main gate, on either side of which were long horizontal walls ("Drawers" to Coleridge). Above and behind each "Drawer" was a structure that resembled the top half of a bottle. The fort Coleridge saw in 1803, of course, was not the same, as it had been partially destroyed during the 1745–46 uprising.
[127] He refers to his incarceration in the prison of the fort in Letter 3, to Southey, and more specifically in Letter 4, to his wife. Coleridge would have fared better if he had arrived with a letter of introduction, as apparently was the custom. When Boswell and Johnson appeared at Fort Augustus in 1773, they met with warm hospitality from a Governor Traupaud. Boswell had sent a guide and the servant Joseph ahead from the General's Hut, with "a card"; as Boswell's father, a judge in the circuit court in Inverness, knew the governor, the name Boswell provided entre. "[T]he governor waited for us at the gate of the fort. We walked to it. He met us, and with much civility conducted us to his house. It was comfortable to find ourselves in a well-built little square, and a neatly furnished house, in good company, and with a good supper before us; in short, with all the conveniences of civilized life in the midst of rude mountains" (*Johnson & Boswell in Scotland, A Journey to the Hebrides*, p. 74). Sarah Murray, travelling over twenty years later, also made sure to have letters of introduction: "The creeping centinels hailed us with 'who goes there?'—I had letters to the worthy Governor, which I sent in; and was admitted over the thundering drawbridge, and through the dark gateway, to the parade and the Governor's door; who, with his lady, received me with every

mark of kindness and hospitality. Alas! Since that period, that good man, Governor Trapaud, is gone from his earthly friends to reap the reward of his numerous virtues!" (*Companion and Useful Guide*, II, p. 272). A new governor, Colonel Brodie, was in charge by the time Stoddart appeared at the fort in 1799. When Stoddart presented his "introductory letter" to Brodie, he "was shown by him whatever was worthy of remark" (*Remarks* II, p. 71).

[128] Taking the military road from the fort toward Inverness on the east side of Loch Ness, he winds up a hill losing sight of Loch Ness and heading into Stratherrick, passing two little lakes, Loch Tarff and Loch Knockie.

[129] While the two lochs may be easily understood to refer to Knockie and Tarff, and Stratherrick merely spelled differently, what Coleridge means in the text from "Easterborlan" on remains a puzzle. Very likely he has read an advertisement for property.

[130] He should have made a turn at Whitebridge in the direction of Foyers, which is on Loch Ness.

[131] The Falls of Foyers (or Fyers), which Coleridge describes in detail on his return the next day, has attracted tourists to the present day. For the Romantics, however, its scale and setting and the element of danger qualified it as sublime. When Burns visited in 1787, he produced a poem "written with a pencil on the spot" entitled "Lines on the Fall of Fyers near Loch Ness." Guide books touted it. Sarah Murray gave an account of what a "bold adventure" it was for a woman to hazard the paths to a promontory for a view of the Fall of Fyers, but acknowledged her reward: "I was in ecstacy with all around me" (*Companion and Useful Guide*, II, p. 263). Stoddart pronounced the falls "the great wonder of this country" in his travel book (*Remarks*, II, p. 74). After Keats and Brown stood before the falls in 1818 Brown boasted to a friend in a letter: "I

Pass a Tairn, almost surrounded by 5 bare-knobby Hills, with 4 Islands in it, covered with Bushes & Heather—continue ascending, the road on the breast, & above the breast, & on the summit of the Heathland Hill, a wild Tarn under bulgy Grey rocks in the bottom on my right—Over the Hill a most extensive area of Heath & Moorland crowded to the right & left & not empty in the middle, of grey Stony Hills with purple Patches, two Tairns in sight.[128]

Loch Nochy—Loch Garth/ Strathheric/ Easterborlan nigh Fort Augustus, let for 80—woman offered 76£, 80 souls maintained on it/ Glendamaer & Tom Vort, all 3 given to one Man.[129]

Having passed thro Strathherick, a broken country, granite rock, & birch Trees in among them & in one place a beautiful round Island of Heath in a circle of granite Rocks—this to my right hand & as the road leaves it, it climbs a small height thro' fine Birch Trees, the lower halves of the Stems split longitudinally in thick rough scales, & now a deep Bason of fine cultivated Land is below me as I descend/ I look down in & upon it thro' a grove of Birch Trees, one large Corn-field walled by a mountain of Granite carpeted with moss & heath on the ledges only of its precipices.

The road turns down into like a winding Staircase,[130] & I face what was before at my back—& see at the head of this Bottom a most lovely Hill of Birches, a rich wood!—overhanging a brook, the bare points of granite mountain towering over the rich wood.—The road turns thus

✳ the wooded hill ＼ the stream

The road passes thro' the bottom, climbs again—still Birches amid Granite Rocks, and on the summit of this ascent I regain Loch Ness & its mountain wall, a stream brawling thro' a *convulsed* channel on my left in a deep Cleft of the Hill—on which my road is—the deep wide Cleft dividing from the birch and granite mountain that forms a part of the left Bank of Lochness— In this deep wide Cleft, I suppose, I am to find the fall of Foyers[131]—some fifty yards on the descent of the Hill I come to a part of the wall built higher and the higher interspace bounded by 2 Gate Heads—& from thence look down, a prodigious Depth! and see a fine narrow fall at the bottom, a volume of smoke the Foam seems, or like the softest plumage of the Eagle or Ostrich. Determined not to go without a guide, for I sadly fear, that I shall be disappointed—so went down thro' woods to a River side, beautifully gliding smooth & broad into Lochness, to a House which I supposed the General's Hut, but which was indeed the house of a Gentleman—of a vera great Gentleman, as a child told me, yan Mr Fraser,[132] and I wound up thro' a wood to the General's Hut where I was received with sufficient & increasing Civility—

~Dined on lean mutton, & good Tea, and supt on Sewens & roasted Potatoes, had a miserable screamy night, & after breakfast Wednesday Morning, Sept. 7, walked back about a mile, & entering by the two pillars wound down to the green beak of a slender Promontory & afterwards still lower/ & tho' the feeling of Disappointment lingered awhile, the Fall at length grew into sublimity & its own dimensions/ on my first calculation I made it not exceed 110 feet, and the whole height of the chasm 220—but it grew upon me, & my feelings at least coincided at length with Stoddart's account/[133] the plumage of the fall, the puffs of Smoke in every direction from the bed of plumy foam

at the bottom, the restless network of Waves on its Pool/ 〉〈 The vase-like Shape of the fracture out of which it comes, as if one side of a huge vase had been chipped out, & this stream flowed out at the rim/ you see up into the vase, and its rim is wreathed with delicate Birches/ the water atoms driving away the myriads of midges, now driven away by a puff of wind/ —the fall & pool in a noble inverted Chamber of 300 feet high, with a long winding antichamber/ only a very few Trees in the Chamber itself, one Oak Tree, where • is on the Vase/ —The enormous walls mossed or bare, but . . . larches are admirable tho' a few Oaks, Ashes, & Mountain Ashes, more Hazels, by far the most were Birches. Four Trees I shall never forget, the Hazel bent down & half uprooted with its broad Canopying head over a flock of mossy Stones—under this I sate/ two Birch Trees, one not very far below the summit of the Precipice, bent like a Bow, with its slender stem, over the channel of the stream/ above this a straight fir, noble & lovely in its singleness—another

Birch ⚘ and a Scotch fir above the Pool thrust out straight like an arm from the oak a strange perplexity & twisting of head & boughs/ Then the Stones, & Trees, & uprooted Trees, & half uprooted & roots of Trees,—one set of these formed half a Cavern, and a hugh root an arched Doorway to it/ —Altogether it is no doubt a glorious Scene/

~. . . Hen, nervously blown forwards, tumbling topsy Turvy, in the strong Wind. General's Hut.

must mention my having seen the grandest fall of water in Europe" (see *Walking North*, p. 216).

[132] Fraser was a common name in the area of Foyers and Stratherrick. Stoddart notes that "in former times" Stratherrick "was occupied by two considerable tribes of Frasers, that of Farraline, and that of Foyers" (*Remarks*, II, p. 73). It was a Fraser of Farraline whose hospitality Stoddart enjoyed and who escorted him about the area to the Falls of Foyers. The old Mansion House, home of the Frasers of Foyers, no longer stands. Nor does the place called General's Hut, a shelter built by General Wade while construction of his military road and bridges went on, around 1732. The present day Foyers Hotel stands on the approximate site of the General's Hut, with the hotel bar, called the General's Hut Bar, reminding travellers of its earlier incarnation, which doubled as an inn, receiving among others, Boswell and Johnson, in 1773 (see note 126 above).

[133] Stoddart described the Falls of Foyers at great length, highlighting what made it sublime: "There is something in the darkness and imprisonment of wild overhanging crags, inexpressibly awful; and in this instance their grandeur is heightened by the kindred impulses around, by the ceaseless toil of the struggling river, by the thundering sound of a thousand echoes . . ." (*Remarks*, II, p. 76). As for the dimensions, Stoddart figured the fall itself to be about 200 feet, and with the rocks above it, 300 feet (p. 78).

[134] The room in the General's Hut Coleridge describes here contains objects and illustrations that have significant reference to war. First, the small Mediterranean island of Malta had been taken by Napoleon and plundered in 1798. The British helped the Maltese, The Order of St. John, resist the French, and in 1800 the French capitulated and Malta came under the protection of the British Crown, having surrendered to Sir Henry Pigot in September 1800. It was to Malta that Stoddart had suggested Coleridge travel for reasons of health before the Scottish tour, and it was to Malta Coleridge would travel only months (in March 1804) after his return from Scotland, to remain there for an extended period in the capacity of secretary to Sir Alexander Bell, Governor of Malta. Second, the picture of the farm house on fire has reference to the violent destruction of Scottish clan property by the government in the course of the Jacobite uprisings. Third, the Storming of Seringapatam shifts the locale to India, where Coleridge's brother Francis was an ensign of infantry in the Indian army. Wounded in an attack on Seringapatam, Francis contracted a fever and in his illness committed suicide, in 1792. Finally, a map of Europe, valuable in following the Napoleonic campaigns, a sergeant's cap, and a cartouch bag continue the military theme in the General's Hut.

[135] The stunning Christopher Wren church of St. Clement Danes, familiarly referred to as St. Clements, stood prominently on the Strand, London until it was destroyed in World War II by a German air raid. Its churchyard would have contained far more artful stones and grave sites than the one Coleridge passed.

~A room, a wooden Bureau locked up, a Sea board on it under shelter of Birchen Boughs, 3 Tables, 11 Chairs. The surrender of the Island of Malta to General Pigot, published by Thomson—the Farm House on Fire, just over the Fire Place, an exact Draught of the City of Jerusalem, by C. Thomson (these three fill up nearly the fire-place side of the wall.) On the other side, under birch boughs, the Storming of Seringpatam/ & on the side opposite the fire a large Map of Europe, a stuffed Roebuck, a week old, lying over Tartary, the Dominions of Russia in Asia, & the Caspian/ & close by them on the same side a wild Duck, & a Sargeant's Cap, *Scarf* & Cartouch Bag—the Birchen Boughs with their moveless Twigs & leaves hanging down in between the Rafters—& the wind moaning above them/[134]

~Over the lower wall of the Chasm you see the lake, its high mountain Bank, the ‿‿‿‿ between/ Pleasing sort of Terrace walk with an enormous descent below it—That descent, so covered with wood as still to see the red soil, & yet no where not to see the woods—and the road climbing up along its Breast even to the summit of the cultivated Hills, into which this mountain bank descends—fields of lovely cultivation are seen crowning as with a bald friars Top the Woody descent to the Lake/ the road from the General's Hut goes between Birch Trees—

That sweet delicate birch with its tri-prong Root—& the other twisty little creature near it. O Christ, it maddens me that I am not a painter or that Painters are not I!—The *chapped Bark* of the lower part of the Trunk, the Bark like a Rhinoceros rolled in mud & exposed to the tropic Heat/ the second Fall to Sheep forced thro' water, & vaulting over each other throwing off the pearly streams from their heavy fleeces.

About $\frac{3}{4}$ of a mile from the General's Hut, divided from the Lake by a Birch Coppice & a cornfield two burnt down Huts bearing every mark as if the owners had burnt them in heart's-spite-Joy before their Emigration—

A Horse, two Birchen Poles with 5 cross rafters with twists of Hazel & Rope—inclosing a few Sheaves of Oats, the poles dragging along the ground, their ends merely flattened.—This I stopped & examined by the Burial Ground of Stratherich, 40 strides long, 35 broad—a grave dugged, 2 spades in it, the bank of Earth, Thigh-bone & shin by it/ tis a wild burial place—contrast it with St Clement's in the Strand/[135] twice I walked round it, & stripped the seeds from a large Dock which I will plant at home in its memory.

Still goes the straight Road, birches, & the ascending Hill on my Right, Birches & the descending Hill & Lake on my Left. O never, never let me forget the beautiful birch stems, like silver tarnished, rising out of the *chapped "Elephantiasis"* bark of the 6 lowermost feet of the Trunk/ O the endless lines of motion of the Trees here/

& now to my right Hand over a thin coppice of Birch is a wall, a rampart-wall, of Granite, Birches growing along its Ledges or Terraces—& a rampart, more bulgy before me, & over the lake on my left the segment of a rainbow on the Hills—So on to a bridge high over a rocky stream overhung with Birch & one other large Tree unknown to me, where the road turns touchingly close to the bulgy rampart; & here over a field of rocks & over the Stream a hugh Mountain like a Castle wall, the lower Half Birch, the higher bare Grey Precipice with a thwart smear of reddish Clay—here I do not see the Lake, but the road ascends to it—Let me not forget the Ode to my Shadow.

The left hand the Lake & its now half copsy half cultivated bank/ the right, birchen Hills, more or less thick, now straight, now bulging, now concave, an Embracement, Heath, Fern, stones white with lichens, Birches of all shapes & Twisture, & white Clouds of many Shapes in the blue Sky above/ S. Rosa had the conifers & chesnut/ I would study the Birch/ it should be my only Tree.

A Break in the Mountain Bank of the Loch Ness, the Interspace green & yellow, but mostly, yellow, with cultivated Ground—& at its foot washed by the Loch, on a rock-ground of its own a mass of Building, Tower, Castle, I know not what/[136] beyond this the Bank of the Lake loses its cultivation, bulgy, & Knobby rocks, with patches of wood/ the other Bank, on wch my right hand rests as rutty rocks as before, & Trees, O in what wild Twistures starting out of the rocks, which their roots split as with a wedge—After this my road, maintaining its character in all other respects, loses its Birches & has Hazels instead, with ash Trees intermixed,—Let me not, in the intense *vividness of the Remembrance, forget to note* down the bridging Rock, cut off alas! from the great fall by the beaked promontory, on which were 4 Cauldrons, & a small one to boot—one at the *head* of a second Fall, the depth of my Stick, reflected all the scene in a Mirror—Gracious God/ —the 4th on the side of the Fall, larger & deeper than all the others together, its low water in unceasing waves & agitation from the Fall *vibrating* its rocky sides—All 4 had the appearance of the Tooth-Sockets of some Mammoth among Mammoths, Fox + Mammoth/ Now approaching the end of the Loch, many Juniper Trees on each side of my Road—The mountain across the Lake—one single Farm excepted, naked, clay Scars—with grey-blue Slate Screes, then a Break & a Dip, just like the former, all cultivated Land & the mountain rising again loses its Slate & is all clay Scar & Patch/ in several places from Top to Bottom, a wooded Hill-ridge runs across the Lake, & I suppose,

[136] Across Loch Ness, at the promontory of a bay, roughly twelve miles from Inverness, stands Urquart Castle, which may be seen, though not always in clear focus, by travellers on the east side of the loch. The castle is a ruin, but well positioned. Stoddart, who took a boat across Loch Ness from Foyers especially to see the castle, noted: "Its position is strong, and appears to have been very early occupied as an important post: first, by the great family of Cummin; then as a royal fort of the kings of Scotland; and, lastly, it was granted by James IV, in 1509, to the Laird of Grant" (*Remarks*, II, p. 83).

137 Coleridge forces his thoughts to return to the Falls of Foyers.

138 He appears to have gone to and returned from Fort George or Culloden or both in this chaise. Both places were on the postal route, and both were in "The Line of the Forts" Coleridge said he would follow.
139 He is now on the military road that runs from Inverness to Moy (called, on one old map, Moy Road) which is well marked with milestones.

140 The mansion Coleridge glimpsed from the road was new, replacing one that had been burned down in 1800. The latter had been built around 1700, replacing the castle of the chief of the Macintosh clan which had stood on an island in the lake. The setting was steeped in the history of Macintosh struggles and resistance to government. The mansion one sees today was remodeled in 1955, with a few elements of the older construction on the side facing the lake. A gate house stands at the entrance to the extensive park of Moy Hall.

terminates it/[137] —a pleasant 100 yards—a fir grove on my right, the Lake, a mass of molten silver, on my left—its own lacustrial Sounds & the fir grove its own! Long may they thus sound together!

Routing South from Inverness through the Grampian Highlands to Perth and Edinburgh

~Left Inverness in a return post Chaise Thursd. Sept. 8. with a mad drunk Post Boy whom I was soon obliged to quit/[138] tho' the mad Blackguard was not so well disposed to quit me/ —I was every way unfortunate—Dancing with Indian Yells to a late Hour at the new Inn in Inverness—however owing perhaps to the Camphor + Ether what sleep I did get was quiet—O anything for quiet Sleep—6 miles from Inverness,[139] the Country rude Moorland, after this the wildest of all wild moorlands—cloven and tossed up into Hills of all shapes & sizes, all of sharp Lines/ the greater number having whole sides stripped of their Heath/ bare Screes of White Clay & rubbishy Pebbles—/ —after this dreariness itself with 1 patch of cultivation, & across the Road a village of strange Peat Hovels—the Road ascending, on my left a high Hill, the pearly white clay staring thro' the purple Heath, & ever so straight before me/ but to my right in a wide & distant semicircle, a glorious circumvallation of Mountains, ridges smooth and billowy, sugar loaves/ triangles, Pyramids, & whatever other misted Shapes these mountain Masses put on to the distant eye—. The 9th mile Stone locks me in compleatly with high Heath-hills, a few Scotch Firs—the hills often black—and the whole Surface tossed about, rising, dipping, bulging & sinking—11th milestone, a water & handsome House, Moy Hall,[140] to my left—/ both under a Hill scurvily planted with mineral-green Scotch Firs. Hovel on my right & enclosed Field, in one field Potatoes, Barley, Oats, & a square Plot of Wheat/ & a Copse of Birches on the other side of the road—Bridges with turf & sod rims, 2 or more every mile, over half viewless streams or none—/ —a good deal of low cowring Juniper with its fruit of various years, purple & green/ beyond the 12th mile stone a Square Furlong of perfect level, thro' which the road runs/ Oats on each side/ no inclosures, but it is inclosed naturally by low Hill-*banks*/ A public House here/ a bell outside of the window ringing in the wind, its Shadow on the Glass quarries—

A Stone throw before the 16th mile Stone a village of Hovels of Turf— some quite green/ one a spinning Wheel reaching above the Eaves, but the roof as high again as the Eaves. 17th milestone past half a mile, my eyes at least get out of their long Prison of Heathland moor, & I gain a view of distant Mountains/ after the 18th Milestone the high Hill to the Left of the Road is cleft—a rent to the Ground, even as Foyers, only not so high/ but what a difference, even from the *materials*/ —*Dirt & dusty Grass*—! *& rocks & Trees!*—Both above & below me the largest quantity of Junipers growing together, that I ever saw/ the whole Hillside from Top to the very bottom, save where the road runs, covered with it, as thick as ever Somersetshire Hills with Furze—/

From the 20th the country changed, mountain & more cultivation/ observed a lazy boy pasturing a miserable rope-legged Horse!

Cross a high Bridge over the River Slugan/[141] a pretty wooded bank/ long field & then a Hill-Bank of Birches—seen till my road comes among Firs, & at last thro' a *noble* Firwood—Remember that bough caught up by the wind, forced over the fork of the Tree, & there growing, its elbows on the side split & naked!—O what work the winds make with these Branches! & yet what noble Creatures! compare them with the stifled ones in favor of Wordsworth's Theory—

The Darkness came on/ I walked thro' a birch grove/ & so on to Aviemore—Left it, Friday morning, Sept. 8. 10 °clock,[142] a dreary Country, seeming drearier for Cultivation—at length gain a view of mountains before me/ once more imprisoned, a little before the 37th mile, a very pleasant Bottom, Bridge shouldering a woody Hill, stream winding away prettily under a woody Bank/ —regain a view of mountains with a noble

outline 〰〰〰—they seem bare from their Bases—the whole Country is very wild—the meagre Oat-harvest, I thought *they were weeding*—low Oats, so meagre!—& the Harvesters so lazy & joyless!—the fields all common/ and the only mock inclosure bleak walls of rocks. 39th mile, a huge house to my Right, Mr Macpherson's[143]—40th new or new-making Village, Kingussie—& a fine Ruin of a Castle to the Left—& so to Pitmaine[144]—the first place where *whisky* was not—& Rum commenced—41 miles from Inverness at Glentruim/ Craig. girls shiv'ring, 2 under a Cloak [gathering] Hay & shearing at the same time/ peas, few & hard, but this is the Season—

Met a girl carrying a lighted Peat to make a fire in the Hay & Harvest Field—Three miles, at least, from Pitmaine, the *wildest* of all countries (N.B. I might have gone 20 miles nearer, had I been earlier & the Day fine). It is not only that the distant Mountains before me,[145] all named "du" black, are of the wildest Shapes, one of them a bridge tumbling topsy Turvy, called mountain Croupean—all dark, of a hundred Shapes, & no shape of Grandeur, none combining—it is not only this, but the whole Land thro' which the Road lies,

[141] Sluggan Bridge, one of General Wade's bridges over the river called not Sluggan but Dulnain, had been replaced once by the time Coleridge crossed it on his route to Aviemore, and it would be replaced again in 1829 after flooding carried away the second one.

[142] Friday would have been September 9.

[143] James Macpherson (1736–96), controversial "translator" of the Ossian poems, was born in a village near Kingussie. Some two miles northeast of Kingussie stands the mansion Macpherson had built to plans of James and Robert Adam. Its name was originally Belleville, but it later received a Gaelic identity as Balavil House.

[144] What was once Pitmaine, a mile southwest of Kingussie, has been subsumed into the Kingussie area. What Coleridge thought was a castle was in fact the massive ruin of Ruthven Barracks, a Hanoverian barracks built 1719–21 and later, in 1734 enlarged on the recommendation of General Wade. A castle and fortification had been built here in the mid-thirteenth century for the lords of Badenoch. In the following centuries the castle belonged to Alexander Stewart, the Wolf of Badenoch, and afterwards the Gordon earls of Huntly, who reconstructed it. By the end of the seventeenth century it was a ruin. After the 1715 Jacobite Rebellion, the government took it over. In 1746 the government barracks were blown up by retaliating Jacobite troops who had retreated to this point after their defeat at Culloden.

[145] The Cairngorm, of the Grampian range.

[146] The building that now houses the Folk Museum of Kingussie is the Pitmaine House of Coleridge's observation. Once Pitmaine Lodge, the house had grounds with trees and gardens which extended well beyond the present railroad tracks to the River Spey, and possibly beyond, in the direction of Ruthven Barracks. It occurs in travel writing of the time as Pitmaine Inn. The Pitmaine family, from which the house took its name, married into the Macpherson family and became part of that formidable clan.

[147] Thirteen miles from Kingussie, Dalwhinnie was on the military road as well as the coaching road. Its stagecoach inn made it a good stopover for travellers between Inverness and Edinburgh. Today a major distillery provides the best reason for stopping.

[148] Saturday would have been September 10.

[149] The Monadhliath.

[150] Grisedale Pike, a mountain in the Lake District, about $4\frac{1}{2}$ miles west of Keswick.

[151] At Dalnacardoch Coleridge would find another building that had been General Wade's headquarters in 1729. Like the General's Hut, its counterpart on Loch Ness, it had developed later into an inn or kingshouse for travellers. The building and its outhouses, stables, and yard have recently been dramatically refurbished and converted into an elegant private residence by a French owner. A plaque over the front lintel reflects its second phase of being a kingshouse, reading: "Dalnacardoch—Public Accommodation, George III, Rex. Constructed 1774 A.D. Rest a Little While."

[152] Crossing one of Wade's bridges, over the River Garry, Coleridge takes the military road from Dalnacardoch to Trinafour (where there had also been a kingshouse), and heads toward Tummel Bridge, at Loch Tummel, where an attractive stone bridge, constructed by John Stewart, a local laird, under contract to Wade, coexists with a more recent bridge geared to modern traffic.

is cloven & cut into a vast room left by Drunkards—short tables, & high Tables, & side Tables, & cushions in confusion—& the hundred Forms that can be brought into no Analogy. In short, I who adore Nature, was kept *grinning* at the Scene—& the Faces of the Highlanders like faces on wooden Sticks.

To be sure, the Gardens at Pitmaine worthy of note/ —a bank, a sloping down Bottom, a semi-ellipse of Trees, form the only inclosure; & many Trees in the Garden itself—beyond it a perfect Level, cultivated Land, perhaps a mile broad—& then wild Banks swelling up into Hills, those into Mountains—4 miles from Pitmaine a House—/[146] Arches that form a rainbow, on sundown on the ridge/ A cragg behind the rainbow—& a solemn sound in the Forground that bids "Listen!"—

~Croupean beck = lesser . . . Croupean muir = a terrace & rocky Stream beneath—a wild & desolate Moorland, with moorfowl, on the Dalwhynny,[147] a good bed, & left it Sat. morn. Sept. 9.[148]—9 °clock—Moors, Streaks & Soils of Green upon the purple Hills. Poles along the roadside as from F. Augustus;—& past the 60 mile Stone, simple Mountains on my right especially[149]—as at Tayndrum/ Half a mile of road landlocks me/ to my left one Hill, heath & fields of Stones & burnt Heath, and a scald Head of stones upon black burnt Heaths—behind three mountains Lines, one under the other, the first horizontal as a wall, the other 2 descending in a furious gust.

A Hill exactly like Grysdale Pike[150] & Bason, two round Hills, the nearest delved with Fast Torrents, in a line with each other—& just beyond the furthest & roundest the mountain wall runs across & locks me in—. Dalna Cardach/[151] & turned off over the Bridge—/ Between the 73 and 74th Stones a Bottom, with a stream, pleasant Fields—& human white Houses. The Bank of the Tummel very beautiful, green & yellow fields.[152] Under the wall-like Hill, purple & pebbly about two miles below the Bank a wood & a blue Lake in a bason, the rim of various outline, & the inside variously brown with cultivation. On ascending the Hill from the Tummel—still Tummel Loch peeping over rocks. I meet my long Absent Friend, the Grundsell/[153] beautiful + wild scene behind the Houses & Hill under the stony ridge, the fields on the other side of the ridge fringes on the little Streams/ Then a

[153] Coleridge would not have regretted the long absence of this fast growing weed, groundsel, with its yellow rayed flower, commonly known as ragweed or ragwort, if he had been a hay fever sufferer. He had last observed goundsel on 18 August, when he was at Brownhill, in Burns country.

laborious Ascent of 3 miles, & on the top of the mountain a Tairn,[154] with a ridge of Hill to the right, far over the ridge a high hill—/ black, of various Outline, not unlike Skiddaw[155]—On the top of this Hill, along wch the road runs, I am landlocked in less than half a mile, landlocked by the summits of Ridges as by walls—The road thro' Oat & potatoe fields, still rainbow waters of Bointon[156] on each side—till to my right the ground is very wildly cleft & rifted, birch Trees clothing the perpendicular walls of the Rift, & a sounding River at the Bottom, wch I can sometimes look down upon from the edge of the Terrace-like Road. The variety of outline, Lines parallel, & crossing, of Mountain, Hill, Hillock, & Rift in each outline—a wall of 13 strides built up against the tremendous precipice. It is one of the loveliest Rifts I have ever seen, the sides chasmy. I walked/ between it & 85 milestone, & it goes beyond the 85th for a $\frac{1}{2}$–1 mile, & then opens out on you a cultivated inclosed Hill to the Right, which has a pleasing effect contrasted with the high bleak mountain in front that closes in the scene, & the dreary Hills on the Left of the Road—& on the breast of which the Road rises when we come in sight of these. The walls of the rift are very high & with shelving Cliffs—& Oatfields & Harvesters on the Top of the right Walls—& here too is the *Stump* of a Castle—and now the Hills on right & left curving enclose the view behind— all is cultivated and it is quite delicious, Houses, Oatfields, Oatsheaves, Clumps of Trees, the old Castle, the playful Outline & the still more playful Surface. Mem. I am just come from Aviemore &c. The Trees on hillocks of their own, or in small Rifts of their own—The darkness came on after I had crossed the Bridge by the Castle/[157] —a fine effect of Larches planted on the summit of a wooded Hill, at right, pointing to the others.

~Left Kenmore, Sunday M. $\frac{1}{2}$ twelve, Sept. 10[158]—for Perth—Taymouth Castle, Park, and Woods. Then a high vast wall of mountain, clothed from top to Bottom with Firs; & above & behind this ridge, the vast range of Mountains—Ben Lawer, Schehellan &c—These I leave behind me, & cross the moorland Hill, & so come out upon a little Lake, & vale, very like Grasmere, as seen from the Raise tho' very inferior, & the Lake without an Island/[159] the extreme Levelness of the vale more like Keswick & Bassenthwaite—pass by, the Lake to my Right, sent out of my way to Amalrhee/[160] the Lake Glen Culoch—/[161] cut across the Hill out of the high road leaving a delved, steep mountain rolling to my right —/ on my

the way to Kenmore Coleridge must have been reminded of the Falls of the Clyde, at Lanark, and in particular the upper fall, Bonnington, also spelled "Boniton" (by Dorothy in her *Recollections*, for example, as in: "We stayed some time at the Boniton Fall..." (p. 65).
[157] A quite poetic 1774 stone bridge with five arches over a narrowing of Loch Tay as it becomes a river bro
ught Coleridge out of the forest called Drummond Hill and into the village of Kenmore, where, in a large park with gates at either extremity of the road that runs though it, Taymouth Castle stood. At the time Coleridge saw
it the castle was undergoing its fifth transformation, from Balloch Castle, built by Sir Colin Campbell in the sixteenth century, to Taymouth Castle, in the Gothic style by John Campbell, 4th Earl of Breadalbane. Well after Coleridge's visit the castle was sold to the Mactaggart family. During World War II it served as a hospital.

The inn, now the Kenmore Hotel, where Coleridge spent the night, dates from 1760, when a sort of model village, in a uniform architectural style, with white stucco and dark wood beams, was developed just outside the park, west of the grounds. The hotel still welcomes guests.
[158] Sunday would have been September 11.
[159] Two mountains, Ben Lawers, to the west of Kenmore, and Schiehallion, to the north, are left behind as he walks through the castle park and exits at the east gate, then, following General Wade's road in the direction of Amulree, passes through Glen Quaich, finding Loch Freuchie on his right and comparing it to Grasmere Lake as seen from the Dunmail Raise at home in the Lake District.
[160] At Amulree, on Wade's road, he would have found an inn that had been a kingshouse to make it worth his going out of his way.
[161] His walk continues through Glen Quaich and past Loch Freuchie.

[154] At the top of Allt Kinardochy he found Loch Kinardochy.
[155] The Lake District mountain especially

enjoyed by visitors to and residents of Keswick.
[156] Having passed the Falls of Keltney on

descent see mountain ridges far before, with 2 remarkable Peaks /\\—the immediate Bottom very prettily tossed about, Oat fields, sheaves, Hay-cocks, Houses, & Stacks. Close to my right one beautiful Spot—a purple mountain sinking down into ragged Burnt-Land, this into inclosures, then all terminating in a deep-rich green Bank—a *square* of cottages at the end, & a rich green path winding up it from the Stream—the sum of the Lines of that green Bank—O how lovely!—

Cross the Bridge of the Almond,[162] steep perpendicular Banks of solid rock—Trees wildly starting from them/ A fall in the river above the Bridge—over such a "blasted Heath" to Methvan, the delights of an inclosed Country felt 2 miles before Methvan.

~Ben Lawr the westermost Hill G . . . , over Drummond vales & so on to. . . .

Rocks exactly like stunted old Massive Trees among Burnt Hether—& the Toes of mountains cross from the opposite Gills—Four Islands in the triangle of the Lake/ many promontories/ Dolphin

~. . . Descartes Proof of Deity discovered by Anselm Archbishop of Canterbury, CICCIX decessit.[163]

Spinoza's System rests on his Deism/ Subst. ad se subsistet. seorsum. His opponents define it "per seorsum subsist." It appears to me, that this Latter was *invented* purely to answer Sp. but "seorsum" clearly involves a mode or accident of sensuous Intellect.

~The weary man's stick often falling & out of his Hand & wearily taking it up/ exhaustion of nervous Power/

~Men noticed in the History of the Dark Ages, as single Hovels are in the Map of the North of Scotland.

~Wherever her eye turned, gladness came, like spots of Sunshine on green Moorland Hills, creating a new field in the Waste/ —spots of sunshine seen thro' floating mists, or thinning Showers—

~Ode to Solitude, Nature, Liberty—the Solitude free & natural, the Nature unmanacled & solitary, the Liberty natural & solitary—/ —I feel here as if I

162 Now in the Sma' Glen, of Glen Almond, Coleridge crosses the River Almond at Newton Bridge and later again, in the area of Millrodgie, as he proceeds in the direction of Methven and on to Perth, still on Wade's road.

163 Anselm, Archbishop of Canterbury died in the year 1109. In his notes Coleridge reverses the second "C," so that the date reads: CIƆCIX.

were here to wander on the winds, a blessed Ghost, till my Beloved came to me/ go back with her & seek my children.

~Ode to Music—the thought I lost was that perhaps Music bringing me back to primary Feelings did really make moral regeneration.

~Such love as mourning Husbands have. To her whose spirit hath been newly given/ To be his guardian Saint in Heaven/ whose Beauty lieth in the Grave Unconquered/ as if the Soul could find no *purer* Tabernacle, nor place of Sojourn, than the virgin Body it had before dwelt in, & wished to stay there till the Resurrection—Far liker to a Flower now than when alive—Cold to the Touch & blooming to the eye—

~   ——Removete, centum
        Rura qui scindunt opulenta bubus:
        Pauperi surgent animi jacentes.[164]
                      Seneca. Troad. v. 1020
applied to large farms.

~Divide your subject? Why, you *pulverize* it.—To the Schoolmen.

~My Love rested among the Heath, & the purple Heath flowers' Shadows played on her naked feet, between the silken ligatures of her Sandals.

~There have been times when looking up beneath the sheltring Trees, I could Invest every leaf with Awe.

~I do not think, that as yet the whole of the *crime*, the cause, nature & consequences of *Sophistry* has been developed. Try it dear Coleridge!

~In extreme low Spirits, indeed it was downright despondency, as I was eating my morsel heartlessly, I thought of my Teeth, of Teeth in general—the Tongue—& the manifest *means & ends* in nature/ I cannot express what a manly comfort + religious resolves I derived from it—It was in the last Days of August, 1803. —I wish, I had preserved the very Day & hour.

~Fall of Clyde. Stand on a precipice—cavern of some amphitheater to the left of gray bare stone coloured or if steep as a wall surmounted with ashes oaks &c and a few firs/ —in front the fall prescribed a self obliquely over a large

[164] "Dig it all up, you with your hundreds of rich acres loaded with cattle. The poor spirits lying dormant will burst forth." (Trans. John Nolan)

177

sheet slope—and above with an intermediate space—another part of fall quietly visible, this on the right a woody bank . . . a great ghost promontory of bare rock rising from a Valley below—Holy rood House palace & Abbey in front form an arch up to the Castle for a mile. Castle quite in the sky. Brodig consisting old & new town—St. Andrews Spire Calton hill/ Observatory on the right above Holyrood house/ purple

O this landscape

Letters of the Scottish Tour*

LETTER 1

To His Wife[1]

Friday Afternoon, 4 o clock. Sept. [2 1803]

My dear Sara

I write from the Ferry of Ball[achullish;] here a Letter may be *lucky* enough to go, & arrive at it's destination. This is the first Post, since the Day I left Glasgow——we went thence to Dumbarton (look at Stoddart's Tour,[2] where there is a very good view of Dumbarton Rock & Tower) thence to Loch Lomond, and a single House, called Luss—horrible Inhospitality & a fiend of a Landlady!—thence 8 miles up the Lake to E. Tarbet—where the Lake is so like Ulswater,[3] that I could scarcely see a difference / crossed over the Lake, & by desolate Moorland walked to another Lake, Loch Ketterin, up to a place called Trossachs, the Borrodale[4] of Scotland & the only thing which really beats us—You must conceive the Lake of Keswick[5] pushing itself up, a mile or two, into Borrodale, winding around Castle Crag,[6] & in & out among all the nooks & promontories—& you must imagine all the mountains more *detachedly* built up, a general Dislocation—every rock it's own precipice, with Trees young & old—& this will give you some faint Idea of the Place—of which the character is extreme intricacy of effect produced by very simple means—one rocky high Island, four or 5 promontories, & a Castle Crag, just like that in the Gorge of Borrodale but not so large— / ——. It rained all the way—all the long day—we slept in a hay loft, that is, Wordsworth, I, and a young man who came in at the Trossachs & joined us—Dorothy had a bed in the Hovel which was varnished *so rich* with peat smoke, an apartment of highly polished [oak] would have been poor to it: it would have wanted the *metallic* Lustre of the smoke-varnished Rafters.—This was [the pleasantest] Evening, I had spent, since my Tour: for [Wordsworth's] Hypochondriacal Feelings keep him silent, & [self]-centered—. The next day it still was rain & rain / the ferry boat was out for the Preaching—& we stayed all day in the Ferry [house] to dry, wet to the skin / O such a wretched Hovel!—but two highland Lasses who kept house in the absence of the Ferry man & his Wife, were very kind—& one of them was beautiful as a Vision / & put both me & Dorothy in mind of the Highland Girl in William's Peter Bell.[7]—We returned to E. Tarbet, I with the rheumatism in my head / and

*© Oxford University Press 1956. Reprinted from *Collected Letters of Samuel Taylor Coleridge, Volume II: 1803–1806*, edited by Earl Leslie Griggs (1956), by permission of Oxford University Press.

[1] This letter and the one that follows were stamped at Fort William.

[2] Sir John Stoddart's *Remarks on Local Scenery and Manners in Scotland during the Years 1799 and 1800* was well known to the Coleridges and their circle.

[3] East of the Coleridge residence, roughly twelve miles, Ullswater is a long lake with curves in it and views of the fells all around, rather like Loch Lomond with its views of Ben Lomond and neighboring mountains.

[4] An area of the Lake District some six miles south of Keswick and beginning at the bottom of Derwentwater, especially impressive for the Jaws of Borrowdale, a point at the southern end of the lake where the slopes of Grange Fell on the east and Scawdel on the west nearly converge, allowing the River Derwent to flow through. The valley through which the river flows is Borrowdale.

[5] Derwentwater.

[6] In the valley of Borrowdale a steep cone of rock, called Castle Crag, appears to fill the dale

[7] Dorothy Wordsworth had said: "There was a single cottage by the brook side; the dell was not heathy, but it was impossible not to think of Peter Bell's Highland Girl" *Recollections*, p. 47). In William Wordsworth's tale "Peter Bell" (Part Third) a remorseful Peter remembers "A sweet and playful Highland girl (1. 888) and her home:

Her dwelling was a lonely house
A cottage in a heathy dell.

(ll. 891–92)

8 Thomas Wilkinson (1751–1863), a Lake District friend, had written an account of his 1787 travels in Scotland which though not yet published was shared with the Coleridges and the Wordsworths. See *Scottish Notes*, p.148, n. above. One sentence from Wilkinson's manuscript, "Passed a female who was reaping alone; the sweetest human voice I ever heard: her strains were tenderly melancholy, and felt delicious, long after they were heard no more," suggested the poem "The Solitary Reaper" to William Wordsworth, according to Dorothy, who incorporated his early version in her *Recollections* (p. 193).

9 Assuming Coleridge means the four forts linked by General Wade's roads, these are, from south to north, through the Great Glen, on along the east side of Lochs Linnhe, Lochy, Oich, and Ness: (1) Fort William, (2) Fort Augustus and (3) Fort George, which until 1746 stood in Inverness on the site of the present Castle, but by the time Coleridge travelled had been rebuilt at a location northeast of Inverness, at Ardersier Point on the Moray Firth; and from Inverness southeast to (4) Ruthven, near Kingussie. Wade's roads and the forts had been built to facilitate the movement of English troops to repress the Scots after the Jacobite uprising of 1715. Of the four forts, only the one in Fort William (where Wade had fortified a preexisting military structure) survived the 1745–46 Jacobite rebellion.

now William proposed to me to leave them, & make my way on foot, to Loch Ketterin, the Trossachs, whence it is only 20 miles to Stirling, where the Coach runs thro' for Edinburgh—He & Dorothy resolved to fight it out—I eagerly caught at the Proposal: for the *sitting* in an open Carriage in the Rain is Death to me, and somehow or other I had not been quite comfortable. So on Monday I accompanied them to Arrochar, on purpose to see THE COB[B]LER, which had impressed me so much in Mr Wilkinson's Drawings[8]—& there I parted with them, having previously sent on all *my* Things to Edinburgh by a Glasgow Carrier who happened to be at E. Tarbet. The worst thing was the money—they took 29 Guineas, and I six— all our remaining Cash! I returned to E. Tarbet, slept there that night—the next day walked to the very head of Loch Lomond to Glen Falloch—where I slept at a Cottage Inn, two degrees below John Stanley's but the good people were very kind—meaning from hence to go over the mountain to the Head of Loch Ketterin again—but hearing from the gude man of the House that it was [40] miles to Glen Coe, of which I had formed an Idea from Wilkinson's Drawings—& having found myself so happy alone—such blessing is there in perfect Liberty!—that I walked off—and have walked 45 miles since then—and except the last mile, I am sure, I may say, I have not met with ten houses. For 18 miles there are but 2 Habitations!—and all that way I met no Sheep, no Cattle—only one Goat!—all thro' Moorlands with huge mountains, some craggy & bare, but the most green with deep pinky channels worn by Torrents—. Glen Coe interested me; but rather disappointed me—there was no *superincumbency* of Crag, the Crags not so bare or precipitous, as I had expected / — / I am now going to cross the Ferry for Fort William—for I have resolved to eke out my Cash by all sorts of self-denial, & to walk along the *whole line of the Forts*.[9] I am unfortunately shoeless—there is no Town where I can get a pair, & I have no money to spare to buy them—so I expect to enter Perth Barefooted—I burnt my shoes in drying them at the Boatman's Hovel on Loch Ketterin / and I have by this mean hurt my heel—likewise my left Leg is a little inflamed / & the Rheumatism in the right of my head afflicts me sorely when I begin to grow warm in my bed, chiefly, my right eye, ear, cheek, & the three Teeth / but nevertheless, I am enjoying myself, having Nature with solitude & liberty; the liberty natural & solitary, the solitude natural & free!——But you must contrive somehow or other to borrow 10£—or if that cannot be—5£, for me—& send it without delay, directed to me at [the Pos]t office, Perth. I guess, I shall be there [in 7] days, or 8 at the furthest—& your Letter will be two days getting thither (counting the day you put it in to the Office at Keswick as nothing)—so you must calculate / and if this Letter does not reach you in time—i.e. within 5 days from the Date hereof—you must then direct the Letter to Edingburgh / (I will *make* 5£ do. You must borrow it of Mr Jackson.—)[10] & I must *beg* my way for the last 3 or 4 days!—It is useless repining; but if I had set off myself, in the Mail for Glasgow or Stirling, & so gone by foot as I am now doing, I should have saved 25£; but then Wordsworth would have lost it.——.

I have said nothing of you or my dear Children—God bless us all!—I have but one untried misery to go thro'—the Loss of Hartley or Derwent[11] —aye, or dear little Sara!——In my health I am middling—While I can walk 24 miles a day, with the excitement of new objects, I can *support* myself— but still my Sleep & Dreams are distressful—& I am hopeless; I take no opiates but when the Looseness with colic comes on; nor have [I] any Temptation: for since my Disorder has taken this asthm[atic turn,] opiates produce none but positively unplea[sant effects. S.T.C.]

[10] William Jackson, owner of Greta Hall, Coleridge's residence in Keswick, was a generous landlord and certain to oblige Mrs. Coleridge's request for a loan.

[11] Hartley, Derwent (named after the neighboring lake), and Sara were the Coleridges' children. Coleridge and his wife Sara had lost one child, Berkeley, their second born, in 1799, while Coleridge was in Germany.

LETTER 2

To His Wife[1]

[1] Also posted at Fort William.

Saturday, Sept. 3.—Fort William. 1803

My dear Sara

I learnt at the Ferry that it would be safer to take my Letter with me to
this place, as the same Post took it, & did not go off till early on Sunday
Morning.—I walked on very briskly, when now Night came on / my road
lay all the way by a great Sea Lake, Rocks or Woods, or Rocks among
woods close by my right hand, great mountains across the Sea on my left
/—and now I had walked 28 miles in the course of the Day, when being
thirsty I drank repeatedly in the palm of my hand, & thinking of writing
to Sir G. Beaumont I was saying to myself—this using one hand instead of
a Cup has one disadvantage that one literally does not know when one has
had enough—and we leave off not because the Thirst is quench'd but
because we are tired of Stooping.—Soon after (in less than a furlong)—a
pain & intense sense of fatigue fell upon me, especially within my Thighs—
& great Torture in my bad Toe—However I dragged myself along; but
when I reached the Town, I was forced to lean on the man that shewed
me my Inn (to which I had been recommended by a Dr Hay Drummond
who met me at Kingshouse, & *created* an acquaintance in the most farcical
manner imaginable—) Mrs Munro, the Landlady, had no room at all—and
I could not stand—however she sent a boy with me to another little Inn,
which I entered—& sitting down . . .
an affair altogether of the Body, not of the mind—that I had, it was true, a
torturing pain in all my limbs, but that this had nothing to do with my
Tears which were hysterical & proceeded from the Stomach— / Just as I
had said this, a kind old man came in to me, who had crossed the Ferry
with me, & being on horseback had been here half an hour before me / and
I had had some chat with him in the Boat, told him of the Gout in my
Stomach, & that this Tour was an experiment for Exercise—&c—/ [']I
never saw a man,['] says he, [']walk so well or so briskly as this young
Gentleman did—and indeed he must have done so, for I rode as hard as I
could, & yet have not been in much more than $\frac{1}{2}$ an hour—or three quarters.'—I told him with faltering voice that I should have been in half an
hour sooner, but that the last mile & a half I could scarcely drag my Limbs

along: & that the Fatigue had come upon me all at once.—'Whoo! Whoo! Whoo! says the old man—[']you drank water by the road-side then?[']—I said, yes!—'And you have Gout in the Stomach—/ indeed, but you are in *peril*.'—By this time they had gotten me a dish of Tea; but before I could touch it, my Bowels were seized violently, & there . . .
Gallon of nasty water——and so went to bed. Had a Bason of hot Tea brought up to me—slept very soon, and more soundly than I have done since I have been in Scotland. I find myself a little stiffish, this morning / 30 miles was perhaps too much for one day—yet I am positive, I should not have felt it, but for that unfortunate Drench of Water!—I might have gone on; but I wished to have a Shirt & Stockings washed / I have but *one* pair of Stockings—& they were so clotted & full of holes that it was a misery to *sit* with them on/. So I have sent them, & sit with none.—I had determined to buy a pair of Shoes whatever befell me, in the way of money distresses; but there are none in the Town ready made—so I shall be obliged to go as far as Inverness with these—perhaps to Perth / & I speak in the simplest earnest when I say, that I expect that I shall be forced to throw them away before I get to Inverness, & to walk barefoot—My bad great Toe, on my left Foot, is a sore Annoyance to me.—

I am bepuzzled about this money. This Letter will not reach you, I fear, till Wednesday Night—However, you must at all events send me the money (I can & will make 5£ do) Mr Coleridge, to be left at the Post Office, Perth, N. Britain.—

I have been so particular in my account of that hysterical Attack, because this is now the third seizure / & the first from mere physical causes. The two former were the effect of agitated Feelings.—I am sure, that neither Mr Edmondson[2] nor you have any adequate notion, how seriously ill I am. If the Complaint does not settle—& very soon too—in my extremities, I do not see how it will be possible for me to avoid a paralytic or apoplectic Stroke. . . . moment . . .

I have no heart to speak of the Children!—God have mercy on them; & raise them up friends when I am in the Grave.—

Remember me affectionately to Mr Jackson and to Mrs Wilson.[3]—Remember me too to Mr Wilkinson & Mrs W.[4]—& tell Mr W. that if I return in tolerable Health, I anticipate a high Feast in looking over his [Drawings.] . . . him for flattering . . .

[2] John Edmundson (1760–1823) was a Keswick surgeon-apothecary whom Coleridge consulted and from whom he borrowed medical journals and obtained medicine. It was Mr. Edmundson (whose name Coleridge spelled Edmondson) who encouraged him to undertake the Scottish tour, urging that the exercise would be good for Coleridge's condition (see Introduction). Wordsworth also routinely purchased prescription medicine from Edmundson.
[3] An older woman, Mrs. Wilson was the housekeeper retained by Coleridge's landlord William Jackson. She lived with Jackson in the rear portion of Greta Hall and played a role in the lives of the Coleridge children.
[4] Thomas Wilkinson's wife.

To Robert Southey[1]

[1] Written in Perth but mailed in Edinburgh the next day, postmarked 12 September 1803, this letter was sent to Southey in care of Mrs. Coleridge. In it Coleridge reacts to two letters he had received from Southey, the first telling him of the impending death of his only child and the second announcing plans to be in Keswick at Greta Hall soon, so that his wife Edith might have the comforting companionship of her sister, Sara Coleridge, and Southey himself comparable companionship from his brother-in-law Coleridge. The poem included in Coleridge's letter was later to be known as "The Pains of Sleep."

[2] In 1724 General Wade was ordered to look into ways of controlling Highlanders who despite having been disarmed after the 1715 Jacobite uprising continued to pose a threat to peace between the Scots and the British government. Wade began building a network of military roads in the Highlands, using as his base the place now called Fort Augustus. He constructed a new fort close to Loch Ness, replacing an older and smaller one, called Killichuimen, located, he felt, too far from the loch. The village had been called Wadesborough until he named the fort Fort Augustus, after William Augustus, Duke of Cumberland. To what must have been the embarrassment of the Hanoverian army, Wade's new fort was captured and largely destroyed when a shell detonated the powder magazine in the Jacobite uprising of 1745–46. In 1876 the fort was given to the Benedictine Order by Lord Lovat, who had purchased

[Perth,] Sunday Night, 9 o clock—Sept. 10. [11]. 1803

My dearest Southey

I arrived here half an hour ago—& have only read your Letters—scarce read them.—O dear friend! It is idle to talk of what I feel—I am stunned at present—& this beginning to write makes a beginning of living feeling within me. Whatever Comfort I can be to you, I will.—I have no Aversions, no dislikes, that interfere with you—whatever is necessary or proper for you, becomes ipso facto agreeable to me. I will not stay a day in Edinburgh—or only one to hunt out my cloathes. I can[not] chit chat with Scotchmen, while you are at Keswick, childless.—Bless you, my dear Southey! I will knit myself far closer to you than I have hitherto done—& my children shall be your's till it please God to send you another.——

I have been a wild Journey—taken up for a spy & clapped into Fort Augustus[2]—& I am afraid, they may [have] frightened poor Sara, by sending her off a scrap of a Letter, I was writing to her.—I have walked 263 miles in eight Days—so I must have strength somewhere / but my spirits are dreadful, owing entirely to the Horrors of every night—I truly dread to sleep / it is no shadow with me, but substantial Misery foot-thick, that makes me sit by my bedside of a morning, & *cry*—. I have abandoned all opiates except Ether be one; & that only in *fits*—& that is a blessed medicine!—& when you see me drink a glass of Spirit & Water, except by prescription of a physician, you shall despise me—but still I can not get quiet rest—

> When on my bed my limbs I lay,
> It hath not been my use to pray
> With moving Lips or bended Knees;
> But silently, by slow degrees,
> My spirit I to Love compose,
> In humble trust my eyelids close,
> With reverential Resignation,
> No Wish conceiv'd, no Thought exprest,

Only a *Sense* of Supplication,
A *Sense* o'er all my soul imprest
That I am weak, yet not unblest:
Since *round* me, *in* me, every where,
Eternal Strength & Goodness are!—

But yesternight I pray'd aloud
In Anguish & in Agony,
Awaking from the fiendish Crowd
Of Shapes & Thoughts that tortur'd me!
Desire with Loathing strangely mixt,
On wild or hateful Objects fixt:
Pangs of Revenge, the powerless Will,
Still baffled, & consuming still,
Sense of intolerable Wrong,
And men whom I despis'd made strong
Vain-glorious Threats, unmanly Vaunting,
Bad men my boasts & fury taunting
Rage, sensual Passion, mad'ning Brawl,
And Shame, and Terror over all!
Deeds to be hid that were not hid,
Which, all confus'd I might not know,
Whether I suffer'd or I did:
For all was Horror, Guilt & Woe,
My own or others, still the same,
Life-stifling Fear, Soul-stifling Shame!

Thus two nights pass'd: the Night's Dismay
Sadden'd and stunn'd the boding Day.
I fear'd to sleep: Sleep seem'd to be
Disease's worst malignity.
The third night when my own loud Scream
Had freed me from the fiendish Dream,
O'ercome by Sufferings dark & wild,
I wept as I had been a Child—
And having thus by Tears subdued
My Trouble to a milder mood—
Such Punishment[s], I thought, were due
To Natures, deepliest stain'd with Sin,

it in 1867. The Benedictines established an elaborate abbey incorporating the remains of the fort. By the end of the twentieth century the abbey welcomed visitors. Of special interest (in terms of Coleridge) was a tour, in a museum setting, of the prison cells of the fort, with mock incarcerated prisoners. The cells were dismal, with thick stone walls, bars, and rats. By 1999 the abbey and remaining fort were closed, the Benedictine Order having run out of funds to maintain the facility, and as of this writing, the prison, in which Coleridge was "clapped" may no longer be visited.

Still to be stirring up anew
The self-created Hell within;
The Horror of their Crimes to view,
To know & loathe, yet wish & do!
With such let Fiends make mockery—
But I—O wherefore this on *me*?
Frail is my Soul, yea, strengthless wholly,
Unequal, restless, melancholy;
But free from Hate, & sensual Folly!
To live belov'd is all I need,
And whom I love, I love indeed—& &c &c &c &c &c—

I do not know how I came to scribble down these verses to you—my heart was aching, my head all confused—but they are, doggrels as they may be, a true portrait of my nights.—What to do, I am at a loss:—for it is hard thus to be withered, having the faculties & attainments, which I have.—

We will soon meet—& I will do all I can to console poor dear Edith.— O dear dear Southey! my head is sadly confused. After a rapid walk of 33 miles your Letters have had the effect of perfect intoxication on my head & eyes—Change! change! change!—O God of Eternity! when shall we all be at rest in thee?—S. T. Coleridge.

LETTER 4

To His Wife[1]

[Perth, 11 September 1803]

For Mrs Coleridge.

My dearest Sara

I was writing you from Fort Augustus when the Governor & his wise Police Constable seized me & my Letter[2]—Since then I have written to nobody. On my return, if God grant! we will take the Map of Scotland, & by help of my pocket Book I will travel my rout over again, from place to place. It has been an instructive tho' melancholy Tour.—At Fort Augustus I got a pair of Shoes—the day before I had walked 36 miles, 20 the WORST in conception, & up a Mountain—so that in point of effort it could not be less than 46 miles / the shoes were all to pieces / and three of my Toes were skinless, & I had a very promising Hole in my Heel.—Since the new Shoes I have walked on briskly—from 30 to 35 miles a day, day after day—& three days I lived wholly on Oat cake, Barley Bannock,[3] Butter, & the poorest of all poor Skim-milk Cheeses—& still I had horrors at night!—I mention all this to shew you, that I have strength somewhere—and at the same time, how deeply this Disease must have rooted itself.—I wrote you my last Letter, overclouded by Despondency—say rather, in a total eclipse of all Hope & Joy—and as all things propagate their Like, you must not wonder, that Misery is a Misery-maker. But do you try, & I will try; & Peace may come at last, & Love with it.—I have not heard of Wordsworth; nor he of me. He will be wondering what can have become of me—. —I have only read the first Letter—& that part of Southey's, containing the 10£ note, which relates to himself—for they have stunned me—and I am afraid of Hysterics, unless a fit of vomiting which I feel coming on, should as I hope it will, turn it off—I must write no more / it is now 10 o clock / & I

[1] This letter to Sara was written on the same sheet as the letter above to Southey.
[2] Coleridge does not, must not, explain why he was seized. However, it is easy to imagine a scenario in which he raised suspicion by making remarks, in conversation or in writing or both, that showed sympathy with the Jacobite cause. He might have gone beyond the political to making a joke about Wade's formidable fort that failed to withstand the attack of the Highland clans in the rebellion of 1745–46. Such looseness of the tongue would have been compounded by the general tension in Britain in 1803 when, the Peace of Amiens having been broken, the country was on guard against attacks from France. Coleridge's Jacobinism (so closely related to the term "Jacobite" but with an entirely different chronological and political reference) in the early years of the French Revolution, though tempered and even reversed later, would have made him especially vulnerable to any waves of anti-French sentiment now. Further, a wandering soul who looked as down-and-out as Coleridge must have, tired, with shoes falling apart, but an educated manner of speech and an accent that was clearly not Scottish might be taken for a spy (as Keats and his friend Charles Brown were on their pedestrian tour of Scotland as late as 1818). In any case, the fact that Coleridge took care not to write any more letters from the area (as he indicates in the next sentence) and remained curiously silent about the Jacobite uprisings, though he continued to travel along the line of the forts, through territory that continued to live and breathe the memories of those uprisings and the bitter defeat of the clans at Culloden, suggests this traveller was holding back. For Coleridge was a politically informed man with strong opinions. His silence in this setting stands in sharp contrast to his outspokenness on his own turf, as when he wrote for the *Watchman* or the *Morning Chronicle*.
[3] A Scottish cake, round, flat, thick, and unsweetened, and baked, in modern times, on a griddle and in 1803 on whatever was the counterpart of the griddle. The bannock might be made with oatmeal or barley meal.

go off in the Mail at 4 in the Morning—. It went against the Grain to pay 18 shillings for what I could have made an easy Day's walk of: & but for my eagerness to be with dear Southey, I should certainly have walked from Edinburgh home / —O Sara! dear Sara!—*try* for all good Things in the spirit of unsuspecting Love / for miseries gather upon us. I shall take this Letter with me to Edinburgh—& leave a space to announce my safe arrival, if so it please God.—Good night, my sweet Children!

S.T. Coleridge

Monday Morning, 12 o clock.

    I am safe in Edinburgh—& now going to seek out news about the Wordsworths & my Cloathes—I do not expect to stay here above this Day—Dear Southey's Letter had the precise effect of intoxication by an overdose of some narcotic Drug—weeping—vomiting—wakefulness the whole night, in a sort of stupid sensuality of Itching from my Head to my Toes, all night.— I had drunken only one pint of weak Porter the whole Day.—This morning I have felt the soberness of grief. God bless you all, & S. T. Coleridge—

LETTER 5

To A. Welles[1]

Tuesday: Feb. [September] 13. 1803. Edinburgh

Dear Sir

I have, but even now, received your very obliging Letter, which comforted as well as amused me. I will give the medicine the fullest, and fairest Trial, yield the most implicit obedience to your Instructions, and add to both every possible attention to Diet and Exercise. My Disorder I believe to be atonic Gout: my Sufferings are often sufficiently great by day; but by patience, effort of mind, and hard walking I can contrive to keep the Fiend at arm's length, as long as I am in possession of Reason & Will. But with Sleep my Horrors commence; & they are such, three nights out of four, as literally to *stun* the intervening Day, so that more often than otherwise I fall asleep, struggling to remain awake. Believe me, Sir! Dreams are no Shadows with me; but real, substantial miseries of Life. If in consequence of your Medicine I should be at length delivered from these sore Visitations, my greatest uneasiness will then [be], how best & most fully I can evince my gratitude:—should I commence Preacher, raise a new Sect to your honor, & make, in short, a greater clamour in your favor, as the Antipodagra,[2] 'that was to come, and is already in the world', than ever the Puritans did against the poor Pope, as the Antichrist—Ho! All ye, who are heavy laden—come, and draw waters of Healing from the *Wells* of Salvation. This in my own opinion I might say without impiety, for if to clear men's body [bodies] from Torture, Lassitude & Captivity, their understandings from mists & broodings, & their very hearts & souls from despair, if to enable them to go about their Duty steadily & quietly, to love God, & be chearful—if all this be not a work of Salvation, I would fain be informed, what is.—

Or I have thought of becoming theorizing Physician of demonstrations, (for that is the fashionable word) that all Diseases are to be arranged under Gout, as the Genus generalissimum / that all our faulty Laws, Regulations, national mismanagements, Rebellions, Invasions, Heresies, Seditions, not to mention public Squabbles & commissions of Bankruptcies have originated in the false Trains of Ideas introduced by diseased Sensations from the Stomach into the Brains of our Senators, Priests, & Merchants—of our

[1] A. Welles was a professional acquaintance of Coleridge's friend and medical advisor Dr. Thomas Beddoes, who lived in Bristol, and was a specialist in pulmonary ailments and an advocate of the use of opium. (He was, in fact, at the center of a drug scene in Bristol that included among others Thomas Wedgwood and Thomas De Quincey.) Beddoes had corresponded with Coleridge about his gout, and Welles, who had received a letter from Beddoes on the same health issue, wrote a hubristic letter to Coleridge with the promise of a miracle cure: "A letter from Dr. Beddoes yesterday informed me you were gouty—he need not have added that you wished to be cured——for I should have supposed it. I have in my possession a kind of Nectar / for it removes pain, & of course promotes pleasure—& may in the end immortalize—me / which I freely offer to you. I will further add the prediction, founded on experience, that you may be relieved from the gout, & your general health improved into the bargain. For confirmation of this you may consult Sir Wilfred Lawson Bart. Brayton Hall Cockermouth, who is near you" (quoted by Griggs, *Collected Letters*, II, p. 986; no source given.) Although the tone of Coleridge's response here is jocular if not satirical, he looked forward to receiving a package from Welles and visited him after he returned from Scotland.

[2] Anti-gout in the foot. (Podagra: gout, especially in the foot).

great & little men / hence to deduce, that all Diseases being Gout & your M. curing the G. your medicine must cure *all* Diseases—then, joining party with Thomas Taylor, the Pagan (for whom I have already a sneaking affection on account of his devout Love of Greek) to re-introduce the Heathen Mythology, to detect in your per[son] another descent & meta-morphosis of the God of the Sun, to erect a Temple to you, as Phoebo Sanatori; & if you have a Wife, to have her deified, by act of Parliament, under the name of the Nymph, Panacea. But probably it would not be agreeable to you to be taken up, like the Tibetan Delha Llama [Dalai Lama], and to be imprisoned during life* for a God. You would rather, I doubt not, find your deserved reward in an ample independent fortune, & your sublunary Immortalization in the praises, & thanks of good and sensible men: of all who have suffered *in* themselves *for* others.—And in sober earnest, my dear Sir! (dropping All Joke, to which your lively & enlivening Letter has led me) to this last reward I shall be most happy to become instrumental, by being first a proof, & ever after an evidence & zealous Witnesser, of the powers & virtues of your discovery.—I leave Edinburgh tomorrow morning, having walked 263 miles in eight days in the hope of forcing the Disease into the extremities: & if the Coachman does not put an end to all my earthly Ills by breaking my neck, I shall be at Greta Hall, Keswick, Thursday Afternoon—at which place I shall wait, with respectful Impatience, for a Letter & Parcel from you. In the mean time, dear Sir! accept the best Thanks & warmest wishes

of your obliged & grateful / humble Servant
S. T. Coleridge

*P.S. Great & well-founded however as your objection may be to my proposed national apotheosis of your Person, yet as whatever, Verse or Prose, I write hereafter, would be chiefly owing to the cure by you performed, at all events 'eris *mihi* magnus Apollo.[']— [Note by S.T.C.]

LETTER 6

To Robert Southey[1]

[1] This letter was addressed to Southey at Greta Hall, where he and his wife were now reunited with Sara Coleridge.

Edinburgh   Tuesday Morning 13 [September 1803]

My dear Southey

I wrote you a strange Letter, I fear: but in truth your's affected my wretched Stomach, & that my head in such a way, that I wrote mechanically in the *wake* of the first vivid Idea. No Conveyance left or leaves this place for Carlisle earlier than tomorrow morning—for which I have taken my place. If the Coachman do not turn Panaceist, and cure all my Ills by breaking my neck, I shall be at Carlisle on Wednesday Midnight—& whether I shall go on in the Coach to Penrith, & walk from thence, or walk off from Carlisle at once, depends on 2 circumstances—whether the Coach goes on with no other than a common Bait to Penrith, & whether—if it should not do so—I can trust my cloathes &c to the Coachman safely, to be left at Penrith—There is but 8 miles difference in the walk—& eight or nine Shillings difference in the expence. At all events, I trust, that I shall be with you on Thursday by dinner time, if you dine at $\frac{1}{2}$ past 2 or 3 o clock.—God bless you! I will go call on Elmsley.[2]—What a wonderful City Edinburgh is!—What alternation of Height & Depth!—a city looked at in the polish'd back of a Brobdignag Spoon,[3] held lengthways—so enormously *stretched-up* are the Houses!—When I first looked down on it, as the Coach drove in on the higher Street, I cannot express what I felt—such a section of a wasp's nest, striking you with a sort of bastard Sublimity from the enormity & infinity of it's littleness—the infinity swelling out the mind, the enormity striking it with wonder. I think I have seen an old Plate of Montserrat,[4] that struck me with the same feeling—and I am sure, I have seen huge Quarries of Lime or Free-Stone, in which the Shafts or Strata have stood perpendicularly instead of horizontally, with the same high Thin Slices, & corresponding Interstices!—I climbed last night to the Crags just below Arthur's Seat, itself a rude triangle-shaped bare Cliff, & looked down on the whole City & Firth, the Sun then setting behind the magnificent rock, crested by the Castle /—the Firth was full of Ships, & I counted 54 heads of mountains, of which at last 44 were cones or pyramids—the smokes rising up from ten thousand houses, each smoke from some one family—it was an affecting

[2] Peter Elmsley (1773–1825) was a classical scholar with whom Southey had been friends since college days at Westminster. Elmsley, Southey, and another friend (William Watkins Wynn) had travelled through Wales together in 1801, a tour that provided Southey with scenery for his *Madoc*.

[3] In Jonathan Swift's *Gulliver's Travels*, Part II, "A Voyage to Brobdignag," Gulliver finds himself a miniature creature among giants, in a land where everything, including eating utensils, was scaled to the giants. "[The] knives were twice as long as a Scythe set straight upon the Handle. The Spoons, Forks, and other Instruments were in the same Proportion" (*Gulliver's Travels, and Other Writings*, ed. Ricardo Quintana; New York: Random House, Modern Library, 1958, p. 78).

[4] Coleridge recalls seeing a drawing or etching of the island in the West Indies called Montserrat.

[5] At the end of Coleridge's "Rime of the Ancient Mariner" the wedding guest who has listened to the mariner's long tale goes away "a sadder and a wiser man."

[6] Scott and his wife Charlotte were spending time in their thatched roof cottage in Lasswade, where, on 17 September, Dorothy and William Wordsworth would call upon them: "Arrived at Lasswade before Mr. And Mrs. Scott had risen, and waited some time in a large sitting room. Breakfasted with them, and stayed till two o'clock . . ." (*Recollections*, p. 199).

[7] Scott lived at 39 Castle Street, found today two blocks north of Princes Street, which was not there at the time of Coleridge's visit. Despite the commercial development of the area, there is still a good line of sight from the corner of Scott's street to the castle, high upon its hill of rock.

[8] In the Skiddaw mountain range is a particular fell called Great Calva, at the foot of which lies the source of Dash Beck, which streams and drops over cascades called Whitewater Dash. However, Calva is above, not below Keswick. Coleridge undoubtedly confused directions as he wrote.

[9] William III, "William of Orange," 1688–1702 (William and Mary, 1688–94) was at the root of the notorious massacre of Glen Coe in 1692 in which the Macdonald clan of Glen Coe was suddenly attacked by Campbell of Glenlyon, who, with his 128 soldiers had been receiving the hospitality of Macdonald for two weeks. Some forty of the 200 Macdonalds, including children and infirm and elderly adults, were slain. The order for this treacherous attack, designed to make an example of Macdonald's insubordination, had been issued by the Under Secretary of State in Edinburgh. Macdonald had been late in signing an oath to William and Mary, whom Highlanders in general had not wanted to accept in place of James VII/II.

sight to me!—I stood gazing at the setting Sun, so tranquil to a passing Look, & so restless & vibrating to one who looks stedfast; & then all at once turning my eyes down upon the City, it & all it's smokes & figures became all at once dipped in the brightest blue-purple—such a sight that I almost grieved when my eyes recovered their natural Tone!—Meantime Arthur's Crag, close behind me, was in dark blood-like Crimson—and the Sharp-shooters were below, exercising minutely, & had chosen that place on account of the fine Thunder-Echo, which indeed it would be scarcely possible for the Ear to distinguish from Thunder. The passing a day or two, quite unknown, in a strange City, does a man's heart good—He rises 'a sadder and a wiser man.'[5]—I had not read that part in your second Letter requesting me to call on Elmsley—else perhaps I should have been talking away instead of learning & feeling. Walter Scott is at Laswade,[6] 5 or 6 miles from Edinburgh—his House in Edinburgh is divinely situated[7]—it looks up a street, a new magnificent Street, full upon the Rock & the Castle, with it's zig-zag Walls like Painters' Lightning—the other way down upon cultivated Fields, a fine expanse of water, either a Lake or not to be distinguished from one, & low pleasing Hills beyond—the Country well-wooded & chearful. I' faith, I exclaimed, the Monks formerly, but the Poets now, know where to fix their Habitations.—There are about four Things worth going into Scotland for, to one who has been in Cumberland & Westmoreland / —the view of all the Islands at the Foot of Loch Lomond from the Top of the highest Island, called Inch devannoc [Inchtavannach]: 2. the Trossachs at the foot of Loch Ketterin 3. The Chamber & anti-chamber of the Falls of Foyers—(the Fall itself is very fine—& so after Rain is White water Dash—7 miles below Keswick[8] & very like it—& how little difference in the feeling a great difference in height makes, you know as well as I—no Fall, of itself, perhaps can be worth go[ing] a long Journey to see, to him who has seen any Fall of Water, but the Pool, & whole Rent of the Mountain is truly magnificent—) 4th & lastly, the City of Edinburgh.—Perhaps, I might add Glen Coe: it is at all events a good Make-weight—& very well worth going to see, if a Man be a Tory & hate the memory of William the Third[9]—which I am very willing to do—for the more of these fellows, dead & living, one hates, the less Spleen & Gall there remains for those, with whom one is likely to have any thing to do, in real Life.

I was very much amused by Welles's Letter—& have written him a droll one enough in return—of which, if I am not too lazy, I will take a Copy.—I am tolerably well, meaning, the Day Time, for my last night was just such a noisy night of horrors, as 3 nights out of 4 are, with me. O God! when a man blesses the loud Scream of Agony that awakes him, night after night; night after night!—& when a man's repeated Night-screams have made him a nuisance in his own House, it is better to die than to live. I have a Joy in Life, that passeth all Understanding; but it is not in it's present Epiphany & Incarnation. Bodily Torture! all who have been with me can bear witness that I bear it, like an Indian / it is constitutional with me to sit still & look earnestly upon it, & ask it, what it is?—Yea often & often, the seeds of Rabelaism[10] germinating in me, I have laughed aloud at my own poor metaphysical Soul.—But these Burrs, by Day, of the Will & the Reason, these total Eclipses by night—O it is hard to bear them. I am complaining bitterly when I should be administering Comfort; but even this is one way of comfort. There are States of mind, in which even a Distraction is still a Diversion. We must none of us *brood*: we were not made to be *Brooders*.— God bless you, dear Friend,

&
S. T. Coleridge

Mrs C. will get clean Flannels ready for me.

The London government had set a deadline of 31 December 1691 for swearing the oath. Macdonald had waited till the last minute, then gone to Fort William, where he did not find a magistrate before whom to swear the oath. He was forced to travel some distance to Inverary, on Loch Fyne. The papers confirming his oath then arrived in Edinburgh too late to meet the deadline, and were in fact suppressed by the same Under Secretary of State, Sir John Dalrymple, Master of Stair, who appears to have been looking for a way to exert vengeful authority. Three years later, after an official investigation, the Scottish parliament declared the killing in Glen Coe a murder. King William was never held accountable, and Dalrymple received the king's protection.

[10] Françoise Rabelais (*c.* 1495–1553), the French satirist who gave the world the unforgettable giants Gargantua and son Pantagruel, wrote in a burlesque narrative with humor that was often crude, broad, and larger than life. If Coleridge sees his sufferings at night as in any way humorous it could be only in the sense that they were Gargantuan—much larger than normal human suffering.

LETTER 7

To Thomas Wedgwood[1]

[1] The letter was addressed to Wedgwood in London, postmarked 19 September 1803, and stamped in Keswick. Thomas Wedgwood, son of the famous pottery maker Josiah Wedgwood, was, along with his brother, the younger Josiah, a trusted friend and generous patron to Coleridge.
[2] Essayist and critic William Hazlitt (1778–1830) had known and admired Coleridge since 1798 when he heard him preach in Shrewsbury and visited him (and Wordsworth) at Nether Stowey and Alfoxden. Hazlitt's aspirations to become a portrait painter took him to Paris, where he studied by copying the old masters at the Louvre. He visited Coleridge and Wordsworth in the Lake District in the summer of 1803, arriving in July, and in fact painted portraits of both poets, which have since been lost. Coleridge's extraordinary verbal portrait of his younger friend in this letter to Wedgwood simulates the brilliant style in which Hazlitt himself executed character studies in his essays. Coleridge's warnings to Wedgwood about Hazlitt's sexual misdemeanors have their foundation in the philandering and generally inappropriate behavior toward local girls of which Hazlitt was guilty on his visit.
[3] Richard Sharp (1759–1835), critic and Member of Parliament, was known in the circle that included the Wedgwood brothers and Thomas Poole but not highly regarded by Coleridge, who once referred to him as "a very shallow man" (in 1801, in a letter to Poole). Sharp was a friend of Samuel Rogers, for whom Coleridge had equally as little admiration.

[4] These are the closing lines of the poem (eventually to be called "The Pains of Sleep") included in the letter to Southey written in Perth (Letter 3).

Greta Hall, Keswick. Sept. 16. [1803.] Friday

My dear Wedgwood

I reached home on yesterday noon; & it was not a Post Day.—William Hazlitt is a thinking, observant, original man,[2] of great power as a Painter of Character Portraits, & far more in the manner of the old Painters, than any living Artist, but the Object must be *before* him / he has no imaginative memory. So much for his Intellectuals.—His manners are to 99 in 100 singularly repulsive—: brow-hanging, shoe-contemplative, *strange* / Sharp[3] seemed to like him / but Sharp saw him only for a half hour, & that walking—he is, I verily believe, kindly-natured—is very fond of, attentive to, & patient with, children / but he is jealous, gloomy, & of an irritable Pride—& addicted to women, as objects of sexual Indulgence. With all this, there is much good in him—he is disinterested, an enthusiastic Lover of the great men, who have been before us—he says things that are his own in a way of his own—& tho' from habitual Shyness & the Outside & bearskin at least of misanthropy, he is strangely confused & dark in his conversation & delivers himself of almost all his conceptions with a Forceps, yet he says more than any man, I ever knew, yourself only excepted, that is his own in a way of his own—& oftentimes when he has warmed his mind, & the synovial juice has come out & spread over his joints he will gallop for half an hour together with real Eloquence. He sends well-headed & well-feathered Thoughts straight forwards to the mark with a Twang of the Bow-string.—If you could recommend him, as a Portrait-painter, I should be glad. To be your Companion he is, in my opinion, utterly unfit. His own Health is fitful.—I have written, as I ought to do, to you most freely imo ex corde / you know me, both head and heart, & will make what deductions, your reason will dictate to you. I can think of no other person. What wonder? For the last years I have been shy of all mere acquaintances—

To live belov'd is all, I need,
And whom I love, I love indeed.[4]

I never had any ambition; & now, I trust, I have almost as little Vanity.—

For 5 months past my mind has been strangely shut up. I have taken the paper with an intention to write to you many times / but it has been all one blank Feeling, one blank idealess Feeling. I had nothing to say, I could say nothing. How deeply I love you, my very Dreams make known to me.—I will not trouble you with the gloomy Tale of my Health. While I am awake, by patience, employment, effort of mind, & walking I can keep the fiend at Arm's length; but the Night is my Hell, Sleep my tormenting Angel. Three Nights out of four I fall asleep, struggling to lie awake—& my frequent Night-screams have almost made me a nuisance in my own House. Dreams with me are no Shadows, but the very Substances & foot-thick Calamities of my Life. Beddoes, who has been to me ever a very kind man, suspects that my Stomach 'brews Vinegar'—it may be so—but I have no other symptom but that of Flatulence / shewing itself by an asthmatic Puffing, & transient paralytic Affections / this Flatulence has never any acid Taste in my mouth / I have now no bowel rumblings. I am too careful of my Diet—the supercarbonated Kali does me no service, nor magnesia— neither have I any headache. But I am grown hysterical.—Meantime my Looks & Strength have improved. I myself fully believe it to be either a tonic, hypochondriacal Gout, or a scrophulous affection of the mesenteric Glands. In hope of driving the Gout, if Gout it should be, into the feet, I walked, previously to getting into the Coach at Perth, 263 miles in eight Days, with no unpleasant fatigue: & if I could do you any service by coming to town, & there were no Coaches, I would undertake to be with you, on foot, in 7 days.—I must have strength somewhere / My head is indefatigably strong, my limbs too are strong—but acid or not acid, Gout or Scrofula, Something there is [in] my stomach or Guts that transubstan- tiates my Bread & Wine into the Body & Blood of the Devil—Meat & Drink I should say—for I eat but little bread, & take nothing, in any form, spirituous or narcotic, stronger than Table Beer.—I am about to try the new Gout Medicine / & if it cures me, I will turn Preacher, form a new Sect in honor of the Discoverer, & make a greater clamour *in his Favor*, as the Anti-podagra, 'that was to come & is already in the world', than ever the Puritans did *against* the poor Pope, as Anti-christ.—All my Family are well. Southey, his Wife & Mrs Lovell[5] are with us. He has lost his little Girl, the unexpected Gift of a long marriage, & stricken to the very Heart is come hither for such poor comforts as my society can afford him.—To diversify this dusky Letter I will write in a Post-script an Epitaph, which I composed in my Sleep for myself, while dreaming that I was dying. To the best of my recollection I have not altered a word—Your's, dear Wedgwood,

[5] Mary Lovell was the second of the five Fricker girls, sister of Edith (Southey's wife) and Sara (Coleridge's wife). Widow of Robert Lovell, a Quaker and a member of the Patisocratic group initiated by Southey and subscribed to by Coleridge, that failed in its scheme to emigrate to America to settle, as a commune, in the Susquehanna Valley of Pennsylvania, Mary lived with the Southeys after her husband's early death in 1796, and came up to Keswick with them in this autumn of 1803 to take up residence at Greta Hall.

The coaching inn called the Black Bull, located in the Grassmarket area of Edinburgh, near the Castle, is not far from the White Hart, where William and Dorothy stayed 15 September. The Black Bull remains a lively pub today and Grassmarket, which in 1803 was not a fashionable part of town in recent years shows signs of becoming upscale.

and of all, that are dear to you at Gunville, gratefully & most affectionately, S. T. Coleridge

Epitaph
Here sleeps at length poor Col, & without Screaming,
Who died, as he had always liv'd, a dreaming:
Shot dead, while sleeping, by the Gout within,
Alone, and all unknown, at E'nbro' in an Inn.

It was on Tuesday Night last at the Black Bull, Edinburgh—6

SELECT BIBLIOGRAPHY

I have listed in this bibliography works cited in the Introduction and Notes well as works I feel would enrich the reader's background just as they did mine as I researched *Breaking Away*.

Ashton, Rosemary. *The Life of Samuel Taylor Coleridge*. Oxford: Blackwell Publishers Ltd., 1996.

Bate, Walter Jackson. *Coleridge*. New York: The Macmillan Company, 1968.

Bragg, Melvyn. *The Maid of Buttermere*. London: Hodder and Stoughton, 1987.

Coleridge, Samuel Taylor. *Biographia Literaria*. Ed. James Engell and W. Jackson Bate. Princeton, New Jersey: Princeton University Press, 1984. (Complete in one paperback volume.) Number 7 in the *Collected Works of Samuel Taylor Coleridge*. Bollingen Series LXXV.

——. *Collected Letters of Samuel Taylor Coleridge, I, 1785–1800; II, 1801–1806*. Ed. Earl Leslie Griggs. 6 vols, Oxford: Clarendon Press, 1956–72.

——. The *Notebooks of Samuel Taylor Coleridge*. Ed. Kathleen Coburn. 4 double vols. New York: Pantheon Books, 1957–; (vols I and II) Bollingen Series L, Princeton University Press (vols III and IV).

——. "Notebook 6," MS 47, 503; "Notebook 7," MS 47, 504; "Notebook 16," MS 47, 513, Manuscripts, The British Library.

——. *The Watchman*. Ed. Lewis Patton. London: Routledge & Kegan Paul, 1970. Vol. II of *The Collected Works of Samuel Taylor Coleridge*. Ed. Kathleen Coburn. Assoc. ed. Bart Winer. Bollingen Series LXXV. 16 vols. Princeton University Press. 1969–.

Elliott, Robert. *The Gretna Green Memoirs*. London: "Published by the Gretna Green Parson," 1842.

Gill, Stephen. *William Wordsworth: A Life*. Oxford: Clarendon Press, 1989.

Gittings, Robert, and Jo Manton. *Dorothy Wordsworth*. Oxford:Oxford University Press, 1988.

Haller, William. *The Early Life of Robert Southey, 1774–1803*. New York: Octagon Books, 1966.

Hazlitt, William. *Selected Writings*. Ed. Ronald Blythe. London and New York: Penguin Books, 1987.

Holmes, Richard. *Coleridge: Early Vision, 1772–1804*. New York: Pantheon Books, 1989.

——. *Coleridge: Darker Reflections, 1804–1834*. New York: Pantheon Books, 1998.

Johnston, Kenneth R. *The Hidden Wordsworth: Poet, Lover, Rebel, Spy*. New York and London: W.W. Norton & Company, 1998.

Lefebure, Molly. *Samuel Taylor Coleridge: A Bondage of Opium*. London: Victor Gollancz Ltd., 1974

——. *The Bondage of Love: A Life of Mrs Samuel Taylor Coleridge*. London: Victor Gollancz, 1988.

Mayberry, Tom. *Coleridge and Wordsworth: The Crucible of Friendship*. Foreward by Richard Holmes. Phoenix Mill · Thrupp · Stroud · Gloucestershire: Sutton Publishing Limited, 2000.

Moorman, Mary. *William Wordsworth, The Early Years, 1770–1803*. London, Oxford, New York: Oxford University Press, 1968.

Murray, Sarah (Aust). *A Companion and Useful Guide to the Beauties of Scotland, and the Hebrides, to the Lakes of Westmoreland, Cumberland, and Lancashire; and to the Curiosities of the District of Craven, in the West Riding of Yorkshire. Also a description of Part of Scotland, Particularly of the Highlands; and the Islands of Mull, Ulva, Staffa, I-Columbkill, Tirii, Coll, Eigg, Rum, Skye, Raza, and Scalpa. To which is Now Added, An account of the New Roads in Scotland, and of a Beautiful Cavern Lately Discovered in the Isle of Skye*. 2 vols. London: published by the author, 1810. (3rd ed.)

A New and Correct Map of Scotland or North Britain with all the Post and Military Roads, Divisions &ca. By Lieutenant Campbell. London: R. Laurie and J. Whittle, 1799. In *A New Universal Atlas*, T. Kitchin. Plate 10, showing northern Scotland from 1794 edition. Maps C.40.f.9. The British Library.

Oram, Richard. *Moray & Badenoch: A Historical Guide*. Edinburgh: Birlinn Ltd., 1996.

Pennant, Thomas. *A Tour in Scotland, 1769*. Intro. Brian D. Osborne. Edinburgh: Birlinn Ltd., 2000.

Prebble, John. *The Highland Clearances*. Harmondsworth, Middlesex: Penguin Books, 1977.

Rambler, A. [Joseph Budworth/Palmer]. *A Fortnight's Ramble into the Lakes In Westmorland, Lancaster, and Cumberland*. London: 1792. (Repr. Basildon, Berkshire: Preston Pupblishing, 1990.)

Rogers, Pat, ed. *Johnson & Boswell in Scotland: A Journey to the Hebrides*. New Haven and London: Yale University Press, 1993.

Rogers, Samuel. *Recollections of the Table Talk of Samuel Rogers*. Ed. Alexander Dyce. New Southgate: H.A. Rogers, 1887.

Skrine, Henry. *Three Successive Tours in the North of England and Great Part of Scotland*. London: W. Blumer, 1795.

Stoddart, Sir John. *Remarks on Local Scenery and Manners in Scotland during the Years 1799 and 1800*. 2 vols. London: W. Miller, 1801.

Summers, Gilbert J. *The Great Glen & General Wade's Roads*. Norwich: Jarrod & Sons Ltd., 1986.

Taylor, Anya. *Bacchus in Romantic England: Writers and Drink, 1780–1830*. New York: St. Martin's Press, Inc., 1999.

Taylor, William. *The Military Roads in Scotland*, revd. ed. Colonsay, Argyll: House of Lochar, 1996.

Tomes, John. *Blue Guide. Scotland*. London: A & C Black, 1996.

Walker, Carol Kyros. *Walking North with Keats*. Introduction, notes and photographs by the author. New Haven and London: Yale University Press, 1992.

Wilkinson, Thomas. *Tours of the British Moutains, with Descriptive Poems of Lowther, and Eamont Vale*. London: Taylor and Hessey, 1824.

Woof, Pamela. *Dorothy Wordsworth, Writer*. Grasmere: The Wordsworth Trust, 1994.

Wordsworth, Dorothy. *The Grasmere Journals*. Ed. Pamela Woof. Oxford and New York: Oxford University Press, 1993.

—— *Recollections of a Tour Made in Scotland*. Introduction, notes, and photographs by Carol Kyros Walker. New Haven and London: Yale University Press, 1997.

Wordsworth, William. *The Fenwick Notes*. Ed. Jared Curtis. London: British Classical Press, 1993.

——. *Poetical Works of William Wordsworth, I–III*. 5 vols. Ed. Ernest de Selincourt and Helen Darbishire. Oxford: Clarendon Press, 1940–49.

Wordsworth, William and Dorothy. *Letters of William and Dorothy Wordsworth, I, The Early Years, 1787–1805*. Arr. and ed. Ernest de Selincourt, revd. Chester L. Shaver. Oxford: Clarendon, 1967, (2nd ed.)

——. *Letters of William and Dorothy Wordsworth, II, The Middle Years, 1806–1811.* Arr. and ed. Ernest de Selincourt, revd, Mary Moorman. Oxford: Clarendon Press, 1969.

Wordsworth, William and Samuel Taylor Coleridge. *Lyrical Ballads.* The text of the 1798 edition with the additional 1800 poems and the Prefaces. Ed. R. L. Brett and A. R. Jones. London: Methuen and Co Ltd, 1963.

——. *Lyrical ballads,* 1798. A Woodstock Facsimile. Oxford and New York: Woodstock Books, 1990.

INDEX OF NAMES AND PLACES

Italicized numbers refer to pages on which illustrations appear.